AMELIA EARHART

THE TURBULENT LIFE OF AN AMERICAN ICON

Kathleen C. Winters

palgrave
macmillan

AMELIA EARHART
Copyright © Kathleen C. Winters, 2010.

All rights reserved.

First published in 2010 by
PALGRAVE MACMILLAN®
in the United States—a division of St. Martin's Press LLC,
175 Fifth Avenue, New York, NY 10010.

Where this book is distributed in the UK, Europe and the rest of the world, this is by
Palgrave Macmillan, a division of Macmillan Publishers Limited, registered in England,
company number 785998, of Houndmills, Basingstoke, Hampshire RG21 6XS.

Palgrave Macmillan is the global academic imprint of the above companies and has
companies and representatives throughout the world.

Palgrave® and Macmillan® are registered trademarks in the United States, the United
Kingdom, Europe and other countries.

ISBN: 978–0–230–61669–1

Library of Congress Cataloging-in-Publication Data

Winters, Kathleen C.
    Amelia Earhart : the turbulent life of an American icon / Kathleen C. Winters.
      p. cm.
    ISBN 978–0–230–61669–1 (hardback)
      1. Earhart, Amelia, 1897–1937. 2. Women air pilots—United States—
    Biography. I. Title.

TL540.E3W57 2010
629.13092—dc22   2010020026
[B]

A catalogue record of the book is available from the British Library.

Design by Newgen Imaging Systems (P) Ltd., Chennai, India.

First edition: December 2010

10 9 8 7 6 5 4 3 2

Printed in the United States of America.

To the memory of my mother and father

CONTENTS

ACKNOWLEDGMENTS

TO THE MANY PEOPLE who helped with this book I am deeply grateful. I wish to thank the staff members of the Purdue University Archives and Special Collections; Schlesinger Library, Radcliffe Institute; International Women's Air and Space Museum; Minnesota Historical Society; Seaver Center for Western History Research; Texas Woman's University; University of Wyoming, American Heritage Center; Library of Congress; San Diego Air and Space Museum; Fédération Aéronautique Internationale; and the Washington County and Hennepin Country libraries in Minnesota.

For reviewing several technical points in the narrative, I thank F. Lee Bradshaw, Jim Hanson, and in particular, Lyle Wheeler. Richard Weil was of immense help in reviewing the entire manuscript. Richard Mullen, Christopher Prince, Bertha Ryan, Ken Scholter, William Menkevich, Lisa Hanson, and Kevin O'Brien also helped in various ways. I am also grateful for the guidance and inspiration given me by others, including friends who provided a spark for the book's beginning.

Among those at Palgrave Macmillan, I thank Airié Stuart and my editor, Christopher Chappell. Chris and I worked together on my previous book, and I was delighted to have the chance to continue our association. I also offer my thanks to Donna Cherry in Production.

I am grateful for the direction and enthusiasm my literary agent, Andrew Zack, gave to the project.

Researching and writing a book is an arduous process, and I owe profound gratitude to my family for their support and encouragement. My daughter, Claire Winters, helped with research in Los Angeles and read portions of the manuscript. My husband, Jim Hard, supported me in all ways possible, and the book could not have been written without his assistance. Jim was my lifeline as I entered the final stretch. He suggested improvements to the manuscript, verified the endnotes, and helped with household chores. My heartfelt thanks.

Kathleen C. Winters
May 2010

INTRODUCTION

YEARS AGO I HEAVED a large red Amelia Earhart suitcase in and out of airports when I traveled. Of course I knew about Earhart. She was spirited, fearless, and a good pilot. Eventually I retired the scruffy bag, but I never forgot the travelers who asked why I carried that particular brand. After all, on her last flight Earhart got lost and crashed at sea. Wasn't that a bad omen?

When I started my own flying lessons I didn't feel a close bond to Earhart, although she had inspired many women to take up aviation, nor did I question her iconic place in American history. I was just too busy living my own life to delve into her legend.

A funny thing happened, though. After I wrote my previous book—a biography of Charles Lindbergh's wife, Anne Morrow Lindbergh—whenever I gave a reading or appeared before aviation groups, members in the audience always asked my opinion of Amelia Earhart: How did she die? Was she an incompetent pilot who tempted fate one too many times? Exactly what role did Earhart's husband, George Palmer Putnam, play in molding her into America's best-known woman pilot? Had Putnam pushed his wife into making her world flight attempt? And so on. Pilots and nonaviators alike were curious about this lovely, charismatic woman who helped to promote American aviation and was a genuine advocate for women's rights.

It seemed everywhere I went I heard mention of Earhart. At the EAA AirVenture/Oshkosh air show, a retired Pan American Airlines pilot told me of his revealing talks with Paul Mantz, the technical adviser to Earhart on her last flight, at a Hawaiian hotel. (Mantz believed she had rushed her departure.) Our conversation was one of many I had with people who had been involved, in one way or another, with Earhart and the ongoing Pacific Ocean searches for her.

My fascination with Earhart was further piqued by reading memoirs, biographies, and studies of other, less-famous pilots and their aerial accomplishments. My long experience flying small aircraft sparked my decision to write a biography of Earhart. I felt a new book, written from a pilot's perspective and updated with fresh research, was long overdue. And thus I began to chip away at the façade surrounding the story of her life.

Myriad surprises unfolded during my attempts to separate myth from fact. I was startled by the enormous help politicians and the military extended to Earhart in her quests for records; by the demands placed upon her by her endless public appearances and publicity stunts; and by her lack of focus and disregard for fundamental details in preparing for record flight attempts. We don't want to admit our heroes have flaws. I confess that I tended to idolize Earhart before starting this book. I had defended her when airmen criticized her flying skills, but as her story unraveled I realized they had a point.

She was not the world's most skilled woman pilot in her day, by any means, nor even the best in America. She was not a "natural stick," in pilots' parlance, and struggled during her flight training. Despite this, George Palmer Putnam catapulted her to fame, controlling her image ferociously and orchestrating the illusion that indeed she was the best. Many of her more accomplished contemporaries claimed that if she had logged more hours, her skills would have been on par with theirs. So I wondered why she hadn't practiced more. Was it because of the demands of upholding her image, or was it something more fundamental to her character?

We can't help but like Earhart, a personable woman who, during the height of an exhausting career, supported her irascible mother and indigent father, wrote hundreds of letters to youngsters wanting advice on aviation careers, and gave generously to friends in need. Maybe she spread herself too thin. Overcommitted and always in a rush, she skimped on preflight planning, bypassing the meticulous work necessary for consistent, successful long-distance flights.

Amelia Earhart often said that "a pilot is a pilot" to make the point that gender is irrelevant in the cockpit. But the reality is that she was, and is today, usually viewed in the context of women in aviation, and this remains one of the reasons for the public's enduring fascination with her. In part as recognition of the era in which she lived, I have continued the tradition of considering her alongside other women pilots, many of whom far surpassed her achievements but have nonetheless been lost to history.

1

ATCHISON

OF AMELIA EARHART'S ANCESTORS, she was most like her grandfather Alfred Otis. Both were extremely ambitious, enjoyed adventure and traveling, and had a strong sense of duty toward family. They were also firstborn children and lived with their grandparents during their formative years. Alfred's parents, Isaac and Caroline Abigail Otis, had moved from the state of New York to Michigan in 1834, among the many thousands lured westward at the time by the promise of available land.[1] Caroline was the daughter of Gideon Curtiss II, a devoutly religious state legislator in New York. The Curtiss family counted among their relatives John Brown, the abolitionist who would stage a bloody raid on Harpers Ferry, West Virginia, in 1859.

The hard-working Alfred strove to be a role model to his twelve siblings, as his granddaughter Amelia later would with her sister and cousins. He studied at night following his farm chores and entered the University of Michigan, graduating in 1852. Amelia's mother, Amy Otis, would later recall that her father spoke Greek and Latin "like a parrot" and tutored her and her school friends in mathematics.[2]

After graduating, Alfred traveled throughout the South, taught, and eventually enrolled at the University of Louisville to study law. His foremost goal during this period was to make money. His correspondence to his brother George during a stay in Mississippi is peppered with descriptions of his wealthy neighbors, including planters with good libraries who were "generally rich, count[ing] up from fifteen to twenty thousand & sometimes double that sum."[3]

After passing the bar, however, he soon found himself struggling to get enough business. In October 1855, Alfred, a poor man with little more than a frockcoat, shirt, trousers, and a few books, moved to Atchison, Kansas, which would later become Amelia Earhart's childhood home. Atchison, on the western bank of the Missouri River between St. Joseph, Missouri, and Leavenworth, Kansas, was at the time a frontier depot, serving as termini for steamboat and ox-team freighters, and outfitting west-bound settlers. The river was at times tame, at times turbulent and fast moving, and in harsh winters portions could freeze over, making navigation impossible. Alfred arrived as part of the first major wave of migrants to set out after Congress passed the Kansas-Nebraska Act in May 1854. After the Civil War, frontier life would lure more than a million more people to Kansas, the greatest number of migrants in its history, encouraged by the Homestead Act of 1862: In return for a small filing fee, settlers gained title to 160 acres of land after five years of residence; wealthier homesteaders paid $1.25 an acre and claimed title after six months of residence. Flour mills, foundries, and woodworking factories would also fuel the town's expansion, and by Amelia's birth its population hovered around fifteen thousand.[4]

Why Alfred selected Atchison over Lawrence, Kansas, or other new settlements is unclear, but he would have known that Atchison was founded by and named for the famous Senator David R. Atchison from Missouri, a powerful champion of the proslavery movement. Whatever Alfred's reasons for choosing Atchison, his correspondence clearly showed that his sympathies lay with the proslavery movement, at least during his first years there.

Alfred's arrival in Atchison coincided with a period of increasingly violent upheaval. The controversial provisions of the Kansas-Nebraska Act had removed legislative barriers to slavery in the West, leaving the question of slavery in the Kansas and Nebraska territories to be determined by popular vote. Consequently, the act intensified the existing disagreement between stunned northern abolitionists and southern slaveholders and helped to precipitate the Civil War. Bitter guerilla warfare erupted between the opposing sides, bringing bloodshed and mayhem to Kansas. When the abolitionist Free Soil Party gained support in the Kansas Territorial Legislature, an angry Senator Atchison retaliated and led a heavily armed mob of Missourians into Kansas. They cast thousands of fraudulent proslavery votes on Election Day, March 30, 1855.

Hostilities expanded, and in early 1856 leaders of the Free Soil Party were indicted for treason and imprisoned after a conflict at Lawrence, Kansas. Shortly after, on May 21, a proslavery mob sacked Lawrence, demolishing its hotel and printing presses. Alfred participated in the sacking of Lawrence but stressed that the hotel was destroyed "under judicial process & orders." (The grand jury had indicted the hotel as a nuisance, claiming it was a fort, just the sort of fighting words needed to provoke an attack.)[5] Only two days later, in retaliation for the Lawrence incident, John Brown and his sons massacred five proslavery men at Pottawatomie Creek, west of Atchison. A large number of northern abolitionists continued to settle in Kansas, and the Free Soil Party captured control of the Territorial government in January 1858. Three years later, in January 1861, Kansas was admitted to the Union as a Free State; in March of the same year, Lincoln was inaugurated as the sixteenth president of the United States; and in April, Confederate soldiers fired on Fort Sumter.

Despite the claims of previous biographers, there is no evidence that Alfred Otis served in the Union Army during the Civil War—or in the Confederacy, for that matter.[6] In a family history, Alfred's daughter Amy, Amelia's mother, would later claim he was an active abolitionist who hid and smuggled runaway slaves. She wove quite a story of his actions, describing his hiding slaves in trunks on his property and carrying them in luggage to safety.[7] This seems highly unlikely, based on the extensive evidence of her father's proslavery sentiments. The idea that the law-abiding Alfred would violate another man's property rights by aiding runaway slaves is difficult to take seriously.[8]

The town of Atchison and Alfred Otis prospered hand in hand despite the political upheaval of these early years. Its rapid growth and prime location at the extreme western bend of the Missouri River convinced him of its promise and reinforced his decision to put down roots there. Throughout the violent struggle between the abolitionist and proslavery factions, he remained loyal to the town, declaring he was an "Atchison man." By April 1856 he had purchased ten lots in town, built his law office, and erected a "smashing log house 12 X 14" on one of his claims.[9] He toiled for long hours and continued to focus on accumulating material wealth. Land litigation powered his law practice, and through this and real estate speculation he reaped his riches. In 1865 he and his partner, George Glick, who later became governor of Kansas, gained a plum client for their practice, the Central Branch of the Union Pacific Railroad.(Four years later the first transcontinental rail line would be established when the Union Pacific and Central Pacific Railroads joined at Promontory Point, Utah.) The two partners would help found the Atchison and Nebraska Railroad, the Atchison Gas Company, and the Atchison Savings Bank.

In the process of becoming wealthy, Alfred had established himself as a revered leader in the community. In 1878 he would be elected Circuit Judge on the Democratic ticket, but after declining a second nomination, he would devote his time to his business enterprises, real estate and banking, and serve as president of the Atchison Savings Bank. He would also serve two terms as Regent of the University of Kansas. By the time of his retirement in 1891, he had earned the sobriquet "the Judge," an emblem of his standing in the community as well as his prominence in the eyes of his children and grandchildren.

IN APRIL 1862 ALFRED Otis married twenty-five-year-old Amelia "Millie" Josephine Harres, a well-connected woman from a prosperous family, who was ten years his junior. After the marriage ceremony in the bride's hometown of Philadelphia, the newlyweds traveled by train to St. Louis and from there on a steamboat up the Missouri River to Atchison. At the time of Millie's arrival in 1862, Atchison was still relatively primitive, with rutted dirt streets, no sidewalks, and an extreme climate. There were few trees to break the force of relentless winds, and temperatures could drop below zero in winter or hover near one hundred in summer. Millie did not embrace the pioneer mindset and, even decades after leaving Philadelphia, held fast to Eastern standards of gentility. She wore long, black brocade gowns, and her daily agenda involved church, afternoon teas, and social calls. Her mother, Maria Grace Harres, a Philadelphia-born Quaker, provided companionship and helped around the household, having moved in after her husband died.

Amy Otis Earhart was born in 1869, the second of six surviving children and the oldest daughter of Alfred and Millie. Slender and pretty, she liked traveling and dancing, and would later regale her own daughters with tales of her youth, when she and a friend were the "undisputed leaders of the young social set" and traveled by chartered steamers to balls and cotillions at Fort Leavenworth and St. Joseph.[10] It was an idyllic and cosmopolitan upbringing. With five brothers, one sister, and myriad cousins in Atchison, Amy did not want for company or material comforts. Her father considered travel crucial to his children's education and organized at least one big trip annually to locations ranging from Colorado to California.

The Otis children partook in daily reading sessions; Grandmother Maria would lead with a page or so of Dickens, followed by the youngsters taking their turn. Alfred urged his children to read domestic and foreign newspapers, as well as history and biographies, and to memorize and recite poetry. Until Amy married she lived at home, organizing a Dickens club and busying herself with other social activities. She was fond of saying that her grandparents and parents drilled into their children that "everything given you is given you to share with others."[11] This notion may have later contributed to her own financial irresponsibility.

All things considered, it was not surprising Alfred balked when poor Edwin Earhart asked for her hand in marriage. Amy had first met Edwin at her debut in 1890, a coming-out party that attracted the elite of Atchison's society to her parent's home. There on a warm June evening, a light breeze scented with heliotrope wafted through the yard, where Japanese lanterns were strung on wires between trees. Hired musicians from St. Joseph played reels and waltzes, and the guests danced atop a wooden floor built especially for the event. It was in this romantic setting that Amy's brother Mark introduced her to Edwin, his tutor and fellow student at the University of Kansas law school. Amy's was a standard of living unknown to Edwin, and its luxury drew him in like a honeyed flower.

Edwin, born in 1867, was the youngest of twelve children of Mary Wells Patton and the Reverend David Earhart, an Evangelical Lutheran who

moved his family from Pennsylvania to Kansas to minister to Indians and
settlers in 1860. Hardship and poverty beset the Earharts, whose meals often
consisted of only corncakes and turnips, and who staved off starvation with
financial help from a local pastor and the Home Missionary Society. The
reverend kept Sabbath strictly, deeming Sunday a day of rest and no activity.
An Earhart family anecdote told of hungry, six-year-old Edwin sneaking off
to fish one Sunday and returning with a catch for supper. Only after his
mother begged that she be allowed to cook the fish did his father give in and
allow it to be eaten.

Despite his difficult childhood, Edwin was charming and erudite, a
natty dresser, and a good dancer with an ear for music; he also sang and
played piano. It is unclear which of his characteristics most annoyed Amy's
father; perhaps it was too much charm, too little substance, and a sense of fri-
volity that put off the stern Alfred Otis. Edwin seemed neither ambitious nor
wealthy enough to adequately provide for Amy. He had a fondness for liquor,
too. His daughter Muriel would later describe him as a man of "humor and
a great *joie de vivre*. He could not say No to his friends whether he was asked
to lend money or to take another drink."[12]

Hoping to dampen Amy's ardor and allow more time for her to meet
suitors in her own social circle, Alfred insisted that Edwin earn at least $50
a month before marrying her.[13] But this only hardened Amy's resolve, and
she stubbornly insisted on waiting. Five long years elapsed before Edwin
met Alfred's demand, and he and Amy wed on October 16, 1895, at Trinity
Episcopal Church in Atchison. After the small wedding, Amy and Edwin
Earhart boarded a train for Kansas City, Kansas, settling in their new, fur-
nished, white frame house at 1021 Ann Avenue, a wedding present from the
Otises.

Amy and Edwin lived only fifty miles from Atchison, but their standard
of living differed sharply from that of Amy's wealthy parents. Amy was no
longer the "pampered debutante" in an affluent family, and she at first found
marriage to Edwin, now a struggling railroad lawyer, to be a tearful, wrench-
ing adjustment.[14] Frequent trips to Atchison helped to alleviate her feelings
of isolation, though Edwin seldom accompanied her, and the rift between
him and his in-laws widened as he continually failed to adequately provide
for his family.

Amy's first pregnancy ended in miscarriage. After becoming pregnant again in 1896, she decided she would retreat to her parents' house for the birth. There the Otises and a staff of Irish servants doted on her, as they had before she married, and a half hour before midnight on July 24, 1897, in a second-story bedroom of the Otises' frame and brick Victorian house, Amelia Mary Earhart was born. It was her great fortune to be born near the cusp of the twentieth century, when enormous technological changes were sweeping across America. Her destiny would later be assured after "aviation fever" gripped the country, and unimagined opportunities would open up to her.

2

CHILDHOOD

AMELIA, THE FIRST OF Amy and Edwin's two daughters, was named for her grandmothers, Amelia "Millie" Harres Otis and Mary Wells Earhart. On October 10, 1897, she was christened at Trinity Episcopal Church in Atchison, Kansas. At the marble font, Reverend John H. Moleneaux touched holy water to her head, intoning a benediction, welcoming her to the faith of her ancestors. The pretty, nine-pound infant, who had a clear complexion and an upturned nose, wore a family heirloom, a long ivory gown fringed with lace. She lay nestled in her mother's arms while other family members clustered near black walnut pews.

Around the church revolved the social lives of Atchison's leading citizens, among them Alfred Otis. He was among the founders of the parish, having drawn up its articles of association in 1857, and served as vestryman and senior warden until resigning the positions before Amelia's birth. He helped select the builder of the stone church, designed in the Gothic Revival style, with a high-pitched roof covered in a patterned slate, its steeple with bell cote topped by a stone cross. In vivid red, blue, green, and yellow, its three soaring stained glass windows depicted the Ascension of Christ, Christ in the home of Martha and Mary, and Christ and the Child.[1]

Amelia grew up in Atchison, not Kansas City. She would later write, "My girlhood was much like that of many another American girl who was growing up at the time I was, with just the kind of fun and good times we all had then," yet in many ways she did not live as other American girls—for she lived apart from her parents.[2] Millie Otis, whose own mother had recently died, longed for the company of her namesake and favorite grandchild, Amelia. Millie's husband had been left with his grandparents until age fourteen; perhaps he encouraged his lonely wife to take in Amelia. In any case, during the school year, from ages three to eleven, Amelia lived with the Otises in Atchison. In the meantime her parents resided in Kansas City with Grace Muriel (known as Muriel and nicknamed "Pidge"), Amelia's sister, younger by two and a half years. When the school year ended, Amelia left the grandeur of her grandparents' home for her parents' small, white frame house, on a small lot, in an ordinary neighborhood in Kansas City, and the two sisters reunited on holidays and spent summer vacations together. Muriel would form an especially close bond with her mother, whereas Amelia was closer to Edwin. She adored her witty and imaginative father, who would entertain the girls and their friends with Western thrillers, complete with bandits, cowboys, Indians, and other made-up characters. She thought him brilliant, too, and a wordsmith familiar with the entire dictionary; she recalled his addressing her in a letter as "Dear Parallelepipedon," and rushing to find its definition.[3] She missed him during the school year, yet she never admitted so publicly. Though a loving and dutiful daughter, she was more independent than Muriel and would grow into a very private woman, shielding herself and hiding any unhappiness with a humorous quip. Her good friend Louise Thaden, also an aviator, would later write, "Amelia, I think, has never been really close to anyone. It has always been difficult for her to break down the barriers of reticence and reserve."[4]

The handsome nine-room house in Atchison that Amelia grew up in had been built in 1861 by her grandfather Alfred for Millie. Its amenities included stained-glass windows, crystal chandeliers, a formal dining room, and a piano in the drawing room, along with a well-stocked library of classic and contemporary literature. A lively child, Amelia much preferred being outdoors, but she would often be found sprawled on the library floor with a book, or curled up in a nook, reading. She and her family "loved the smell of a book," she would later say.[5]

Meanwhile, Edwin worked as a railroad lawyer in Kansas City, handling claims on a contingency basis, so he was not paid unless he successfully defended the railroad. In the hierarchy of railroad lawyers, his job was near the bottom rung. He didn't apply himself diligently to his career, in contrast to his hard-working father-in-law and own father. In 1903 there occurred an irreparable rift in his relationship with his in-laws. After having spent all his spare time and the family's dwindling resources inventing a device to hold signal flags on the rear of trains, he traveled to the patent office in Washington, D.C. He tramped about for two days attempting to have it categorized and finally wrote Amy that a "man from Colorado had filed a patent on an identical holder two years ago. . . . This news is a terrible blow, because I had been counting on receiving several hundred dollars from the railroad for my flag holder."[6] The funds he expended on this doomed venture had been earmarked to pay the Earharts' property taxes, and he created another fiasco when, to pay the tax bill, he sold a collection of valuable law books that had been a gift from Judge Otis. The Judge was livid.

Nor was the Judge appeased the following year, when Edwin took his family to the 1904 World's Fair in St. Louis, where they stayed for a full week. The Judge thought the excursion an extravagant waste of money and further proof of Edwin's spendthrift habits. Still, the Earharts loved the adventure. Spread out over 1,200 acres in the heart of St. Louis and featuring 75 miles of roadways, it was at the time the largest fair ever held. The extravagant exhibits in its twelve palaces and fifteen hundred buildings were all lit by electricity—still a new phenomenon—and showcased the latest developments in technology, fine arts, manufacturing, science, and education. By the time it closed, on December 1, 1904, an estimated twenty million people had visited.[7] What most fascinated seven-year-old Amelia were the amusement rides on the mile-long midway called the Pike, particularly the Ferris wheel, which she rode with her father, and the roller coaster, which served as a model for a short-lived "rolly-coaster" she built upon returning home.

LOOKING BACK ON HER childhood—in her second book, *The Fun of It*, which was published in 1932, four years after she achieved fame—Amelia singled out three important "threads" attracting her to aviation: an interest in mechanical pursuits, the many railroad trips she took with her father, and a tendency to experiment with all types of sports and games.[8] Both her parents had an enlightened attitude toward rearing their daughters, and encouraged their interest in pursuits that at the time were unconventional for women.

Amelia loved seeing new places and meeting new people. "Because I selected a father who was a railroad man it has been my fortune to roll," she would later write.[9] The Earharts traveled throughout the country and as far as California, sometimes by private rail car fitted out with a chef and luxurious accoutrements, a perquisite later given to Edwin in his position as a railroad claims agent. Not until Amelia was sixteen did she have to purchase a railroad ticket. Both Earhart parents prioritized travel over their children's classroom study, but Amelia and Muriel got good grades despite missing school days.

When not actually traveling, Amelia enjoyed playing Bogie, in which she and her cousins Lucy and Kathryn Challiss imagined journeying around the world. The threesome sat in an old abandoned carriage in the Otis barn looking over maps of faraway continents. Unknown terrors lurked in the barn's empty stalls, waiting to pounce on them. Even years later, the game evoked memories for Amelia. "For me the dreams of long ago had come true," she wrote in 1937 as her Lockheed Electra flew over the Middle East on her last flight. "Only, back in Atchison, our imaginary African treks were on camels or elephants. Then airplanes were of another day."[10]

Early on, Amelia was a daredevil and liked taking risks. As ringleader of her neighborhood playmates, she shrugged off near accidents as if she were immune to danger. During the Christmas holidays following the excursion to the World's Fair, the Earhart girls were given low-slung sleds fitted with steel runners. They allowed the girls to lie flat, belly-style, instead of sitting upright, the more sedate fashion preferred for little girls. A few days later Amelia, showing off, took off down a steep, icy slope on her new sled, as Muriel looked on from atop. Midway down, a junk dealer's horse rounded a corner at the foot of the hill—directly in Amelia's path. She couldn't stop or turn on the ice, and no one heard her warning cries, so she ducked her head and coasted between the horse's front and hind legs. The same Christmas Edwin also gave his girls a .22 Hamilton rifle, which they used to shoot rats in the Atchison barn, until the Otises confiscated it.

All sports attracted Amelia—softball, basketball, skating, horseback riding, and tennis, among others—but she later begrudged the limited guidance given to young girls at the time, saying they were not formally trained until attaining college age and by then had developed bad habits. Likewise, she loved the outdoors, but complained about the restrictions imposed on her gender. "Unfortunately I lived at a time when girls were still girls. Though reading was considered proper, many of my outdoor exercises were not."[11] Compared to town girls, Amelia may have been a tomboy, but outside the narrow confines of her Atchison neighborhood, country girls played rough and worked with their hands. In the prairies west of town, they farmed their family's claim, ploughed, lived in mud dugouts, and helped cook, garden, rear children, and were hired out to wealthier families as servants. Later in life, Amelia's publicity machine would portray her as a dedicated tomboy, ignoring mannish female pilots such as Bobbi Trout and Florence "Pancho" Barnes who outdid her in this respect.

Amelia and Muriel appreciated the unconventional behavior their parents encouraged, their father who indulged their tastes for boys' games, and a "forward-looking mother who endured the neighbors' raised eyebrows with equanimity" while her girls wore dark blue flannel bloomers gathered at the knees for play, rather than the customary dresses and pinafores.[12] Grandmother Otis was scandalized by the girls' costumes and conduct. Seeing young Amelia jump over a fence, she pointedly said she had done nothing more strenuous than roll a hoop in the public square during her childhood.

UNTIL MOVING FROM ATCHISON, Amelia attended the town's private College Preparatory School, which taught a coed student body totaling thirty to forty students. "Millie" Earhart, as she was known, earned good grades, although she didn't conform to her teachers' expectations. She wasn't rebellious but seemed indifferent to academic recognition. "Amelia's mind is brilliant," commented one teacher, "but she refuses to do the plodding necessary to win honor prizes. She deduces the correct answers to complex arithmetic problems, but hates to put down the steps by which she arrived at the results."[13] Whether owing to impatience on Amelia's part or an aversion to details, this childhood trait would carry over into her adult life.

In August 1906, when Amelia was nine, her family joined the summer exodus of city dwellers seeking a cooler, drier climate away from the heat and humidity of Kansas City, traveling to the shores of Lake Okabena in Worthington, a small farming community in southwestern Minnesota. In those days before air conditioning, families of even limited means tried to escape to cooler climates during summer months. This marked the first of four Augusts the Earharts would spend in Worthington. There they roomed with the local postmaster, Mr. J. P. Mann, and his family and took meals at a boarding house run by Mrs. Twitchell, a wonderful Swedish cook. The girls delighted in these annual excursions north, which they considered perfect summer vacations. They swam in the lake, rowed, played tennis, caught garter snakes and turtles, and helped to harvest hay and milk cows on the Mann farm. Edwin joined them on weekends or longer when he could leave his law practice, leading the girls in fishing trips, catching sunfish. Best of all, Amelia indulged her passion for horses, for Mr. Mann allowed the girls the use of Prince, an old but spry Indian pony that "could be bribed by cookies to do almost anything."[14] The children rode him bareback and fed him pies made of Mrs. Twitchell's delicious sugar cookies topped with grass and clover leaves.

It was in Worthington where the Earharts first rode in automobiles, an REO and Stoddard Dayton, to a picnic twenty miles distant; having no tire punctures to delay them, they arrived in two hours. Along the way, Clinton Mann, driver of the REO, told them about a driver named De Palma who reached an amazing 74 miles an hour on a Florida race track, a speed that astonished the girls. Amelia would later become an excellent driver, fond of speedy automobiles.

THE EARHARTS' APPARENTLY COMFORTABLE standard of living— characterized by extended vacations and lavish gifts—belied persistent financial difficulties. Amy's parents were obviously scornful of Edwin's extravagance and inability to earn a substantial salary. Money ran like water through his hands, and Amy, likewise impractical, had little success budgeting the household funds. Apparent from early on, Edwin's desultory behavior showed no signs of abating during the first years of the marriage.

Despite his troubles, slowly, over the next few years, Edwin transformed himself into a respected railroad lawyer and in 1906 was offered a permanent position in the claims department of the Rock Island Lines. The new position required that he move to Des Moines, Iowa, and he and Amy set off right away to find a suitable house, leaving the girls with their grandparents. Muriel joined her sister at the College Preparatory School and in playing Bogie and other games with the Challiss cousins next door. As always, reading figured prominently in their leisure time, and when confined indoors they reveled in their grandfather's library, reading *Harper's Young People*, *Puck*, works by Charles Dickens, and Oliver Optic's success books for boys.

Although the separation had been intended to last only a month, it was more than a year before they reunited permanently with their parents. Not that their grandmother minded. Writing to her "dear brother Charlie" (he was her brother-in-law) on March 6, 1906, she delighted that "my little grandchildren help to keep us merry this winter and are a special pleasure to us."[15]

In 1907, at the Iowa State Fair in Des Moines, Amelia saw her first airplane, "a thing of rusty wire and wood" that didn't interest her.[16] She much preferred her fifteen-cent purchase of a hat shaped like an inverted peach basket. She would later write she didn't know how psychoanalysts would interpret this preference, given her subsequent career. (She also grew to dislike hats.) The same year, *Scientific American* magazine had applauded the advent of "mechanical aeroplane flight," forecasting its use in military service. "In all probability," the magazine continued, "its chief development ultimately will be in the field of sport, where it should enjoy a popularity equal to that of the automobile."[17] At the time neither automobiles nor airplanes were predicted to become functional means of transportation.

By 1908 Amelia and Muriel had joined their parents in Des Moines and thereafter began a peripatetic life. Moving to a strange city, they were no longer members of the Atchison aristocracy as the Judge's granddaughters, and they faced a tumultuous adjustment. Eleven-year-old Amelia felt the loss of her school, friends, and beloved cousins as a terrible blow, but no one could have foreseen how the move would precipitate the family's eventual decline into poverty and disgrace.

In Des Moines Amelia and Muriel entered public schools, despite their mother's wishes and social aspirations. Having heard reports of lice in the public schools, Amy had first hired a young widow, Mrs. Florence Gardiner, as a live-in governess and teacher. A former teacher at the College Preparatory School whose husband had drowned at the seashore on their honeymoon, Mrs. Gardiner's curricula emphasized French and fine arts. She and Edwin found themselves in frequent arguments, however. Their disagreements came to a head during the 1908 Christmas holidays, when he gave the girls a football instead of a sewing basket, her idea of an appropriate gift for young ladies. Mrs. Gardiner departed, and Amy was forced to enroll the girls in public school. Undoubtedly the Otises would have provided tuition money for private schools, had they been confident Amy and her husband would not spend the funds elsewhere.

Shortly after the move, Edwin was promoted to lead claims agent at the Rock Island Lines, with his salary doubled and his name displayed on the company letterhead. He was given frequent access to a private rail car equipped with a kitchen, dining room, and Tokimo, a Japanese chef and butler. Edwin often called the car into service, using it to transport family and guests in style to Worthington, Atchison, and points west. The Judge and Mrs. Otis even dined aboard at one point, with Tokimo serving them a delectable lamb entrée.

Amy lost no time in again hiring a cook and a maid and locating a more suitable, upscale residence, at 3002 Cottage Grove Avenue, in a fashionable neighborhood one block from Drake University. The Earharts regularly attended art exhibits and concerts sponsored by the Drake Conservatory of Music, and they joined a neighborhood pool of families who subscribed to ten magazines, including *The Atlantic Monthly, Scribner's, Outlook*, and *The Century*. For cultural events the girls wore high-necked silk frocks, or white dotted Swiss with pastel sashes during summer months, and Amy a silk dress with velvet bows and a "sweep" to her long skirt, which rustled behind her. Edwin's costume usually consisted of a white shirt with high stiff collar, dark gray trousers, and Prince Albert coat. After returning home from concerts, Amelia and Edwin would often sit at the piano, playing by ear the music they had heard.

Sadly, these halcyon days were short-lived. On October 14, 1911, both the Judge and Mrs. Otis had attached codicils to their wills to safeguard the inheritances of Amy Earhart and her younger brother, Theodore H.

Otis, who had sustained a brain injury at birth. The mentally handicapped Theodore lived on the family homestead in Atchison, where he would later own a cottage. The documents read in part:

> It is my *will* that only the net income of the shares of my estate devised to my children Amy O. Earhart and Theodore H. Otis shall be paid over to them annually and that the entire principal or capital thereof shall be held, managed and controled [*sic*] by my said trustee, Mark E. Otis, for the said period of fifteen years after my death, upon the trusts, hereontofore prescribed.[18]

The codicils, witnessed by their loyal servants Charles Parks and Mary Brashay, appointed Margaret Otis Balis, Amy's younger sister, to act as successor trustee to Mark, secretary of the Otis Real Estate Company. (At Amy's request, in 1912 both Mark and Margaret would resign as trustees of her bequest, and the court-appointed Northern Trust Company would fulfill this role.)

At their signing Amelia Otis was seriously ill with a heart ailment, from which she would die in a few months. The Judge would die shortly after her, in May 1912, at age eighty-five. As the four surviving children, Amy, Mark, Margaret, and Theodore shared equally in their parents' estates, and each inherited approximately $41,400.00. In today's dollars, this substantial sum would be close to a million dollars; Amy was a wealthy woman indeed.[19]

Nonetheless, the trustee provisions of the codicils shocked and humiliated the Earharts, dealing a blow that eventually severed the marriage. Both looked on the codicils as a condemnation of their character. Edwin was insulted by their terms, and his social drinking soon escalated to public drunkenness, which Muriel gave as one reason for the "loss of our material prosperity and the beginning of the disintegration of the family. I find it difficult to write of the deterioration of Dad's character and yet I know that the hardship and mental suffering that Amelia and I endured as adolescents made an indelible impression upon us and help to explain some of Amelia's actions and attitudes in her later life."[20]

In 1912 many states were "dry," and the rapidly growing temperance movement promoted sobriety nationwide. (Prohibition would go into effect on January 17, 1920.) Middle-class families were ashamed and aghast at public displays of drunkenness. "What would the neighbors think?" was the standard by which people were measured. Edwin's first major incident occurred on a fall afternoon in Des Moines, when Amelia, Muriel, and ten of their friends had congregated near the Earharts' home, awaiting his appearance for a rousing game of cowboys and Indians. All eyes were on him as he stepped down from the streetcar and wobbled from one foot to the other, weaving toward his house. When Amy opened the door and saw his condition, she yanked him inside. The group outside dispersed, and the children went home to tell their parents of the ugly scene. Edwin begged forgiveness the next morning, promised to abstain, and dutifully accompanied his family to church. But his drinking worsened, and he began coming home drunk and in a black temper several times a week, railing against his wife's family, the railroad, and the high household expenses.

There came a point when his staff could no longer hide his sloppy work and errors, and when the company's claim agent arrived from Chicago to investigate, he found Edwin in his office, drunk, with an open bottle on his desk. The company recommended he undergo a four-week program at a branch of the Keeley Institute, nationally known for treating alcoholics. Despite his stay there, he began drinking heavily only a few days after returning home. He soon lost his job in Des Moines and was unable to secure another for more than a year, despite writing numerous letters to railroad companies. He now had a reputation in the business, and firms couldn't chance hiring him.

In effect Amy became head of the household, watching over finances and slashing superfluous amenities. (Like her grandmother, mother, and many women of her social class, Amy was never gainfully employed.) Muriel recalled missing magazine subscriptions the most, their participation in the neighborhood pool having been cut. As an intelligent adolescent of fifteen, Amelia was undoubtedly dispirited over the family's change in circumstances, although she would seldom write or say anything of substance regarding her teenage years.

The terms of her parents' wills prohibited Amy's drawing on the principal of her inheritance for fifteen years, but occasional dividends augmented her income. She suspected her brother Mark had misrepresented the principal, including a list of properties he submitted to the trust company upon his resignation in 1912, and asked her uncle Charles Otis to audit the list and present an inventory. An eminent lawyer in St. Paul, Minnesota, Charles hired an accountant to perform the audit and in 1913 reassured Amy that all was in order. She replied in March: "I cannot tell you what comfort your letter has given me, a comfort no one else could have given me, for there is no one on whose judgment I so thoroughly rely." She concluded the letter by thanking him for his "kind offer to have your door open to me wherever you are."[21]

Amy would soon act on this offer, to his surprise. Providentially, Edwin secured a job in St. Paul, although it was a menial one clerking for the Great Northern Railway, and they rushed to pack and vacate their house. They were nearly destitute, with Amy's money close to running out, and were eager to start anew. Whereas the Earharts had joyfully moved to Des Moines five years earlier, believing it was but one stop on Edwin's climb up the career ladder, now their departure was a depressing one, and boarding the railroad car to St. Paul, Amy shed tears of frustration.

3

ON THE MOVE

THE EARHARTS' ARRIVAL in St. Paul, in the fall of 1913, was not without irony. Amy hoped to parlay her birthright into social status in St. Paul, where the Otis name was known. Edwin, too, looked toward a brighter future, believing his clerk position was but a mere stepping stone to a permanent job in the legal department of the Great Northern. Once again their optimism overrode common sense. Amy unwisely signed a $45-a-month, two-year lease for a house at 825 Fairmount Avenue in St. Paul, large enough to hold all her furniture, and exceptionally expensive to heat.

The Earharts had told no one of their impending move, and Uncle Charles was astounded when Amy showed up on his doorstep asking him to endorse a check to the movers. She was so poor that when she saw him again, on September 20, 1913, he had to advance her money to pay her rent, in addition to funds for insurance premiums, coal, and groceries, in all amounting to $100. He wrote the checks to Amy on the advice of her brother Mark, to whom he wrote on September 23 explaining her situation:

> With strictest economy she will require in monthly installments, as it seems to me, at least $100 and perhaps $125 per month. To secure this she is willing to make any assignment or adjustment that we may deem proper with reference to the trust

fund. She volunteered the suggestion furthermore that she would be glad to deposit such funds in the bank and check the same out as might be necessary and submit such checks to you that you might see that proper expenditures had been made and nothing wasted or expended in a manner that would not meet your approval.[1]

Amy had told him, Charlie continued, of her plans to take in boarders, having one application from an elderly lady who would pay $25 monthly, with another woman interested. She had also informed him that her daughters "are taking the teacher's course with the view of teaching as soon as they are prepared for such work and so helping out the family." Rounding out his letter to Mark were scathing remarks about Edwin, a "cypher" who had been "gallivanting" about the country squandering his wife's money.[2]

Whether Amy was paid every month thereafter, according to Charles's suggestion, is unknown. His grandson James Otis would later write that Edwin was an "alcoholic and apparently abandoned the family so that grandfather Charles had to support them until Amy's brother Mark could rescue them."[3] It seems likely she received financial aid from the Otises, because the Earharts' sole earned income, from Edwin's meager salary, would not have covered more than the rent. Certainly Amy never took in boarders in St. Paul, and her daughters did not soon become teachers to help the family.

In any event, Amy's delusions about entering St. Paul society were destroyed, and the family eked out an existence, barely making ends meet. During the long, cold winter in St. Paul, where temperatures often remained below freezing for months, they lived in only two rooms to save heating costs, and rather than ride streetcars the girls sometimes walked to save on fares. Edwin again took refuge in the bottle as the winter progressed. On one occasion, after rushing home to pack for a business trip, he discovered that Amelia had found a bottle of whiskey in his suitcase and emptied it in the kitchen sink. Infuriated, Edwin tried to slap Amelia, but Amy stopped him. At Christmas his condition deteriorated. After promising to escort the girls to a Twelfth Night celebration at St. Clement's, the neighborhood church where their dates awaited, he stumbled home inebriated and three hours late. Crying, Muriel ran off to bed, while Amelia stoically gathered up the festive holiday decorations, cookies, and cocoa she and Muriel had carefully laid out for the boys. Amelia was becoming inured to her father's mood swings and irresponsible behavior, while Amy maintained the pretense of a tolerable marriage.

In spite of these hardships, sixteen-year-old Amelia, a junior at Central High School, and Muriel, a freshman, earned good grades and made new friends. Amelia's favorite subjects were Latin and mathematics, especially geometry, and under the tutelage of a gifted instructor, she developed a keen interest in chemistry and physics. She also played on the school's basketball team, but her extracurricular activities primarily revolved around the church: the Altar Guild and the choir.

Despite her brave front, Amelia would never hold a leadership position in any groups or clubs during high school. The constant moves her family undertook during her teen years left her feeling rootless and insecure; gone were her childhood days when, as a granddaughter of Judge Otis, she was assured of her place in Atchison society. She did not discuss her problems but instead focused her ambitions. She and Virginia Park, a school friend in Atchison, had planned to later attend Bryn Mawr together, and in 1914 she wrote her: "Of course I'm going to B.M. [Bryn Mawr] if I have to drive a grocery wagon to accumulate the cash."[4]

LESS THAN A YEAR after arriving in St. Paul, the family endured another move, to Springfield, Missouri, where Edwin believed a position awaited him in the claims department of the Burlington Railroad. He had lost his job in St. Paul after staggering into the path of an automobile and being briefly hospitalized. The move was a disaster. Exhausted after a seven-hour train journey to Springfield, the family learned the job vacancy had been filled, news that sent Amy, already ill from stress, into a tailspin. She insisted on a trial separation, and she and the girls moved to Chicago, having been invited there by the Shedds, old friends from better times when Edwin's influence had helped Mr. Shedd secure a position with the Rock Island Line. Edwin returned to Fairmount Street in St. Paul and spent his days attempting to revive his law practice. Amy had asked Charles Otis if she could pay Edwin's expenses from the monies advanced her to help him if they had to live apart, but it's unknown if she was able to do so.

In Chicago Amelia shouldered responsibility for her mother and sister as head of the household, and her behavior and appearance changed dramatically. She was reticent and depressed, a condition not at all surprising considering the family was reduced to renting rooms in a small apartment shared with two disagreeable spinster sisters. Although Amelia attended Hyde Park, the best public high school in Chicago—as Muriel recalled, Amelia herself had interviewed school principals to determine which school most suited *her*—she did not participate in any of the numerous clubs the school offered, nor did she play on any of the sports teams she so loved.

It was a year of hardships for Amelia, or A.E., as she now called herself. The semester began badly; she alienated her classmates in an attempt to oust an incompetent, deaf English teacher who was rumored to be a relative of the corrupt mayor. Students used the class as a recreation period, doing whatever they wanted, and refused to sign Amelia's petition to have her replaced. Instead of attending the English class, Amelia holed up reading in the library until the semester ended. She refused to attend the senior banquet and the graduation ceremony in June. A loner preoccupied with her family and her parents' disintegrating marriage, she was later described by a classmate: "She always walked to school alone and we merely thought of her as a dreamer.... We were even afraid to say hello to her, she was so shy." Muriel later wrote that the caption under Amelia's yearbook picture described her as "the girl in brown who walks alone."[5]

The fall of 1915 brought some renewed optimism to the beleaguered Earharts, for Edwin had stopped drinking and was diligently reviewing the legalities of the Otises' wills and his wife's inheritance. The family reunited in Kansas City, leasing a small house at 3621 Charlotte Street, where Amelia lived an entire year without attending school or working. (Most likely her mother would not permit her to get a job.) By this time she was acting as a buffer between her parents, working to prolong the marriage, and Amy must have welcomed her company.

Edwin convinced Amy to contest the terms of the wills, and in September 1915 she filed suit. Supported by testimony from Amelia J. Otis's doctor, who ruled she was incompetent when she added the codicil to her will, the court ruled for dissolution of the trust. Finally, the principal of Amy's inheritance was in her hands. Humiliated and emotionally wounded by the vagaries of the past few years, Amy determined to educate her daughters in private schools with her newly acquired funds. Amelia acquiesced to her mother's wish that she attend the Ogontz School, on the outskirts of Philadelphia, an exclusive finishing school on the Jay Cooke estate near Bryn Mawr. The school was also conveniently near Margaret Balis, Amelia's aunt, who could keep an eye out for her niece and have her visit.

Why did Amy insist on Ogontz rather than a four-year college for Amelia? Perhaps Charles Otis recommended the school, since his cousin had taught at Ogontz. (He and his wife visited her there in 1895.)[6] On the other hand, Amy's renewed social aspirations could have guided her decision because Ogontz was fashionable and well known in society circles. Amelia might have thought it a compromise, but she adamantly favored furthering her education, and at Ogontz she was nearing her objective of attending Bryn Mawr.

Ogontz turned out to be an excellent choice. It was there that Amelia polished her social graces, which would allow her to move with ease and poise among all segments of society after she became famous. She was nineteen, among the oldest of Ogontz students when she entered in the fall of 1916, and a willowy five feet eight inches tall, with penetrating gray eyes and blond hair. She was given the nicknames "Meelie" and "Butterball," the latter a play on her slender frame. At $600 a semester, the boarding school strained Amy Earhart's budget, and Amelia accounted for all her expenditures to Amy, unlike the majority of her affluent, overindulged classmates.

Ogontz was owned and ruled by a formidable disciplinarian, headmistress Abby Sutherland. With supervised excursions to symphony concerts and the theater, and renowned artists, musicians, and writers visiting the campus regularly, the program placed a strong emphasis on culture and fine arts. But a rigorous exercise regimen was also in place, and outdoor activities, including field hockey, baseball, and military drills complete with wooden guns, figured prominently in the week's schedule. The curriculum was based on that of Vassar College and the grading system incorporated marks of E, G, and F for excellent, good, and fair; there were no failures. The girls awoke to a cow bell at 7:00 in the morning, after which followed prayers, exercises, breakfast, and a short walk until classes, which were held from 9:00 A.M. to 1:15 P.M. After lunch and sports, there was study hall, and then dinner and prayers, which were followed by a variety of evening classes, usually foreign languages. Saturday mornings found the girls busy studying current events—"What do you think of the railroad strike and the abdication of the Czar?" Amelia asked her mother—and the Bible, and performing afternoon exercises outdoors before beginning study hall; and on Sunday, prayers and a lecture comprised the day. As Amelia observed, "Your every minute is accounted for and you have to go by schedule."[7]

Throughout the year Amelia kept up a lively correspondence with her mother, writing of her new friends, classes, and Miss Sutherland, who, she observed, had "many chances of matrimony because she is brilliant but she passes them all by." Early in the fall, she wrote, "Did I tell you I have a reputation for brains?" By February Amelia had found her niche, leading Miss Sutherland to comment on her happiness and remark that she had "made a very warm place for herself in the hearts of her schoolmates and teachers by her charm of manners." Amelia boasted to her mother of a school party wherein she and fifteen girls feasted on sandwiches and hot chocolate with marshmallows while playing ukuleles till midnight.[8]

By virtue of her athletic prowess, Amelia was invited to join the Alpha Phi sorority, but once a member she came to dislike the unfairness of secret societies and argued for creating more to allow membership for all. Her stubbornness surfaced when she insisted more societies be formed, but Miss Sutherland refused to budge and instead chose to disband them entirely. Miss Sutherland created an Honor Board composed of five students, Amelia among them, to monitor the sorority girls and prevent them from meeting secretly. Activities such as the Honor Board honed her leadership skills, and she was voted class vice president after returning to Ogontz in the fall of 1917. As class motto Amelia chose "Honor is the foundation of courage." She also served as secretary of the Ogontz Red Cross chapter and a group named Christian Endeavor.

ON SUMMER BREAK THAT year, Amelia went back to Kansas City, then she vacationed for two weeks at Camp Gray, in Saugatuck, on the eastern shore of Lake Michigan, some forty miles from the old Isaac Otis homestead at Prairieville. Echoing her mother's fastidiousness, she complained about the primitive conditions at the camp—no electricity and substandard food, margarine instead of butter. She grumbled about missing swimming the first week because she was menstruating, although she avoided explicitly saying so in a letter to her mother, being prudish like most of her girlfriends. The camp opened a new world to Amelia, offering her the freedom to choose companions her own age who were not cousins or classmates. It was at Camp Gray that she met Gordon Pollack, who would enlist in the Army Air Corps, and Kenneth Merrill, her first boyfriend, with whom she would correspond for years to come.

Amy Earhart continued to monitor her daughter during her second year at the school, embarrassing Amelia with her barrage of letters to Miss Sutherland. Amelia wrote to her mother on October 31, 1917, "Dear Hen, don't write Miss S. letters of advice and warning. They go thru the whole faculty and come to me and I just shrivel. I am not overdoing [things] and all that is needed to bouncing health is plenty to eat and happiness. Consider me bursting."[9] Amy's concern for her daughter's low weight would continue for years, despite Amelia's good health.

While she was at Ogontz Amelia's feminist proclivities grew; she kept a newspaper clipping file of accomplished women, many of them a "first" or "only" in their fields. Among them were Mrs. E. E. Abernathy, Oklahoma's only woman bank president, and Helen H. Gardner, the first woman to hold the position of United States Civil Service Commissioner. However, Amelia held her own views on women's issues. Next to an article that urged legislators to pass laws removing discrimination against women in holding property and inheritances, she wrote, "This method is not sound. Women will gain economic justice by proving themselves in all lines of endeavor, not by having laws passed for them."[10] She clipped no notices of suffragettes.

In her school files were poems by Edna St. Vincent Millay (such as "First Fig": "My candle burns at both ends...") and Claude McKay, among others. Amelia wrote her first poem at age five and would continue to write them throughout her life, but she rarely succeeded in having them published. In her papers were a letter she sent to *Poetry* magazine on April 16, 1921, in which she wrote, "enclosed are four small efforts of a novice," signed with her pen name, Emil Harte, and a rejection slip sent by the magazine a month latter commenting on the "unusually promising" poems and asking "him" to send more later. Also in her files was a copy of *The Market Place for Manuscripts: A Guide for Successful Authors*.[11] Her often-quoted poem "Courage" would be published when she became famous.

In these voluminous files Amelia included no clippings of American women pilots, even though their daring feats and record flights captured national headlines before, during, and after her tenure at Ogontz. Two female trailblazers of this era were Ruth Law and Katherine Stinson. Ruth Law, ten years older than Amelia, was licensed in 1912 and flew in her first exhibition the same year, afterward becoming a skilled stunt flyer. Her greatest flight took place on November 19–

20, 1916, when she set three records flying nonstop 590 miles from Chicago to Hornell, New York. Offers poured in for her to endorse products and go on lecture tours, and boys and girls idolized her. She earned as much as $9,000 a week for stunting, and used her celebrity to support suffragettes and to advocate for her gender.[12] Daredevil stunt pilot Katherine Stinson, only six years older than Amelia, toured the States and Asia and also flew record flights. During the First World War both she and Ruth flew in fund-raising drives for the Red Cross and Liberty Loan Bonds. Although their accomplishments dazzled the public, they apparently held no interest for Amelia.

OVER THE CHRISTMAS HOLIDAYS, Amelia joined her sister and mother in Toronto, where Muriel attended St. Margaret's College, a preparatory school, while Edwin remained in Kansas City. What started as a holiday interlude became a life-changing event, as Amelia witnessed the ravages of the First World War: soldiers without limbs, blinded, or wounded in other horrific ways. After Great Britain had declared war on Germany on August 4, 1914, Canada and the other parts of the British Empire joined the hostilities. What cinched her decision to help in some way was the spectacle of four one-legged men holding onto each other while walking down the road.

Amelia returned to Ogontz in January, wracked by the tragedies she had seen. "I can't bear the thought of going back to school and being so useless," she wrote to her mother.[13] She ultimately left the school, dismissing all thoughts of graduating.[14] Returning to Toronto, she enrolled in a course to join a Voluntary Aid Detachment, or VAD, a group of civilians who served as assistant nurses, ambulance drivers, and cooks. These volunteer postings were not for the fainthearted; overseas, they worked on the front, too. The VAD British commander instructed her charges: "You are being sent to work for the Red Cross. You have to perform a task which will need your courage, your energy, your patience, your humility, your determination to overcome all difficulties."[15]

After training several months, Sister Amelia ("Sister" being the honorific title given female nurses) was posted to Spadina Military Hospital, located on what is now the campus of the University of Toronto, and worked there until shortly before the Armistice in November 1918. She cared for soldiers poisoned by gas and otherwise injured in trenches along the lethal Western Front. She also tended to pilots who had crashed in Europe and near Toronto, the center for the Royal Flying Corps Canada, during training exercises.

Amelia first fell for aviation in Toronto. Seeing the planes, hearing the airmen converse in the hospital, she became enamored with their spirit and the idea of flight. The flying activity was intense, with hundreds of planes buzzing around the hangars and grass fields in Toronto. Civilians were forbidden to fly in the planes, but on her free days, she, Muriel, and their friends spent time with the pilots and went to aerial exhibitions. At one such event she watched a stunt pilot perform loops, then dive low, toward her, and observed that "his little red airplane said something to me as it swished by." She also wrote that, unlike her friend who ran, she "stood her ground" with "mingled fear and pleasure" as the plane dove, thinking it might crash into her.[16]

Looking back in 1937 on this period, Amelia would claim "aviation in those days was very limited," and observe "about all a pilot could do was to joy-hop. . . . The idea that airplanes could be transportation as today entered nobody's noggin." Oddly, she omitted the stupendous role aviation had played in the First World War: bombing, surveillance and observation, and other technological advances, particularly in range and endurance, which soon translated into commercial air service. Even before the Armistice was signed, Europeans were planning commercial air routes to be flown when the war ended; in 1916 George Holt Thomas, founder of the De Havilland

Aircraft Company, organized an airline company that would first see service, from London to Paris, in 1919. The British R34 airship made the first trans-atlantic roundtrip flight in July 1919, flying from East Fortune, Scotland, to Newfoundland, Canada, and from there to Mineola, New York, before returning to Pulham, England. The French and the Germans, among others, had also laid plans to fly commercial passengers and would do so as early as 1919. Indeed, there were scheduled passenger flights as early as 1914 in the United States, $5 hops across Tampa Bay.[17]

As Amelia's grueling hospital job progressed, there was little time for visiting airfields and other pursuits. She worked twelve-hour shifts (with two hours off during afternoons), performing chores such as emptying bed pans, serving meals, and changing dressings on suppurating wounds and bloody stumps. Working with patients and witnessing their suffering contributed to her later becoming a pacifist. Adding to the overall distress and Amelia's workload was the outbreak of the Spanish influenza pandemic of 1918. The virus was capable of killing its victims within twenty-four hours, and world-wide an estimated fifty million people perished from the disease.

Run down and overworked, Amelia soon fell victim to influenza and then pneumonia, which required hospitalization. As a result of her illness she developed painful sinusitis. Its treatment in 1918, before antibiotics came into use, was an irrigation of the sinus cavities, or "washing outs," as she called them. She would endure chronic sinus infections throughout the rest of her life, seemingly aggravated by stress and general debilitation, sometimes after her longer flights.

In need of a lengthy convalescence, Amelia went to Northampton, Massachusetts, and stayed with her mother and Muriel, who was then study-ing in preparation for exams to enter Smith College. Though she complained of boredom to her friend Kenneth, she soon bought a banjo and took a course in automobile mechanics for female ambulance drivers, held at a local garage. She temporarily abandoned her interest in airplanes; Muriel would later write that Amelia was not interested in an aviation career while visiting Toronto, and that it was instead her insatiable curiosity that drew her to fly-ing exhibitions.

Edwin Earhart, meanwhile, wanted to leave the Midwest and move to California. He had begun to have health problems, and perhaps the warmer climate drew him to the West Coast. He asked his wife to join him in Los Angeles in the fall of 1919, after he settled in. Amy first wanted to splurge on a summer vacation, having received her portion of the proceeds from the recent sale of the Otis house in Atchison. By this time she was deferring many decisions to Amelia and asked her to locate a good area. Amelia chose to rent a cottage at Lake George in upstate New York, in the beautiful Adirondacks, a site popular with the well-heeled. There she and Muriel played tennis, canoed, swam, read poetry, and danced to phonograph records with their neighbors, Frank Stabler and his sister Marian. Tall, slender, and at twenty-three a year older than Amelia, Marian had graduated from Vassar the previous year and was studying art, and the two of them developed what would become a lifelong friendship.

As summer neared its close, Amelia, whose interest in medicine had developed in Toronto, decided to register at Columbia University in the University Extension Program. Courses she studied included biology, chemistry, and zoology, as well as French literature and psychology. While registering she changed her birth date to 1898; later, around 1926, she would try to shave another year off her age. She looked young but may have felt self-conscious around younger students, or perhaps it was vanity that led her to amend her date of birth. She rented a large, well-appointed room at 106 Morningside Drive in New York City, living frugally on an allowance her mother provided. In the zoology class she was one of only two women, the other being Louise de Schweinitz, a graduate of Smith College studying to fulfill the requirements needed to enter the Johns Hopkins School of Medicine. Amelia led Louise, a willing follower, in adventures at Columbia, notably climbing atop the dome of a library and exploring subterranean passages. Not that she gained useful knowledge exploring the tunnels, Amelia wrote, but "that could be said of other things one learns at college, too." Louise would later become a physician whose specialty was research, and she and Amelia remained close friends.[18]

Although burdened with a heavy course load, Amelia left Thursday evenings free to dine at the Stablers' apartment, after which she and Marian went to concerts at Carnegie Hall. As the year went on Marian became alarmed at Amelia's declining health and exhausting work habits. She developed dark circles under her eyes, lost weight, and got little sleep, establishing a pattern that would continue throughout the rest of her life. She was frail, but her endurance was remarkable at times. She shared this trait with her father, who, even when utterly fatigued, would awake refreshed from a short nap.

At the end of spring term, Amelia quit school, although she had earned good grades. She would later say she had simply decided against a medical career and make light of her decision. But in reality she didn't have the temperament to plod through years of higher education, and it's unlikely she would have remained a student even if her parents had not begged her to join them in Los Angeles. She was restless and ready for a change. She wrote her sister that she would try to keep her parents together until Muriel finished college and would then return to the East and live independently. Perhaps she said so with twinges of regret at leaving the East, but she could not know then how integrated her life would become with the burgeoning aviation industry in California.

4

FLYING LESSONS

WHEN AMELIA EARHART TRAVELED by train to Los Angeles, California, in 1920, she left behind all vestiges of her childhood. She was entering the postwar decade, a revolutionary period in which a disillusioned segment of American society cast off lingering bourgeois cultural norms and welcomed a new era. Aboard the train Amelia would have appeared demure, perhaps wearing a modest traveling suit, her golden waist-length hair likely pinned up in braided coils around her head. She had yet to encounter the decade's new fashions—skirt-length hems, long-waisted dresses of sheer silk or rayon fabrics, flesh-colored stockings, and bobbed hair. By the mid-1920s, though, her slender, boyish form, with no apparent hips or breasts, would perfectly epitomize the ideal feminine physique. This new style was but one sign of women's growing freedom and economic independence, which had been largely brought about by their wartime employment. The increasing popularity of the automobile, movies, and radio broadcasting hastened further changes.

In Los Angeles the Earharts lived at 1334 West Fourth Street in a large two-story house not far from Edwin's law office. Before Amy arrived, and well before Amelia did, Edwin had been befriended by a Christian Scientist neighbor, with whose support he finally conquered his addiction to alcohol. As in St. Paul, the house was much too large for the family, but this time Amy would actually take in boarders, renting rooms to three young men. One was handsome Sam Chapman, tall and dark haired, an engineering graduate from Tufts University and a native of Massachusetts. Serious and well read, he and Amelia shared many of the same interests, including the theater, swimming, tennis, and exploring local attractions, but not aviation. The two began dating, but Amelia also went out with other male friends.

Within a year after Amelia arrived on the West Coast, she would take her first paying job, learn to drive a car, and fly her first plane. "Aviation caught me," she wrote later about her transformation from eastern college student to West Coast pilot.[1] Southern California, popular with pilots because of its year-round temperate climate of dry, balmy air, was ideal for aircraft and flying. Local aviator Bobbi Trout, who would hold many records, said pilots learned the joy of flying most in this area.

Ten years before Amelia had disembarked from the train in Los Angeles, America's first international air meet was held over ten days in January 1910, at Dominquez Hill in the Los Angeles area. The exhibition, sanctioned by the Aero Club of America, drew an estimated two hundred thousand spectators, who thrilled to watch biplanes and monoplanes hurtle skyward. Daredevil pilots were flying the fastest, farthest, and highest as they set records in speed, endurance, and altitude, while capturing a portion of $70,000 in prize winnings. Hot-air balloons and dirigibles also competed. The famous French aviator Louis Paulhan, having brought two Blériot monoplanes and two Farman biplanes, reached a record altitude of 4,165 feet; American plane builder Glenn Curtiss, winner of the Gordon Bennett Trophy at Reims, France, the previous year, set a speed record of 55 miles per hour. Airman Lincoln Beachey, who would soon become popular for his death-defying stunts, also competed. One of the many spectators craving a ride but unable to get one was the future airplane builder, industrialist William Boeing, who learned to fly in a Martin biplane upon his return to Seattle.[2]

Of course more than climate attracted aviators to the region. An entrepreneurial spirit and a can-do attitude infused the area and fostered innovative ideas and experimentation, exactly what the new industry needed. In the area were brothers and airplane builders Allan and Malcolm Loughead, who changed their surname to the phonetic pronunciation Lockheed; and Donald Douglas, who would become famous as an airplane manufacturer. Before long, Amelia would cross paths with these luminaries. She and her first flight instructor, Neta Snook, would drop in on Douglas in 1921 to see his new plane, the Cloudster; after 1928 Amelia would use only Lockheed aircraft in her quest for records.

Los Angeles was also full of barnstormers, pilots who stunted in air circuses and gave rides to often terrified passengers. Many were war veterans hanging on to their dream of making a paying career in aviation by stunting in meets and establishing rustic airfields. The air circuses, the excitement, the buzzing of planes in the air, all would affect Amelia. The seed of her dream of taking to the skies had been planted in Toronto two years earlier. In December 1920 she and her father went to an air rodeo at Earl Daugherty's field in Long Beach, where pilots performed spins, loops, and dives amid a crowd of spectators. She urged her father to ask an official the cost of flying lessons and time required to learn. It took from five to ten hours, depending on the student's ability, and cost $1,000, Edwin reported to Amelia.[3] (In truth, at the time flight schools usually asked $250 to $500 for training.)

To satisfy her curiosity, the following day Edwin took her to Rogers Field, a small dirt strip near Wilshire Boulevard, and handed over $10 for her first passenger flight, a ten-minute joy ride with Frank Hawks, a former Army Air Corps pilot later famous for his speed records. Hawks looked her over and turned to a male bystander, telling him to sit in the cockpit with her. She didn't protest, figuring he did so lest she lose her nerve and attempt to jump from his plane. Besides, she reckoned it was unlikely he would listen to her, a woman, much less trust her. She put on a leather helmet and goggles before settling down for a ride to an altitude of 2,000 feet, with panoramic views of the Hollywood Hills and Pacific coastline.

For Amelia life crystallized the moment the little plane leaped into the air. "As soon as we left the ground, I knew I myself had to fly," she later wrote.[4] She had found her calling: it offered an exciting challenge, not to mention the thrill of being carried up from the earth into the air, where her destiny lay in her hands alone.

That evening she casually mentioned to her parents her desire to learn to fly, "knowing full well I'd die if I didn't."[5] They didn't take her seriously until a few days later, after she had signed up for lessons and proposed they pay for them. Neither Amy nor Edwin were inclined to subsidize their daughter's latest obsession, and Amelia took a job for the first time in her twenty-three years, working as a telephone company clerk to pay for her lessons. It was the first of several jobs she would hold in Los Angeles.

Amelia believed she would learn better from a woman flight instructor, and she heard of Anita "Neta" Snook, who was working at Kinner Field, on the east side of Los Angeles. In Iowa Neta had bought and rebuilt a Canuck, the Canadian version of the JN4 Jenny in which 90 percent of Americans had trained during the war years. In this machine she taught herself to fly, then barnstormed. She was licensed by the Fédération Aéronautique Internationale (FAI) around 1920. (In the United States neither pilots nor aircraft were required to be licensed until after 1926, but aviators needed an FAI license to obtain approval for their record flights.) Shortly afterward, Neta moved west and met the mechanical wizard Winfield Bertram Kinner. On his 210-acre field were a hangar, a small filling station serving both cars and planes, and a hamburger stand. His aircraft company, Kinner Airplane & Motor Corporation, built its first Airster, a biplane, in 1920, but would struggle mightily to survive in its first years.[6]

Both Neta Snook and Bert's wife, Cora Kinner, distinctly recalled Amelia and Edwin's first appearance at Kinner Field. Edwin wore a blue serge business suit, and Amelia, a brown suit and white gloves. They were the antithesis of the motley collection hanging around the field: grimy mechanics in coveralls and pilots in stained breeches. Twenty-four-year-old Neta looked the part, too. Dressed in dirty coveralls, her frizzy red hair falling about her face, she served as test pilot for the Kinner Airster, instructed new aviators, gave rides, and did aerial advertising. Neta may have been the only female instructor in California then.

Amelia appeared at her first lesson on January 3, 1921, toting a library book on aeronautics, the first of many technical books she would study at home and at the field. Amelia spent her weekends at Kinner Field, flying if weather and her budget permitted, since scrounging up enough money to fly and fill a gas tank was always a problem. While grounded, she and the other pilots rambled on about all things aviation. Slowly, she underwent a transformation from genteel woman to airfield hanger-on, cropping her long hair and wearing breeches, boots, and an oil-stained leather jacket.

She first trained with Neta in her Canuck, a dual-controlled biplane with tandem seating, the instructor occupying the rear seat. Neta explained the flight controls before taking her up, demonstrating the stick, which moved the ailerons on the wings (used for banking in the air) and the elevator on the tail (used to move the nose up or down). She also showed Amelia the rudder bar on the floor (rudders steer the plane on the ground, and move the nose left or right in the air to correct for yaw in turns). The Canuck was more than adequate, but soon the Kinner Airster caught Amelia's heart.

The lightweight Airster featured a 28-foot wingspan and a length of 21 feet 4 inches, with dimensions and weight considerably less than those of the Canuck and Jenny. Amelia would later describe the hardships of financing her training as "no pay, no fly, and no work, no pay," but she forked over $2,000 for a used Airster (the second one ever built), a purchase price four times that of the ubiquitous war-surplus Jennies.[7] The pretty Airster, painted yellow, had beckoned to Amelia, and she named it the *Canary*. No one could dissuade her from its purchase; Neta and her colleagues felt it was underpowered and a poor choice for a beginner. Its three-cylinder engine tended to clog with oil, contributing to the likelihood of stoppages. And compared to the Canuck and Jenny, it was difficult to land, with a tendency to ground loop (turn uncontrollably on the ground) in the lightest of crosswinds. Amelia rationalized the purchase by promoting its light weight: she could easily pick up the tail and move it around without a dolly. Its air-cooled engine, which weighed less than the Jenny's water-cooled engine, resulted in a lower gross weight. Amelia later wrote that hers was the first air-cooled motor in the country, but they had been used abroad before and during the First World War.

Amy Earhart paid for the Airster, using part of her inheritance, although Amelia and Muriel contributed a small portion toward its cost. Amy later said Edwin didn't think aviation safe and "refused to go up...his attitude was against it. I realized that if she [Amelia] wanted to be a flyer someone in the family had to be interested and had to go with her and help her out."[8] Still, $2,000 could have paid for many hours of advanced training and bought a few Jennies. Bert softened the financial blow by providing hangar space and mechanical work in exchange for the right to use Amelia's Airster for demonstrations. Amelia began training in the Airster after four hours of lessons in the Canuck and had to learn to fly all over again, according to Neta. After Amelia had trained 8 hours and 45 minutes, Neta wanted her to fly alone, but she obstinately refused.

Contradictions about Amelia's training, which appear in the books she published in 1928 and 1932, could stem from her aversion to keeping accurate logbook records. She loathed paperwork throughout her career. In Amelia's first book she wrote that Neta instructed her for only a few hours. Neta, writing many years later, disagreed with Amelia's version of her training. Neta stated that she gave Amelia twenty hours of dual instruction before 1921, when she left aviation at her fiancé's insistence. (After marrying, Neta never returned to flying.)[9] In 1932, Amelia wrote that she spent "about the conventional ten hours" with her instructors before she soloed.[10] At least they agreed that after Neta departed Amelia underwent flight instruction with John Montijo, one of Bert Kinner's best pilots and a movie stuntman. Amelia insisted John teach her aerobatics before she soloed.

John thought Amelia was a good, attentive pilot with a keen interest in navigation and aerobatics and soloed her after an additional seven hours of instruction. Neta, on the other hand, thought Amelia took excessive risks—for example, wanting to land between power lines instead of over them—and described her as an occasional daydreamer whose concentration lapsed while flying. Cora Kinner also thought Amelia was prone to accidents and said her flying frightened her.

On one instruction flight, Amelia had pointed the nose of the Airster toward Long Beach into a strong headwind and assured Neta the gas tank was full because "Mr. Kinner always keeps it full." Neta immediately turned the small craft back to Kinner Field, where Bert was waiting anxiously. He had not filled the tank, and it turned out Amelia had not physically checked it during the preflight inspection, one of the most important duties assigned to students at the start of their training. Recalling this incident years later, Neta wrote, "I was almost angry at her. Perhaps I had misjudged her abilities." Some instructors, not as lenient as Neta, might have dropped her as a student. On another occasion, the Airster engine quit because Amelia had not refueled it, requiring a forced landing in a cabbage patch. Amelia had again shirked her responsibility but admitted no wrong doing when she later wrote of the incident in *20 Hrs., 40 Min.,* published in 1928. Indeed, reading her description one comes away believing that it was Neta who had erred.[11]

To be sure, in the early 1920s engines were unreliable, with failures being commonplace and emergency landings frequent, and at times Amelia showed better judgment. On another flight with Neta to observe the huge Cloudster, Donald Douglas's new aircraft at Goodyear Field, the Airster developed engine trouble at takeoff. Seeing they wouldn't clear a eucalyptus grove at the end of the strip, Amelia pulled the nose up and stalled the plane to avoid the trees. They landed hard, damaging the undercarriage and propeller, but Neta admitted she would have done the same. She crawled out of the plane only to see Amelia calmly powdering her nose—should reporters turn up, she said.

While flying alone, Amelia would experience similar incidents. She once nosed over in a muddy field; on another unexpected landing she hit six-foot-tall dry weeds with such force that the plane flipped over, her seat belt broke, and she was thrown from the cockpit. She walked away unhurt and continued her training in spite of her mishaps.

AMELIA WOULD LATER WRITE about these early years, "For me flying was a sport and not a circus....I appeared in public only on special occasions."[12] She went on to say she wasn't good enough for racing or other public flying at the time. But her humility didn't preclude a few appearances at air shows and two attempts at record-setting in the Los Angeles area.

She was also getting press as one of the few women flyers in the area. In August 1922, the *Los Angeles Examiner* ran a picture of Amelia in her flying togs, a leather coat, and goggles, with accompanying text noting that she hoped to fly across the continent the next year and drop in at Vassar College to take a postgraduate course. Talking about her proposed trip, she voiced what was to become a familiar refrain: "I don't crave publicity or anything but it seems to me it would be the greatest fun..."[13] Throughout her career she would claim that "fun" was what compelled her to fly and establish records, and she even titled her second book *The Fun of It.*

In October 1922 Amelia made her first attempt at a record flight. According to Muriel, who was visiting her family at the time, Amelia

accompanied her and their father to an air meet at Rogers Field then disappeared, saying she couldn't sit with them. The mystery unfolded when they
learned Amelia had set an unofficial women's altitude record of 14,000 feet
at the meet. A barograph installed in her *Canary* and sealed by the Aero
Club of Southern California confirmed the altitude. (Despite Amelia's claim
of a record, Ruth Law had set a women's altitude record of 14,700 feet on
September 28, 1917, five years before Amelia's flight; and Baroness de la
Roche had reached 15,700 feet in 1919, her claim having been certified by the
Aero Club of France. All of these records were unofficial, however, because
the FAI did not establish women's records until 1928.)[14]

Amelia felt confident she could achieve a higher altitude—her Airster
engine had started to falter at 12,000 feet on the first attempt—and set
about trying for a new record some weeks later at Rogers Field, in the fall
of 1922. At 10,000 feet she ran into clouds and sleet, and then dense fog
2,000 feet higher. She was totally enveloped in fog, confused, and without instruments to help orient her. "I kicked the ship into a tail spin," she
would write in 1928, and emerged into clear air at 3,000 feet above the
ground before landing. She was lucky she lived, said one of the old-timers
after looking at her barograph trace. "Suppose the fog had lasted all the
way to the ground," he commented.[15] She shrugged him off, but despite
her nonchalance, she undoubtedly would have known that she should have
descended at the first glimpse of thick clouds rather than climbing into
murk. It's possible the craft had gone into a spin involuntarily, though her
instructor John had taught her spin entries and recoveries. A spin occurs
when an aircraft's wings lose lift and stall, and the aircraft then rotates
downward. A spin is a safe maneuver if executed properly because its low
speed does not put excessive stress on the airframe. In contrast, had she
entered a high-speed spiral dive, stresses on the Airster could have pulled
it apart.

Two months before her flight examination, on March 17, Amelia flew
in an air rodeo celebrating the grand opening of the new Glendale Airport,
located about 7 miles from downtown, near the Los Angeles River. The
billing read: LADIES SPORT PLANE SPECIAL: MISS AMELIA EARHART FLYING KIN-
NER AIRSTER AND MISS ANDREE PYRE FLYING A SPORT FARMAN. Bert Kinner,
given attractive lease terms, had already moved to the field and built a hangar

where he manufactured Airsters. Two months later, Amelia earned her flying license, as reported in the June 4, 1923, issue of *Aviation*:

KANSAS GIRL AVIATOR LICENSED

Miss Amelia M. Earhart, a native of Atchison, Kans., was granted an airplane pilot certificate by the National Aeronautic Association on May 16. Miss Earhart, who resides in Los Angeles, is the first woman licensed by the N.A.A., although several American women hold F.A.I. pilot certificates issued by the former Aero Club of America. The first American woman to obtain a pilot certificate was Miss Harriet Quimby, a Californian, who was breveted in 1911. Miss Earhart used on her qualifying flights a Kinner Airster airplane with 60 h. p. motor.

That Amelia held the first NAA license was owing merely to the date it was issued. The NAA was incorporated in 1922 as the Aero Club's successor, after which it issued all pilot licenses in the United States, until the Department of Commerce assumed this responsibility. Eleven American women had earned FAI licenses by 1917.

From her first lesson in 1921 until she was licensed in 1923, Amelia had turned into a confident pilot, at least comfortable enough to fly as a featured attraction at public events. Learning to fly is not an easy task, requiring confidence and the ability to make quick decisions. An aviator must accurately picture herself in three dimensions, knowing her position and altitude, and though today instruments aid in this, they can't replace the intuitive "feel" of flight. Amelia was not a natural flyer and had struggled throughout her instruction. In contrast, in 1928 her friend Louise Thaden would be licensed after only 5 hours and 15 minutes of flight time. Neta Snook had taught herself to fly, as did many early aviators. When Amelia learned to fly, trainer airplanes were basic with little instrumentation and no radios, and there were no regulations affecting pilots. Becoming a pilot then was easier than it is today. Many women and men were better pilots than Amelia, but her persistence and bravery set her apart. And despite her risk-taking and occasional flippancy, she never lost sight of the inherent danger in flying.

5

TO BOSTON

IN 1923 THE REMAINDER of Amy Earhart's inheritance was lost in an ill-fated investment. She was looking to replenish her rapidly depleting capital, and Amelia's friend Sam Chapman recommended a scheme to give a quick return on her investment. He knew of a young civil engineer and his partner, Californians who were trying to start a new business hauling gypsum near Moapa, Nevada. They could find no bank willing to extend a loan, but after Edwin and Amelia gave the project their stamp of approval, Amy loaned the two men $20,000, virtually all the money she had.

Within a year a flash flood submerged the gypsum mine in Moapa, and the engineer drowned when a bridge collapsed in rushing water, wiping out most of Amy's outlay. The tragedy was partly preventable, too. The local Ute Indians had predicted the storm and told the men, but they were rushing to fulfill a contract and ignored the warning.

The Earharts were stunned by the loss. Muriel was forced to drop out of Smith College at the end of her junior year, move in with her family, and take a teaching position in Huntington Beach. She wrote later, "When a substantial legacy comes into a family, one expects to see the end to all financial worries and also to find that the capital sum remains intact, no matter how

often it is drawn upon."[1] She seemed not to understand the basic arithmetic
by which a debit reduces a balance. One has to wonder how the Earharts
spent $25,000 in five years at a time when a middle-class family of four could
live well on $1,500 a year. Amy had financed the girls' college and Amelia's
plane, but perhaps other foolish investments had depleted her funds.

Feeling overwhelmed and guilty for having supported the ill-fated min-
ing venture, Amelia sold her *Canary* to help rescue the family finances. A
former war pilot, Maynard Morley, bought the Airster and on his first flight
flew stunts at only 300 feet above ground. Amelia and Bert Kinner stood
rooted, watching his antics, and becoming alarmed, Bert called for an ambulance. Minutes later the plane dove to the ground, exploded into fire, and
killed Morley and his passenger. Amelia thought the accident was appalling
and attributed it to Morley's overconfidence and his desire to show off.

The Airster was the last plane she would own for five years, though she
soon bought a new engine Bert was designing that was not ready for production. Amelia had hoped to find an airframe and other parts to combine with
the engine but her budget didn't allow it. Occasionally she flew other small
planes, but as a former plane owner she found having to rent demeaning.
Besides, being short of cash, she couldn't afford to spend much money on
flying. Even buying gasoline was usually out of the question. Still, the field
was a sanctuary from the gloom of the Earhart household, where Amy had
become bitter and argumentative after losing her money, and Edwin's health
was declining. Amelia felt adrift but called forth sufficient initiative to rent a
small apartment on Sunset Boulevard in Hollywood, closer to the field.

She also befriended various men at the field, including mechanic Lloyd
Royer, who partnered with her in a local hauling business, using a truck
salvaged from the mine disaster. Smitten with her, in 1923 Lloyd proposed,
but she told him she wasn't interested in marrying anyone. In the same year,
though, she became engaged to Sam Chapman, according to Muriel. Amelia
would never write about Sam, and she did not wear a ring, but she dated him
until 1928, when she became famous and announced to the press that she
was no longer engaged. Muriel thought highly of Sam, as did Amy, but he
was a staid New Englander, no match for Amelia's pluck and courage. He
was loving and patient and devoted to Amelia but didn't condone her flying,
and Muriel was certain he would insist Amelia stay home if they married.

IN EARLY 1924 EDWIN decided he had enough of his marriage and sued for an uncontested divorce. Amy was devastated. Her upbringing had led her to regard divorce as unthinkable, and she found the very thought traumatizing. She'd had grounds to leave Edwin decades earlier because of his alcoholism, and her parents had offered to support her and her children, had she done so. He had helped to spend most of her inheritance, while she had sustained him in all ways during his various troubles, and now that she was being cast aside, she would bear the stigma that branded a divorcée.

Distraught, Amy moved into Amelia's apartment on Sunset Boulevard. More than ever before, Amelia acted as a mother to Amy and would do so for the remainder of her life. Amy remained childlike, unable to maintain a budget, to live within her means, to say no to a friend or relative wanting money. Throughout Amy's long life she would financially help family members and friends, even when she had little to give—and even when it was Amelia's money. Amelia rarely complained of the burden her relatives imposed, although their behavior was exasperating, to say the least, and she would continue to give generously of her money.

HER PARENT'S MARRIAGE ENDED, Amelia saw no reason to remain in Los Angeles. In 1920 she had told her sister she would eventually return east, and now Muriel and Amy prepared to join her in the move. Edwin would stay behind, comfortably employed and cultivating his spiritual side with his new Christian Scientist friends. Regardless of his failings as a parent Amelia still loved him and would remain loyal to him for the rest of his life, providing him with financial support in his later years, even after he remarried.

Before the summer was upon them, the Earhart women made plans to relocate to the Boston area. Intent on furthering her teaching credentials, Muriel boarded a train to Boston, where she would take a summer course at Harvard. Sam Chapman also headed to Massachusetts and would soon be employed as an engineer. Amelia, whose chronic sinusitis had returned with a vengeance, underwent an operation before leaving and had no qualms about letting the $500 medical bill remain unpaid for over a year. She had more important uses for her money.

She and her mother bought a used 1922 Kissel Speedster Gold Bug, a beautiful roadster renowned for its long, low design, popular with sportsmen and movie stars. Painted "Kissel chrome yellow," the six-cylinder, 61-horse-power automobile was known for its pep and good steering qualities. As before, Amy and Amelia used their scarce resources to splurge when less expensive alternatives were available. In 1924 a new Gold Bug retailed for $2,085, and Amelia would have paid at least $1,000 for her used roadster, a much higher price than a new Model T Ford, which could be purchased for about $300.[2] Amelia sold her Kinner engine, and Amy offered to pay for the trip from what little remained of her inheritance.

Traveling in automobiles over long distances in 1924 posed countless problems: most roads were unpaved; U.S. highway route numbers didn't exist; filling stations were infrequent. The 1924 Rand McNally *Road Atlas* recommended that motorists carry shellac to fix a leaky radiator and cork to jerry rig a blown gasket, and suggested rubbing an onion on the windshield to keep the glass free of mist.[3]

The six-week odyssey took them to Sequoia, Yosemite, and Crater Lake, then north into the Canadian Rockies, where they visited Banff and Lake Louise before heading to Glacier Park, Montana, and Yellowstone in Wyoming. It was a leisurely 7,000-mile drive, open to changes in the itinerary. As Amy recalled, they diverted "if we saw a road sometime that looked interesting." Amelia would fondly remember seeing the airmail beacons at Cheyenne, Wyoming, a stop on the U.S. Post Office's airmail route.[4] Amelia's Kissel arrived in Boston plastered with tourist stickers, around which curious people gathered to inquire about her itinerary and the road conditions—such travel was still very much a novelty.

In the latter weeks of the trip headaches and pain began to torment Amelia, a condition exacerbated from driving in the open air. Within a week after arriving in Boston, she underwent a successful operation at Massachusetts General Hospital, whereby a small piece of cartilage was removed from her nasal passage to allow better drainage of the sinuses. Following a lengthy convalescence with Amy and Muriel, Amelia moved to New York, renting a room in Manhattan. With her was her car, a luxury she refused to part with. She renewed her friendship with Marian Stabler, spending many weekends and once an entire month at her family's house at Great Neck, Long Island, while still struggling to regain her strength after the surgery.

IN FEBRUARY 1925 AMELIA again enrolled at Columbia, taking two courses toward a major in engineering: elementary physics and intermediate algebra. She earned a B in the former, but a C- in the latter jeopardized her status as a student. In April she left school, broke. With her beloved Kissel, she returned to Medford, a suburb of Boston, where Muriel was teaching in a junior high school. To beef up her grade average Amelia went to summer school at Harvard, getting an A in trigonometry, which put her back on track toward her major. Right away she applied to Massachusetts Institute of Technology for a scholarship but was turned down, and it was this rejection that finally brought an end to her college ambitions. She wrote to Marian, "No, I did not get into MIT, as planned, owing to financial difficulties. No, I am not coming to New York, much, ah, much as I should like doing it. When I leave Boston I think I'll never go back."[5]

Amelia would claim in 1932 that she had worked twenty-eight different jobs and hoped to have another 228: "Experiment! Meet new people. That's better than any college education. You will find the unexpected everywhere as you go through life. By adventuring about, you become accustomed to the unexpected."[6] Perhaps this was rationalization on her part, but she was probably sincere: hers was to become a brilliant success story—and she had no degree. At age twenty-eight, she had abandoned nursing, flying, college, and a plethora of part-time jobs. Now she tried teaching, following in her sister's lead. Marian learned she was tutoring "blind guys in Trig."[7]

Over the next two years a series of part-time jobs occupied Amelia, as she taught English to foreign students in the Massachusetts University Extension program and served as a nurse-companion at a sanatorium. (She left after three months, wanting a higher salary.) It was through her position as a social worker at Denison House, a settlement house in Boston, that Amelia found her next calling.

The settlement house had been founded in 1892 by three college-educated women who looked forward to a "time when there should be no more barriers between workers of any kind and the so-called 'leisure class.'" It was located at 93 Tyler Street in the Old South Cove area of Boston, where old row houses were joined together in a polyglot neighborhood of Italians, Greeks, Syrians, and Chinese. The facilities offered sports for boys and girls, clubs, a library, a clinic, dancing, a gymnasium, and classes in English literature. Although Amelia was inexperienced as a social worker, she so impressed Marion Perkins, the head worker at Denison, with her "poise and charm...her quiet sense of humor, the frank direct look in her grey eyes," that she was hired for half-time work in the early fall of 1926.[8]

During her first year there Amelia taught English to foreign-born men and women and made home visits. A year after she started, in October 1927, Perkins promoted her to a full-time position, which came with living quarters and a change of duties, supervising the pre-kindergarten children and girls ages five through fourteen. She was appointed secretary of the staff and elected to secretary of the settlement's board of directors. Amelia treated the children well and in turn was adored by them and their parents. She gave her charges rides in the Kissel, piling them in and dashing around the neighborhood or transporting them to their medical appointments. As Muriel recalled, however, she retained her aversion to paperwork, "and it irked her to have to fill out forms and answer questionnaires."[9]

Amelia and Sam Chapman were still engaged at this time, and they often double-dated with friends as well as with Muriel and her boyfriend, but Sam considered her social work at the settlement house beneath her. Muriel, Amy, and Sam expected Amelia to eventually tire of life as a single woman—or spinster, in their eyes—but she had no such intentions, as she told her family: "I know what I want to do and I expect to do it—married or single!" There had been no mention of a wedding.[10]

THE BENEFITS OF A permanent job, with weekends off, enabled Amelia to return to flying in 1927. Her interest in aviation was renewed when Bert Kinner asked her to find an agency in Boston for his new airplane and air-cooled engines. She found no takers, though her contact with businessmen at the Boston Chamber of Commerce would later prove helpful, and she soon joined the Boston chapter of the National Aeronautic Association, to which she would be appointed an officer that year. Shortly after, Bert hired an agent, a young architect named Harold T. Dennison, who already owned land on which to build a commercial airport in the Boston suburb of Quincy.

Amelia's maturity and flying background impressed Dennison, and he signed her on as one of five incorporators of his concern, after she scraped together a few dollars to buy shares. She wrote to Marian Stabler on August 1 that she had helped decorate the new office and the hangar, using "orange, black and blue, with a few spots of lavender and green thrown in.... Though I haven't a real job for the summer, I am kept pretty busy doing things for Denison House and Dennison Airport. The field opens on Tuesday next for flying in full force."[11]

She was also flying with local pilots and making a name for herself in Boston newspapers. She seemed to have drummed up some of the press coverage herself, and she was not at all averse to publicity. Most articles inflated Amelia's aeronautical achievements, but there is no record of her attempting to correct reporters. Perhaps she felt it was not necessary or that it was just plain impossible. One article claimed she had logged 500 hours of flight time, a high amount of hours considering what she and her friends said of her background and lack of money in Los Angeles. Another identified her as a member of the flying staff at Dennison and said she had soloed after less than ten hours' instruction in 1918—and had established a woman's altitude record two years later. She was "very much a feminist," the piece continued, and the only licensed woman pilot in New England. She may have been a feminist, but the other statements were not true, as her friends and fellow pilots could attest.[12]

By now Amelia had assumed a new mission—promoting women in all their endeavors, particularly in aviation—and she freely expressed it to the press. In September she wrote to Ruth Nichols, an attractive Wellesley College graduate and socialite from Rye, New York, who had received her FAI certificate a year after Amelia did, in 1924. After introducing herself as a fellow FAI licensee, Amelia solicited her opinion: "What do you think about the advisability of forming an organization composed of women who fly?" She asked too whether the club should include women nonpilots who worked in the aviation industry and concluded the letter saying, "I can not claim to be a feminist but do rather enjoy seeing women tackling all kind of new problems—new for them, that is." Ruth replied positively and countered by asking Amelia to clarify her ideas, and nominated her as chairperson of a governing committee for a forthcoming group, which would become the Ninety-Nines.[13]

In January 1928, Ruth herself would garner publicity for a twelve-hour nonstop flight from Rockaway Naval Station, New York, to Biscayne Bay, Miami—about 1,200 miles. Copilot Harry Rogers, owner of the Fairchild pontoon plane used on the trip, accompanied her, as well as businessman Major M. K. Lee. From that point on Ruth and Amelia would become friendly rivals in their record attempts.

Amelia was a natural leader, at ease mingling with both superiors and peers. Her awkward young adult years behind her, she was discovering an increased sense of purpose, becoming more independent, and winning praise in her job and in aviation. She had transcended the limits imposed by her demanding family and was relishing her newfound freedom. She was in many respects finally her own woman, confident and happy.

In 1922 the *Los Angeles Examiner* had quoted Amelia as saying she wanted to fly a plane across the country. Whether she spoke seriously or whimsically, at that time long-distance flying was in its infancy, although definitely possible. Established air fields in America were sparse and navigation consisted of using a compass, road maps, and the "iron compass"—railroad tracks. In 1923 the very experienced Lieutenant John Macready and Lieutenant Oakley Kelley, flying a Fokker T-2 airplane, had made the first nonstop transcontinental flight, in twenty-seven hours, navigating solely with a compass and railroad maps. It is possible Amelia could have flown a comparably long journey in 1924, but it was highly unlikely she would have succeeded without a financial sponsor and mechanical help along the way. When she was finally to fly across America in 1928, she would be plagued by problems— and aviation had advanced immensely by that time. Even mechanical wizard Bert Kinner encountered problems when flying a plane from Los Angeles to Boston in 1927; when a cylinder blew, he was forced to wait a week for the factory to express a replacement to him.

In Boston, Amelia's growing local celebrity, boosted by her membership in the local chapter of the NAA and her earnest pleas to local businessmen to support aviation, would set the stage for what was to become a life-changing flying opportunity. In April 1928 Captain Hilton H. Railey—a former Army Air Corps pilot, a public relations man, and a friend of George Palmer Putnam— was seeking a woman pilot to join a remarkable adventure soon to unfold. He received a suggestion from a member of the NAA, retired Rear Admiral Reginald K. Belknap: "I know a young social worker who flies. I'm not sure how many hours she's had, but I do know that she's deeply interested in aviation—and a thoroughly fine person. Call Denison House and ask for Amelia Earhart."[14]

6

PREPARATIONS

ON AN AFTERNOON IN early April 1928 at Denison House, Amelia brushed off a young messenger asking her to take a telephone call. Only when he persisted did she reluctantly leave the group of children clamoring for her attention. Over the phone Hilton Railey identified himself and inquired if she were willing to undertake "something for aviation which might be hazardous."[1] Amelia began to grill him, asking for details about the proposal and about him personally, including two references. He provided the latter but refused to divulge more until meeting her in person. Curious, she agreed to see him in his office that evening, but took along her employer Miss Perkins as a precaution.

The moment Amelia entered his office Railey was struck by her resemblance to Colonel Charles A. Lindbergh, in particular her slim build, Nordic blond hair, fair complexion, and Midwestern manner of speaking: confident yet soft spoken. After probing her background, he knew she was the right sort of person the project's sponsor required, representative of American women.

"I might as well lay the cards on the table," said Railey. "Would you fly the Atlantic?"[2] He was seeking a replacement for a transatlantic flight; the previous pilot—whose identity he kept secret for the time being—had had to abandon the expedition for personal reasons and insisted on a woman substitute.

"Yes," Amelia blurted out after a minute's thought. She had conditions and questions, but these would be addressed at a later formal interview, Railey said.

The man Railey thought she resembled, Charles Lindbergh, had flown solo from New York to Paris in his single-engine *Spirit of St. Louis*, landing at Le Bourget aerodrome on May 21, 1927, just a year earlier.[3] He had been the first person to fly the Atlantic solo, and the good looking, twenty-five-year-old Minnesotan's takeoff had been captured and depicted worldwide on newsreels, a relatively new medium. Overnight, he became an international hero, having bested all the other Atlantic contenders, and assumed an almost mythic status. Offers worth millions of dollars followed, including requests for endorsements, but he declined most, having negotiated an exclusive series of articles with the *New York Times* and a book deal with G. P. Putnam's Sons.

ALTHOUGH OTHER PILOTS HAD flown the Atlantic before Lindbergh, his was the first solo flight and, at 3,600 miles nonstop, was much farther than previous crossings from Newfoundland, a popular launch site. In early May, before his flight, two Frenchmen had disappeared attempting a flight from Le Bourget to New York in hopes of winning the $25,000 Orteig prize, which was to be awarded to the first pilot to fly nonstop between New York and Paris. Many others perished in takeoff accidents on both sides of the Atlantic.

"Atlantic fever" still raged throughout the world in 1928, but not on the grand scale that had preceded Lindbergh's Orteig-winning flight. Several women resolved to be the first woman to cross the Atlantic, an accomplishment that would bestow instant international celebrity and riches. As an active flyer in 1927, Amelia would have experienced the enormous repercussions of Lindbergh's flight and possibly witnessed his reception in Boston. Although she would not write of his visit or influence, she probably harbored a secret ambition to make an Atlantic flight—what pilot would not?—so it was not surprising she had seized the opportunity Railey presented. She would have been watching closely the dangerous attempts made by other women.

On August 31, 1927, Princess Anne Lowenstein-Wertheim, age sixty-two, and her skilled crew departed England on a westward flight toward New York. Their Fokker disappeared over the ocean. Just over a month later, two American women, licensed pilot Ruth Elder and real-estate broker Frances Wilson Grayson, made separate attempts to accomplish the flight, despite the advice of experienced pilots to wait until the following spring. The window for making a successful crossing was narrow, with meteorological considerations being paramount. Storms and snow and icing conditions could bring down a flying machine in minutes.

On October 11, Ruth Elder, a vivacious twenty-three-year-old, departed New York with her good friend and flight instructor George Haldeman in poor weather, flying a Stinson. When no word was received from them after three days, people feared the worst, but a day later news broke. After they had traveled some 2,600 miles, engine trouble had developed, forcing Elder and Haldeman to ditch beside a Dutch freighter, which took them aboard. (They had taken the wise precaution of flying over shipping routes.) Minutes later their Stinson exploded in flames. It was Ruth's last attempt to cross, and she eventually turned to a career in vaudeville and the movies.

Ruth was roundly criticized for the failure of the flight, which was deemed a publicity stunt by newspapers and the public alike. The press scorned her "flashy flying costume, orange rouge, and carmined lips," and the *Literary Digest* quoted one journalist as saying, "Men in the summer may strive to equal Lindbergh. Women should stay home."[4]

Meanwhile, Frances Grayson impudently promised success, saying she would be the first woman to cross the Atlantic. In October, after two attempts in a Sikorsky amphibian aircraft, the last reaching 500 miles out, her pilot Wilmer Stultz refused to try again so late in the year. Furious with his decision, she assembled another crew and on December 23 launched from New York, headed for Newfoundland. Two hours later her Sikorsky was sighted off the coast of Cape Cod, but was never seen again.[5]

While Grayson and Elder were planning their flights, Mabel Boll, an American adventurer living in Paris, was adding to the bedlam, declaring she would be the first woman to make an east-to-west crossing of the Atlantic.

Attractive and brash, Mabel was not a pilot, claiming that flying was men's work. The press fawned over her because she knew the value of publicity and readily exploited her name. Preening for pictures, she wore two huge diamond rings, one of 62 karats and the other of 48, and an assortment of other baubles, a getup that earned her the nickname Queen of Diamonds. While in Europe she offered promoter Charles Levine $50,000 for the use of his machine, a Bellanca plane that had successfully crossed in June 1927, and he grudgingly agreed. But his offer was conditioned on the plane being crated on a ship back to America, from where they would launch to Europe. In the fall she sailed back to the States, where she awaited her chance for fame. On March 5, 1928, she accompanied Levine and his pilot, Wilmer Stultz (who had sensibly not caved in to Frances Grayson's demands the previous year), on the first nonstop flight from New York to Havana, Cuba, 1,400 miles, in the Bellanca. She made the front page of the *New York Times* with this feat, a first for a woman, but it merely whetted her appetite for a transatlantic flight.

A week later, on March 13, the Honourable Elsie Mackay, spirited daughter of a peer and a former actress admired for her silver Rolls-Royce, fast horses, and jewelry, "muffled herself almost beyond recognition and stealthily departed" from England for America with the one-eyed veteran pilot Captain Walter G. R. Hinchliffe. Fearing reprisal, she had not informed her family of the proposed takeoff. Despite their extensive aviation backgrounds—she, licensed five years; he, a former military pilot—they disappeared over the Atlantic in their Stinson, parts of which washed up in Donegal, Ireland, months later. Aviators were stunned at their departure: it was too early in the season for such air travel, and icing and fog had likely caused their demise.[6]

This latest vanishing act increased Charles Levine's concerns about making another crossing, and he promptly canceled his agreement with Mabel Boll. She in turn went to Wilmer Stultz, who committed to serving as her pilot on an Atlantic crossing. Now they needed an aircraft, and Mabel told reporters they were in the process of purchasing a Fokker from Commander Richard Byrd for a flight attempt in May. Commander Byrd, a pilot and explorer, was famous for making the first flight over the North Pole, in 1927. (Whether he was actually first was later disputed.)

In the face of these transatlantic disasters, it was remarkable that Amy Phipps Guest remained determined to become the first woman to cross the

Atlantic. The fifty-five-year-old American heiress, daughter of Henry Phipps, a former partner in Carnegie Steel, was an aviation enthusiast, although not a pilot. In her youth she was an avid sportswoman, an excellent rider, and a keen participant in Kenyan safaris led by the great hunter Baron Bror Von Blixen. Following the lead of other rich young American girls, she married into the British aristocracy. Her husband, the Right Honourable Frederick Guest, was a first cousin and a close friend of Winston S. Churchill, and briefly held the position of British Secretary of State for Air. A licensed aviator, in the early 1930s he served a prestigious posting as Master in the Guild of Air Pilots and Air Navigators.

Amy Guest surreptitiously went about the task of procuring an aircraft and pilot for her mission, and told no one in her family except her younger brother Howard. On her behalf, David T. Layman, the Phipps family lawyer, began negotiations with the Fokker's owner, Jell-O millionaire Donald Woodward, the sponsor of Commander Byrd's forthcoming expedition to the Antarctic. Byrd had decided to use a donated Ford Trimotor instead.

But within two weeks of Mabel's appearance in the *Times*, Amy Guest had leased the Fokker through Layman and assembled a crew chosen by Commander Byrd. Wilmer Stultz had decamped, agreeing to fly for Amy. He enlisted Louis Gordon as copilot and mechanic, and they flew the Fokker to Boston, where it was converted to a seaplane and otherwise equipped for the journey. Wilmer "Bill" Stultz, at twenty-eight, was a veteran of both the Army Air Corps and the Navy, a former employee of the Curtiss Export Company who had delivered forty planes to Rio de Janeiro and trained Brazilian military pilots to fly them, and a test pilot for Fokker. Louis "Slim" Gordon was also an Army Air Corps veteran. Mrs. Guest had named the craft *Friendship* to signify goodwill in Anglo-American relations.

After another two weeks Howard Phipps became more fretful as his sister's proposed flight neared. Finally he told her son Winston of her plans, and a furor erupted on both sides of the Atlantic, from her husband in England and her children attending American schools. Absolutely not, they decreed. Winston even threatened to drop out of college. Whether Amy was deterred by this or was having second thoughts herself, she was determined that if she could not go, she would find a replacement and foot all the bills. Again she summoned David Layman, instructing him to choose in her place an attractive, educated American woman, preferably a pilot. She had to possess pleasing manners and be above reproach to the more discerning English she would meet upon her arrival.

BESIDES AMELIA EARHART, THERE were other American women aviators who clearly fit the description given by Amy Guest. The most likely candidate would have been Ruth Nichols, the well-known pilot with whom Amelia had been corresponding. There exist two different published reasons as to why she was not chosen for the flight: In her autobiography Ruth wrote that "this striking likeness [to Charles Lindbergh] . . . won Amelia the opportunity for her first trans-Atlantic flight." Mrs. Guest, Ruth explained, had asked George Palmer Putnam to find "a girl who looked like Lindbergh." Yet Muriel Earhart claimed Ruth had been ill and needed time to recover, thus she missed the chance.[7]

One of the key figures in realizing Amy Guest's vision was George Palmer Putnam. Born in 1887 in Rye, New York, he was the scion of the illustrious publishing firm G. P. Putnam's Sons. A brilliant promoter with a knack for showmanship, and a hustler of unparalleled talent, George revolutionized the company's business strategies. Among his innovations were books written to order—whereby the publisher sought out an author for a specific idea—and books that were ghostwritten for celebrities. His successes included true-life adventure books written in the first person, such as *Skyward* by Richard Byrd, and Lindbergh's "*WE*." In Putnam's home was displayed a framed canceled check made out to Lindbergh for the phenomenal figure of $100,000, which represented his *initial* royalty payment.[8]

The humorist Corey Ford would describe Putnam, otherwise known as "Gyp" or G. P., as a "skilled conjurer who could palm an author, pull a best seller out of a hat, flourish his wand and transform a channel swimmer or explorer or aviator into a national sensation."[9] His entrepreneurial skills had bloomed at age twenty-four, in 1909, after he moved to Bend, Oregon, for fortune, adventure, and the "roar of the West." There he purchased the local newspaper (mostly on credit), became mayor, wrote two books, and served as secretary to Oregon's governor before enlisting in the Army.

His striking bride, Dorothy Binney Putnam, a Wellesley College graduate and wealthy daughter of the Crayola crayon inventor, shared his love for the outdoors. She was also a renowned dinner hostess and entertained her husband's associates at the couple's swank Rye, New York, home, with or without George, since often he worked until midnight. The duo cut a handsome figure, she brunette and tall, he with close-cropped dark hair and standing six feet two, radiating charisma. It was said of George that a person either liked him or loathed him. He couldn't tolerate laziness and incompetence, and his explosive temper had severed many a friendship.

Not one to leave the glory of exploits to others, he himself explored Greenland in 1926, with his resultant scoops about his "battle" with a walrus and solving an old Arctic crime headlining major newspapers. A year later he took an expedition to Baffin Land. In both instances George's thirteen-year-old son David accompanied him and wrote about the trips as part of a series of best-selling adventure books he penned for boys.

According to Putnam, the entire selection for the transatlantic flight was based on happenstance when he "stumbled on an adventure-in-the-making which, once completed, certainly should provide a book." As George recounted, when he heard of the sale of Commander Byrd's Fokker to a wealthy woman planning a long flight, with the aircraft now located at a field in East Boston, he contacted his friend Hilton Railey. Within a day Railey had tracked down the Fokker and Wilmer Stultz, who—feeling loquacious after a few drinks—told him David Layman was the point person for the flight's sponsor. George recalled that Layman was "visibly relieved" at his offer to find a suitable American woman to fly the Atlantic. George again called Railey into action, which led to his discovery of Amelia Earhart.[10]

AND SO BEGAN AN interlude as Amelia impatiently awaited the formal interview Hilton Railey promised. After the initial meeting she sent him a note on May 2: "It is very kind of you to keep me informed, as far as you are able, concerning developments of the contemplated flight. As you may imagine my suspense is very great indeed."[11] Her work at Denison House occupied most of her time but she increased her aviation activities, too: Corresponding again with Ruth Nichols about forming a women's pilots' organization;

submitting an article about flying to *The Bostonian;* and writing a three-page letter to the local Chamber of Commerce suggesting methods of publicizing aviation.

Finally Amelia was invited to New York City for the interview by David Layman, John S. Phipps, and George Putnam. She arranged to stay overnight with Marian Stabler in Great Neck. The next day she proceeded to the meeting, a delicate balancing act about which she later wrote, "If I were found wanting on too many counts I should be deprived of a trip" but if "too fascinating the gallant gentlemen might be loath to drown me." At the meeting she learned of the proposed flight's crew and Mrs. Guest's involvement and agreed to receive no remuneration for her participation, not even income from newspaper articles. Wilmer Stultz was to receive $20,000, Lou Gordon $5,000. Another airman, Louis Gower, was added as standby pilot. The flight in itself, Amelia knew, would open up myriad opportunities in aviation, while providing her much sought-after "fun." To Marian Stabler she soon wrote, "You may grant me pardon when you hear, in a little while, what all the mysterious business is. I have had a large struggle to do anything of a personal nature for some weeks. Yes, my performance in N.Y. was successful—at least, it gives me a chance at success of a kind."[12]

Amelia's poise and warm yet calm manner had won over the flight's backers, but her first impression of George Putnam perplexed her. He had kept her waiting an hour in his office and appeared brusque, she later told Muriel. On the other hand, she later said, "before I had talked to him for very long I was conscious of the brilliant mind and the keen insight of the man." For his part, George was bedazzled, immediately recognizing her potential in addition to her resemblance to Charles Lindbergh, but he maintained an unruffled composure. As Corey Ford might say, his magic wand had turned up another sizzling property.[13]

7

ACROSS THE
ATLANTIC

A WEEK PASSED BEFORE Amelia first saw the Fokker *Friendship*. Jacked up in a hangar in East Boston, it was startlingly huge compared to the small plane she flew. The Fokker's 72-foot wing span was two and a half times that of little Kinner Airsters. Amelia noticed, too, the artistry of its color scheme: a reddish-orange fuselage and golden wings, creating a vivid contrast intended to aid rescuers if the craft were downed at sea. Nearby, mechanics and welders worked on the struts of metal pontoons that were soon to replace its wheeled landing gear.

A feeling of immense satisfaction must have swept over thirty-year-old Amelia as she surveyed the hectic hangar. In less than a year she had gone from a virtual nonentity among Boston's aeronautical leaders to the commander of a proposed flight across the Atlantic. In a document addressed to the *Friendship*'s crew on May 18, 1928, Amy Guest's lawyer, David Layman, confirmed Amelia's status as commander: her decisions on policy, procedure, and personnel would be final. She would later write that the flight was a "feminine expedition, originated and financed by a woman, whose wish was to emphasize what her sex stood ready to do."[1] Amelia had requested that she be allowed a turn at the controls during the flight. The project's backers told her it was a possibility, weather permitting, since she was unable to fly "blind," using only instruments. Nor had she ever handled a seaplane or multi-engine aircraft.

The modified Fokker seaplane was equipped with fuel tanks in the wings and cabin for a capacity of 900 gallons, the fuel alone weighing slightly over 5,500 pounds. Although the *Friendship* was the first trimotor equipped with pontoons (or "floats") for long-distance flying, their use was not new to trans-oceanic flights.[2] They were both a blessing and a curse—there were more difficult takeoffs, but easier landings. A pilot could land on water, of course, and also on land, should that be necessary. Moreover, at a time when airports were sparse, it was a decided advantage to have the ability to land on lakes, rivers, and oceans. But seaplanes could not carry the fuel a conventional undercarriage-equipped craft could bear and therefore required more stops.

There was no passenger seating in the Fokker, the seats having been removed to accommodate extra fuel tanks. Three Wright Whirlwind J5 Cyclone nine-cylinder, air-cooled radial engines powered the plane at 200 horsepower each. Its state-of-the-art cockpit instruments included a Pioneer earth induction compass, an instrument far superior to a regular magnetic compass. (According to its manufacturer, "Once the course is set the pilot has only to keep the plane so headed that the hand of the compass always remains on zero, and he will always be on the correct course.")[3] Also onboard were a Cardwell radio with a range of 1,000 miles and an emergency radio set with a range of 50 to 100 miles, the latter designed to work independently of the plane if it went down. Neither Slim Gordon nor Amelia understood radio operation, so Bill Stultz would handle all communication. He would also perform speed and drift calculations based on observations made from a hatchway that opened from the cabin floor. A superb aviator, navigator, and radio man, Bill offered the flight its highest odds of succeeding.

AMELIA SAW THE *FRIENDSHIP* only twice more before the actual take-off. She kept out of sight, knowing the backers wanted to keep the plans secret lest reporters spill the beans and inspire competitors. Ostensibly the plane was being prepared for Commander Byrd's Antarctic expedition. She maintained almost complete secrecy at Denison House and confided her plans only to Marion Perkins and a few coworkers; otherwise she said only that she would be away from work for a few weeks. She tasked her loyal fiancé Sam, who remained an exceedingly patient bystander to all her adventures, with informing her mother and Muriel about the flight at its departure—not before.

She also drew up a will calculating her major debts at $1,000, which a life insurance policy and a bond would satisfy. She owed smaller amounts to the Boston department stores Jordan Marsh and Filene's for clothing (including a $140 fur coat), plus garage-rental fees and an assortment of other miscellaneous bills. She directed her car to be sold to pay remaining debts. To each of her parents she wrote "popping-off" letters, which she entrusted to Putnam to deliver in the event she did not return. "Even tho' I have lost, the adventure was worthwhile. Our family tends to be too secure," she wrote her mother. "Hooray for the last grand adventure!" read her message to her father. "I wish I had won, but it was worthwhile anyway. You know that."[4]

Amelia wrapped up her personal preparations for the journey by assembling her flying costume: high-laced boots, brown breeches, a white silk blouse with a red necktie, and a brown sweater topped with a scuffed and aged leather coat that she had bought to celebrate her first solo flight. A fabric flying helmet, goggles, and white-and-brown silk scarf completed the ensemble. Major Charles H. Woolley of Boston loaned her his heavy, fur-lined flying suit, believing she needed it for an altitude attempt. In a small army knapsack she carried a toothbrush and comb, handkerchiefs, a tube of cold cream, a camera on loan from Layman, and, also on loan, George Putnam's expedition binoculars. Rounding out her scanty possessions were an autographed copy of Byrd's *Skyward* for personal delivery to Amy Guest, now in London for her daughter's presentation at Court, and a handful of personal messages others had asked her to convey.

FROM A HUMAN PERSPECTIVE, all looked in order for departure from Boston, with the Fokker well equipped and tested and the crew ready. They would fly from Boston to Trepassey, Newfoundland, then across the ocean to England. Hilton Railey, assigned as European coordinator of the flight, had sailed to London to await its arrival. Amy Guest had spared no expense in hiring meteorologist Dr. James H. "Doc" Kimball of the United States Weather Bureau in New York, adviser to Charles Lindbergh and Commander Byrd on their flights, and the best in the industry. At his Manhattan office, weather data poured in from ocean-going vessels and weather stations in the United States, Canada, and the Grand Banks, among other locales, as well as wires from England reporting on the eastern Atlantic and Europe; he plotted all this information on a map of the North Atlantic. With the onset of fog and rain, it was on his recommendation that the launch, originally planned for May 20, was delayed.

The twentieth of May was the anniversary of Lindbergh's transatlantic hop a year earlier and had been Putnam's first choice. More than a week of waiting followed, although it was interspersed with lively comings and goings, trips to Boston restaurants and the theater, as well as local sight-seeing excursions to the shore. Occasionally Mrs. Guest's sons, Winston and Raymond, showed up. The Copley Plaza Hotel in Boston housed the key participants, including Amelia; Stultz; Layman and Gower, accompanied by their wives; Gordon and his fiancé; Commander Robert Elmer (technical director of the flight); and George Putnam and his wife. G. P. had asked his wife to join them in order to provide female companionship for his protégé. Dorothy Binney Putnam welcomed the adventure and the chance to meet Amelia, whose intelligence, good looks, and quick laughter had made such an impression on her husband.

By the time of their arrival in Boston, the Putnam marriage was unraveling, an estrangement that had made physical intimacy between husband and wife rare. "Soon we'll see each other by appointment only if this goes on. Well it suits me," Dorothy noted in her diary as early as January 1927. Shortly after this entry she had begun a passionate affair with George Weymouth, a Yale undergraduate nineteen years her junior, who had been brought to Rocknoll, the Putnam estate in Rye, by G. P. to tutor their son David; he had also gone along on the Baffin Land expedition. Dorothy later found evidence of her husband's own infidelity, a "compromising affair and his penciled acceptance," but admitted no jealousy over his brief tryst. (The details of what Dorothy called his "affair" are unknown.) Although their marriage was clearly teetering, the Putnams had not yet considered ending it.[5]

Amelia's friendliness quickly won over Dorothy during her six-day visit to Boston. In the Kissel car, dubbed the Yellow Peril by G. P., Amelia drove the Putnams to a lobster dinner at Kimball's, to the shore, and to lunch with the Byrds—"utterly beguiling," wrote Dorothy of Commander Byrd. For the most part the two women chatted like magpies about their life stories. But the affability didn't stop Dorothy from noticing that Amelia had registered at the Copley under the name "Dorothy Binney." In her journal she also recorded that her husband and Amelia once "talked nearly all night long" even though there was a scheduled takeoff—later canceled—the following day.[6]

Amelia's reputation as "Lady Lindy" was also cemented at the Copley Plaza, where Putnam had cannily hired Jake Coolidge of Paramount News to shoot photographs of her. On the Copley's roof, in a session titled "Remember Lindbergh," Amelia posed in her rakish, masculine flying costume. (Coolidge later said he used camera angles to create the illusion of a resemblance between Earhart and Lindbergh; he didn't think the two looked alike.) Putnam had also worked out an exclusive deal with Paramount for newsreel coverage in Boston and in Trepassey, Newfoundland, and another with the *New York Times* for exclusive, syndicated rights to Amelia's articles.

AT 4:30 IN THE morning of Sunday, June 3, the *Friendship*'s crew boarded the tugboat *Sadie Ross* at Boston's T Wharf, headed for the seaplane moored off the Jeffrey Yacht Club for what would be their third takeoff attempt. Too much fog and rain or too little wind had barred earlier efforts. Their destination was Trepassey, where they planned an overnight stop before the actual ocean crossing. Doc's weather forecast over the entire route looked promising.

After Amelia, Stultz, Gordon, and Gower climbed aboard the craft, Gordon leapt on to the starboard pontoon and crossed to the other to get all three motors turning over. Bill Stultz, meanwhile, fiddled with the radio and checked the cockpit. In the rear of the plane were eight cans of gasoline and a picnic basket of food provisions, including coffee for the boys, cocoa for Amelia, sandwiches, and oranges provided by Putnam.

Stultz headed the lumbering, boxlike plane into the wind and gave it full throttle, but the pontoons remained stuck to the water's surface. Out went six five-gallon cans of gas to lighten the load by 184 pounds, and Amelia, Slim, and Gower moved to the rear of the plane, hoping the shift in weight would help raise the nose. But again the plane stuck. Slim called for a tug-boat, and Gower, the standby pilot, bade farewell and deplaned quietly. Less his 150 pounds, the plane eased off in 67 seconds at the next run. As they took off, the cabin door popped open and wind began rushing in. Amelia jumped up and held the door shut as Slim came aft to help, and both almost tumbled out of the plane in the scramble to fasten it.

An hour out, at 7:30, the Fokker was cruising at 2,500 feet near Cash's Ledge in haze and a blinding sun. "Hooray! Nova Scotia at 8:55," Amelia dutifully recorded in the flight logbook, a gift from G. P. that would form the basis of her first book, *20 Hrs., 40 Min.*[7] In it she scrawled penciled notes and the crew's remarks, in block handwriting. A tailwind pushed the plane's speed to 114 miles per hour, but north of Halifax, halfway to Trepassey, a solid blanket of fog cut off all landmarks beneath it. Bill was forced to turn around and put in at Halifax, telling Amelia the "Newfoundland coast is bad enough but in a fog won't be tried." Shortly after, he took off again, impatient to get going, but in thickening clouds he had to return to Halifax, where the threesome stayed in a small hotel, sleeping atop mattresses stuffed with straw.[8]

Overnight, the fog rolled back and dawn hastened in a bright blue sky and scattering of clouds. The *Friendship* launched easily, in less than a minute. Amelia, perched on a gas can by the window, watched fishing vessels and shoals on the water below. At 11:55 the plane was off Cape Canso, cruising low in minor turbulence. "I hope the air improves for I should like the controls a while," wrote Amelia in her log. On the entire crossing she would not fly the plane. While Bill flew and worked the radio, sending and receiving position reports, Slim spelled him or went aft for "endless" ham sandwiches provided by the Copley Plaza. (Too late, the crew discovered layers of delicious chicken and tongue sandwiches beneath the ham.) Watching Bill and Slim, with little else to do, Amelia noted their good grooming: "Men who care about their appearance on this trip. They both wear silk socks and are fussy."[9]

That morning, readers had picked up the *New York Times* to see front-page photographs of Amelia accompanying the headline: WOMAN TO

BE CO-PILOT: MISS EARHART, SOCIAL WORKER AND FLIER, TO AID WILMER STULTZ. The article detailed the proposed itinerary to England and the take-off at Boston, and described Amelia as looking "more like Lindbergh than Lindbergh himself." The irrepressible George Palmer Putnam had pulled off another publicity coup. Flipping to the second page, readers might have noted another piece praising Amelia's "striking" physique and flying skills, an article stunning in its hyperbole. It announced she was the female counterpart of Charles Lindbergh and "regarded by many as the greatest woman aviator in the country." The articles claimed she had 500 solo hours, an altitude record, and "took to aviation like a baby to milk" when she learned to fly in 1918. The inflation of Amelia's accomplishments would continue to snowball and create high expectations of her that became a significant burden because of her inexperience. She would feel it acutely while in the company of well-known pilots.[10]

Unfortunately Sam Chapman's plan to alert Amy and Muriel of the *Friendship*'s takeoff went awry when a local reporter visited the women at home and broke the news to Amy, who snapped, "I think she is too smart to try it!" She would later write, "Later on, when I found she wasn't...[I] had to eat my words."[11]

In the early afternoon of June 4 the *Friendship* landed at Trepassey to refuel and take on refreshments, on its last stop before the Atlantic crossing. As Amelia, Bill, and Slim stepped ashore at Trepassey, they were greeted with three rip-roaring cheers. The following day, however, brought a howling wind, and conditions forbade loading fuel onboard, let alone a launch. Over the next days countless cables would come in from George Putnam, David Layman, and Commander Byrd. Back and forth went the wires, from New York to Trepassey and back again. The messages, printed on single pages of yellowed paper, offered various ideas on continuing the flight. Wind was the culprit: too much wind, or too little, or from the wrong direction for the takeoff run. The plane was severely overloaded with fuel, too. Added to these problems were a cracked oil tank and a leaking pontoon, both of which ace mechanic Slim ultimately repaired.

Before the thirteen-day wait at Trepassey ended Putnam suggested removing Slim from the crew to save weight, Layman recommended they set a new course to the Azores and abandon England as a destination, and

Byrd offered up ideas to improve the plane's performance. The *Friendship*'s crew discarded these—how could Slim possibly remain behind?—though in desperation Amelia briefly entertained Layman's idea. "Once in Trepassey we were trapped."[12]

WHILE IN TREPASSEY THEY boarded in the home of Mrs. Deveraux, the proprietor of a general store whose children were farmed out with relatives to accommodate the crew. Those in Trepassey lived a harsh existence. "Lives are almost as barren as the country. Physically the people don't look robust but they have endured," Amelia noted, though she praised their kindheartedness. Although clean, the town's houses had no running water, and the crew foreswore the luxury of hot baths while there. Decorative touches in dwellings included silver cutlery and furniture scavenged from wrecks washed ashore. Each resident maintained a garden, a few sheep, and a cow, but the meager soil gave up little other than cabbages, potatoes, and turnips. The monotonous diet wore on the crew. Slim, a Texan who hated fish (a Trepassey dietary staple), lived off chocolate purchased in town. By the end, the slender crew members appeared, in Amelia's words, "distinctly Gothic."[13]

Two days after their arrival Amelia's troubles with the boys began. Claud Frazer, a friend of Paramount cameraman Andy Fulgoni, bought himself some liquor, and though Amelia asked Andy to keep the purchase quiet, his commitment fell flat when that evening the four men congregated in Andy's room. Amelia fretted about the free-flowing booze, concerned that "Stultz's judgment be good in the crisis." There was a respite of sorts the next few days, when the men were occupied with wholesome activities. Amelia joined them in games of rummy and walks along the shore. Books were scarce and live entertainment scanty, and Bill Stultz taught himself to play what Amelia called a guitar harp, attempting versions of "Jingle Bells" and other tunes to help pass the time.[14]

In good weather on June 7 they failed three times trying to launch because the plane was overloaded, and five more days would pass before weather conditions permitted another attempt. Meanwhile, they received word of competitors. Mabel Boll and pilot Thea Rasche were hard on their heels, threatening to make an Atlantic crossing in top-notch airplanes as soon as they had a chance to take off. "Rasche is the one to fear. I wish we'd have a break," Amelia jotted in her log.[15] An accomplished pilot, the German Thea Rasche and her crew dallied at Roosevelt Field in New York, waiting for the rain-soaked dirt runway to dry out. Mabel Boll, having finally snared Charles Levine's plane *Miss Columbia*, would soon arrive with her crew at Harbour Grace, Newfoundland.[16] Both women had planes that were equipped with conventional undercarriages and could easily outperform the *Friendship* by flying faster and carrying more fuel.

"We are just managing to keep from suicide," Amelia observed at the end of Sunday, June 10. "My telegrams imply N. Y. papers think we are bluffing."[17] The launch delay confounded the press, the crew, and the flight's backers. Overseas correspondents also observed the lack of progress. The British *Flight* magazine wrote that Amelia's many attempts to take off with her pilot had failed, "apparently due to overloading."[18] A bright glimmer in the otherwise dismal delay occurred when the crew heard the Fokker trimotor *Southern Cross* had arrived in Brisbane, Australia, having flown 7,388 miles from California with two stops, a feat securing its place in aviation history as the first transpacific flight. The Australian Charles Kingsford-Smith had piloted the craft, assisted by a three-man crew.

Later, Amelia's worries over the "bad booze" resurfaced when the boys went out in search of liquor in a car they had to push 8 miles after its belt broke. "I could choke Frazer," she wrote. Memories of her father's alcoholism couldn't have been far from her mind when she wrote, "I loathe watching men. Why can't they be more responsible?" Nonetheless, Amelia's tact, maturity, and past experience handling Edwin ultimately defused what could have been an even worse situation.[19]

On the morning of June 12, the *Friendship* went at it again, its pontoons spanking the surface for three hours trying to lift off, but spray from heavy seas had soaked the engines. There was not enough thrust to get the plane in the air. The following day, in perfect conditions, the seaplane again refused to take off. The crew was incredulous. After removing 300 pounds of fuel from the tanks, Bill telegrammed Byrd: CANNOT UNDERSTAND MYSELF WHY UNLESS CAUSED BY DOWNWARD AIR CURRENTS OVER MOUNTAINS HERE HAVE REDUCED LOAD TO 850 BUT STILL COULD NOT GET ON STEP.[20] By now the pontoons' struts had begun to bend from the heavy load and numerous failed takeoff attempts.

On June 14 Bill told Amelia that he thought he could make Ireland with only 700 gallons of fuel. With the reduced amount of fuel, however, the margin of safety was narrowing. Even so, although Amelia wanted to launch, Bill refused because of the wind, saying he would obtain ship and weather reports at midnight and use these to make his own weather map. "Had I been alone," she wrote, "I certainly should have gone."[21]

A dreary rain pelted Trepassey on Friday, June 15, and continued into the following day. Amelia made no further log entries until Sunday, June 17, when, at 11:51 A.M. local time, the *Friendship* finally lumbered off from Trepassey. In his book *Soaring Wings*, George Putnam claimed that Bill Stultz was probably drunk when the plane took off and that Amelia "simply got hold of her pilot and all but dragged him to the plane."[22] In her log Amelia made no mention of any such incident, though she did describe the boys' drinking the previous night.

At takeoff Bill was like a demon at the controls, plowing the craft recklessly on a wild, three-mile ride over rough water. He got the plane aloft on his third attempt, after Slim tossed out the remaining cans of fuel, leaving only 700 gallons in the tanks. "I worried awfully," Amelia confided in her log. She also wasn't sure what to expect from Bill in the cockpit "after the loquacity disappeared."[23]

AS THE PLANE CLIMBED to 1,500 feet, Amelia looked down at the many lakes dotting the terrain, describing two as "gigantic foot prints" and another, a dinosaur. From Trepassey a half hour later a wire went out to George Putnam reading VIOLET, signed "Cheerio" and "A.E." The prearranged code word signified a successful launch.[24]

Bill had studied all available ship and weather reports that morning and told the crew he expected the entire flight to alternate between storms and clear skies. About two hours after the launch he reported passing over the Grand Banks, 60 miles east of Cape Race. By now Amelia was sitting on top of three bulky flight suits, the cabin's cushions having been tossed to reduce weight. A little later she took a brief nap, trying to shake off what had become a debilitating headache. The food aboard the craft included huge egg sandwiches, oranges, chocolate, oatmeal cookies, tins of pemmican, malted milk tablets, mineral water, and a small thermos of coffee. Amelia would eat only three oranges and a dozen malted tablets during the entire flight.

Soon the fog thickened to overcast of 5,000 feet, forcing Bill to climb higher, but on top he ran into turbulent storms that shook the 11,000-pound plane as sheets of heavy rain pounded down. Bill pushed the nose down to exit the area, while Amelia marveled at the tempest, the heaviest storm she had ever experienced aloft. After the craft descended 2,000 feet, Amelia saw what seemed to be a calm sea, and Slim came aft to tell her of snow in the air.

Shortly afterward Bill and Amelia changed positions, with her sitting up front. She "didn't take controls 'cause Slim had 'em and Bill wouldn't let him alone a minute about its course." She went on to describe the scenario in her logbook. Bill would tell Slim "to keep at 106 [degrees] and then comes racing up and pushes the rudder bar slightly to one side." She added, "I think I'll try my hand when Bill is up." But she didn't press to fly, and it was unlikely she could have held course because of her inexperience with navigation, and with the plane and its flight instruments.[25]

After a spell in sunny skies, cruising at a groundspeed of 140 miles per hour, the plane came upon a long line of clouds and thick fog, which it climbed above. At 8:45 P.M. London time Bill made contact with the Liverpool steamer *Rexmore,* which reported its position as 48 degrees north latitude and 39 west longitude. Shortly afterward the *Friendship*'s radio went on the blink, ending all further radio contact for the remainder of the trip. Meanwhile, a setting sun cast a pink glow upon the billowing mountains of fog. Amelia reveled in the "vast and lonely" vista, but her long stretch kneeling at the port window left her with sore knees.[26]

There followed a night of stars—the North Star appeared next to the wingtip—along with a meteoric display of sparks from the engines' exhausts. Again they climbed to get above fog and rough air, at full throttle, finally topping out at 10,000 feet. Amelia described the engines as having "picked up too much water." Probably she was describing carburetor icing, a potentially dangerous situation that could cause the engines to stop, since conditions were ideal for its formation.[27]

Bill began a slow descent, pulling the power back before putting the plane in a rapid descent down to 5,000 feet to get out of the icing areas. He was now flying solely on instruments through a foggy murk. Water droplets ran down the windows as the port motor began to cough. Soon all three engines were emitting a staccato sound like muted gun fire, then Bill applied full throttle to clear the icing. Dropping down to 3,000 feet, they encountered more clouds, which began to fuse together, but when the gray, bulbous masses separated, the *Friendship* found itself over the sea, with a reddish dawn rising far in the distance. Amelia figured they were "somewhat into range of our destination if we are on the course." Soon she logged "ten boats!!!!" But fuel was running precariously low. Nearby they saw the liner U.S.S. *America*, which, unknown to them, was only 72 miles east of Queenstown, Ireland.[28] Bill scribbled notes asking the sailors to paint its coordinates on the deck, a courtesy commonly extended to aviators. Amelia weighed them down with oranges and tossed them down, but twice missed the mark. Rather than landing beside the liner to ask its position and risk another takeoff, Bill and the crew elected to backtrack to their original course and go on.

As they flew on, a ceiling of wispy fog clamped lower and lower, forcing the plane to a mere 500 feet above the water, leaving them barely enough room to maneuver, had they come upon any obstructions. By their calculations, less than an hour of fuel remained. Still, there was no land in sight. A half hour later they noticed a fleet of fishing vessels paralleling their course. Then, gradually, an unmistakable blue shadow began to emerge out of the mists. Slim yelled, "Land!" and threw his sandwich out the window, while Bill simply smiled. Inching along in mist with dwindling fuel, they finally found themselves over terrain resembling English countryside. After spotting the mouth of a river alongside what appeared to be a factory town, Bill swooped down to land on the surface of the Loughor estuary at 12:40 P.M. on June 18. In drizzling rain Slim jumped onto a pontoon and made fast to a buoy at what the crew soon learned was the town of Burry Port, Wales.

8

THE HEROINE

THE *FRIENDSHIP'S* LANDING AT Burry Port went unnoticed, ending the remarkable oceanic flight as if it were an everyday occurrence. More than an hour passed before Bill learned where they were and enticed a local into rowing him ashore to telephone Hilton Railey, who was awaiting their landing at Southampton, England, with Amy Guest, her husband, and son Raymond. "A tremendous triumph," was Amy's response.

Three hours later, after a journey in fog from Southampton, a seaplane bearing Railey and Allen Raymond, a *New York Times* correspondent, dropped down at Burry Port. Railey boarded a motor boat to the *Friendship*, where Amelia sat cross-legged and dour at the door. In an exuberant greeting he tossed his hat into the estuary. He couldn't understand her disappointed expression.

"Aren't you excited?" he asked.

"No," she replied. "I was just baggage, like a sack of potatoes. Maybe someday I'll try it alone."[1]

The seaplane had flown about 2,000 miles in 20 hours and 49 minutes. Less than 50 gallons of fuel remained aboard. It was decided they would fly on to Southampton in the morning.

By this time news had spread to surrounding areas, and a frenzied mob of two thousand people was gathered on the shore of Burry Port awaiting Amelia, the girl flyer whose transatlantic feat had heaped honor on their small and sleepy town. Not since the men returned after the First World War had there been such an outpouring of emotion. Wanting to touch her, to get her autograph, to partake in history, townspeople grabbed at Amelia as soon as she stepped ashore. One ripped a silk scarf from her head. Others yelled and surged forward. So hysterical was the greeting that the *New York Times* later reported "it seemed for a few minutes as if she would not outlive her triumph."[2] Quick-thinking policemen formed a cordon encircling her, moving her to a factory (the Frickers Metal Company), where cheers from the crowd impelled her to wave royally three times. Meanwhile, they virtually ignored Bill Stultz and Slim Gordon.

That afternoon began the transformation of Amelia into an international star. Ever afterward she would live in the limelight, inhabiting a stratosphere of adulation and hero worship. Denison House expected her back at work, but George Putnam had already begun to emphasize to his new "property" the commercial value of her achievement. His publicity machine revved up immediately after she landed, and he told the *New York Times* the flight's success "testifies to the indomitable will and extraordinary courage of Miss Earhart. I picked her for the flight."[3]

Under a tight escort the crew headed off to a local hotel for hot baths (their first in weeks), food, and rest. Earlier Bill had told Raymond the crossing wasn't a "pleasant experience, although everything went perfectly. I had to steer solely by the instruments and luckily none of them went wrong."[4] Bill and Slim slept after eating, but to Amelia fell the task of reliving the Atlantic crossing in an interview with Raymond. The account, edited by Raymond and wired to New York while she snatched five hours of rest, would be published under her byline.

All sorts of articles about Amelia soon appeared, and no item was too trivial to relate: she had no interest in fashion or makeup; she enjoyed driving her car, fencing, and horse riding; she couldn't care less about money unless it advanced her interests in flying. Journalists portrayed her as a wholesome American girl, one who stood in contrast to the gin drinking, cigarette-smoking flapper. When asked if she had ever thought to renege on the flight she replied that the idea had never crossed her mind.

Overnight, congratulatory telegrams poured in to Burry Port from President Coolidge, the Fokker Aircraft Company in Amsterdam, and various celebrities. Back home, the *New York American* heralded the triumphs of "Lindbergh and the lady who most nearly resembles him in character, appearance and achievement."[5] That she never touched the controls on a flight more than a thousand miles *shorter* than Lindbergh's solo transatlantic journey went unmentioned. In fact, the hubbub left Amelia smarting because all the glory was attributed to her. "I was a passenger on the journey—just a passenger," she reiterated candidly.[6] To Secretary of State Frank B. Kellogg in Washington, D.C., she wired, "It is my earnest wish that the people of the United States understand that the success was entirely due to the great skill of Mr. Stultz."[7] But try as she might, she simply could not impress upon the public that the accolades belonged to her pilot and navigator, not her.

Not everyone extolled her role in the flight. For the little good she did, read one British newspaper, she was likened to a sheep in the cabin.[8] The most stinging remarks appeared in Britain's *Flight* magazine, whose petulant editor never minced words at what he perceived as stunts: "Compared with the solo flights of lady *pilots* as Lady Bailey and Lady Heath, the crossing of the Atlantic as *a passenger* does not seem to us to prove anything in particular."[9] Bailey and Heath were both Irishwomen who had been recognized worldwide for their epic flights, but could hardly have differed more in personality and background. The formidable and aristocratic Lady Mary Bailey grew up in a castle, and was married off at a young age to a South African millionaire because her father had squandered the family's money; whereas the flamboyant Lady Mary Heath, whose mentally unbalanced father had murdered her mother, was reared by her aunts and gained her title through marriage. In 1928 the two women achieved their greatest honors, when Lady Heath flew solo from South Africa to England in an Avro Avian, and Lady Bailey flew alone in a De Havilland Moth from England to South Africa and back.[10]

It is interesting to note that Lady Mary Heath's African odyssey might have been the deciding factor that nudged Amy Guest into considering the transatlantic flight. On April 11, 1928, the London *Times* published a letter from Amy's husband, Frederick Guest, lauding Heath's "tremendous individual feat." Describing the "scrubby desolation" of Africa's bush country, he remarked that the "chances of rescue if a forced landing occurred are little less hopeless than if it took place in the Atlantic."[11]

Right after Amelia arrived in Southampton Lady Heath sent a welcoming letter offering assistance and support, and four years later, after Amelia completed a flight to Ireland, Lady Bailey and other female pilots would greet her.

Certainly Amelia knew that her flying experience paled beside that of some other women aviators. "Stung by stray criticisms" is how the *New York Times* described her reaction to those who dismissed her.[12] At home she had flown only on local jaunts and thus had not developed the ability to navigate or interpret weather. Nor had she experience with repairing her own planes. She had at one point laid claim to having 500 hours of solo flight experience, which she later corrected to several hundred. But, either way, what better determines competence in a pilot is the variety of flight hours over changing terrain and in different circumstances, and in this Amelia was likewise limited.

UPON LANDING AT SOUTHAMPTON, Amelia met for the first time her sponsor, Amy Guest, and along with Bill and Slim was whisked to the Hyde Park Hotel in London. Thereafter she was subjected to a relentless agenda of social events and interviews, which would continue throughout her visit. In London grasping correspondents besieged her, and after one barged unannounced into her hotel room, Amy convinced her to move to her Park Lane mansion. Even so, there the bustle continued as shopkeepers fitted Amelia with a new wardrobe, and she and Hilton Railey, aided by four secretaries, dealt with the invitations, letters, and various offers that arrived daily. These included a marriage proposal from a farmer in Kent—provided she was financially secure.

Amelia had become a media sensation and society darling feted at lunches and dinner parties hosted by Lord Lonsdale and Lady Astor. She visited Wimbledon, the Olympic Horse Show, and the settlement house Toynbee Hall, and on June 23 the Women's Committee of the Air League of the British Empire sponsored a luncheon for Stultz, Gordon, and Amelia, which was attended by Lady Heath, Winston Churchill, and a plethora of other distinguished guests. There Amelia gave a speech that painted an optimistic future for aviation, including women pilots who could become rich with the right job. Exhibiting some political savvy, she credited Britain's aeronautical industry as being "far ahead of America in many ways, particularly in the number of passengers carried and the use of light aeroplanes."[13] Her modest demeanor endeared her to the audience, as did her self-deprecating humor, which she would sharpen to a fine art in the coming years. Hilton Railey hovered near her at social functions, providing her with support and advice if questions arose about protocol.

Bill and Slim were fortunate to escape the notice of the fashion plates who criticized Amelia's borrowed, oversized silk dresses, and of the upper-crust socialites who were claiming Amelia as one of their own. Bill and Slim were considered hired men whose job was done and done well, and they were free to pursue what they best liked: chatting with airmen, visiting the Croydon and Le Bourget aerodromes in London and Paris, and hopping a flight to Manchester to lay wreaths at the grave of Sir John Alcock, who had first flown the Atlantic nonstop in 1919, with Arthur Whitten Brown. Besides, Bill lacked certain social graces. His English hosts couldn't help but be annoyed when he told the press he preferred to sail home on an American ship because they were safer than their British counterparts.

If Amelia regretted the fullness of her social calendar she didn't complain, but she leaped at the chance Lady Heath proposed: an early morning flying rendezvous at Croydon. The two aviators flew together in Lady Heath's little Avro Avian biplane, which was studded with plaques and stickers from its travels through Africa and Europe. Amelia impulsively offered to purchase the responsive Avian that so reminded her of her beloved Kinner Airster plane. It's unclear why, but Lady Heath immediately accepted; some have suggested she simply needed the cash.[14] Nor is it known how Amelia financed the purchase. It was possible George Putnam advanced her the money, knowing her future earnings—he foresaw a book about the flight, public appearances, endorsements, and articles—would more than cover the expense. The silver and blue Avian, which had been completely reconditioned at the factory before its sale, was crated and shipped to the States, where Amelia would later fly it across the country.

DURING THIS TIME, in America Putnam had been orchestrating the *Friendship* crew's homecoming, scheduling a welcoming tour and other events. While the crew was returning to the States on the S.S. *President Roosevelt*, Amelia received a cable from Putnam asking whether she would accept invitations to civic receptions at thirty-two cities. She trimmed the proposed hectic agenda and agreed to visit only New York, Boston, and Chicago. On the rainy day of July 6, the crew arrived in New York City to a crowd of five thousand. During a parade up Broadway, shredded paper rained down on Amelia, Bill, and Slim as they waved from their open car at the adoring crowd. Amelia wore a blue silk suit and a feathered cloche, a distinctive style of hat she would soon discard because G. P. deemed it hideous. Her fans would come to prefer seeing her signature coif of tousled blond curls, and she rarely wore hats thereafter. Between gala events held in their honor, including a luncheon sponsored by Commander Byrd, the crew gave interviews, although Bill Stultz continued to retreat from the limelight and find solace in the bottle. Often his hosts at events had to send out a scout to round him up.[15]

Notably absent from the New York festivities was Amelia's fiancé, Sam Chapman. At Amelia's suite in the Biltmore a reporter asked if it were true she was going to marry him, and she appeared embarrassed. "That's a personal matter," she replied, ending further questions about Sam.[16]

Three days later the City of Boston pulled out all the stops to bestow honors on the *Friendship* flyers, with welcoming crowds estimated at 250,000 for a parade and other public appearances. The crew had arrived in trimotors, Amelia as a passenger in a Ford, Stultz at the controls of a Fokker. At the airport Amelia, her arms laden with flowers, greeted her mother and sister for the first time in over a month. She then spent a day at Medford, where she was showered with more thunderous acclaim, before joining Bill and Slim at Madison Square Garden in New York for a nationwide NBC radio broadcast about the Atlantic flight, one of the many events arranged by Putnam. Chrysler gave her a blue roadster for her involvement, the first of many products she would accept for her appearances and endorsements. Shortly after, the trio went by private rail car to Chicago, where another round of festivities awaited, starting on July 19.

Occasionally George's schemes went awry. Such was the case when he arranged for Amelia's endorsement of Lucky Strike cigarettes, a brand used by Bill and Slim. She protested the endorsement because she didn't smoke, but George persuaded her to take the $1,500 fee and contribute it to Byrd's Antarctic expedition. Bill and Slim had agreed to the endorsement, needing the money, and without her approval the deal would fall through. The four-color advertisement featured Amelia wearing a flying helmet, with copy below urging, "For a slender figure—Reach for a *Lucky* instead of a sweet." However, George didn't foresee the public disapproval that would occur in an era when "proper women" didn't use tobacco. An irate reader sent Amelia a tear sheet with a note reading, "Is this the face of a lady! What price glory!"[17] After seeing the ad, the management of *McCall's* magazine, who had offered her an editorial position, withdrew the job, but within a week George finagled to have her hired as aviation editor at *Hearst's International Cosmopolitan* magazine. Still, the hoopla bothered Amelia; on August 16 she wrote her friend Marian Stabler of her plans to relocate to New York because she had a "swell new lucrative job. You gotta help me. Don't throw me over on acct. of cigarette ad. I'll explain that."[18]

AMELIA WAS MOSTLY ENJOYING the praise and publicity heaped on her, along with her blossoming status as the predominant American spokeswoman for aviation. With Putnam's guidance, her future seemed secure, leaving her finally free from financial worry. She was earning money from articles and endorsements, and it was likely Putnam had given her an advance on royalties for her forthcoming book. Among the first to benefit from her largesse was her mother, for whom Amelia opened a department store charge account at Filene's. "Please throw away rags and get items you need," she wrote. "I can do it now, and the pleasure is mine."[19]

All thoughts of her returning to Denison House had gone by the wayside; her fame precluded employment as a social worker, but she maintained a strong interest in the field. Her new life of luxury and commitment to aviation demanded she fulfill certain contractual obligations, and looming large on her agenda was the book she had promised George. As July progressed she accepted the hospitality extended by George and his wife to stay at their sixteen-room Rye, New York, estate while writing *20 Hrs., 40 Min.: Our Flight in the Friendship.* George had chosen the title, and he made it a

bit snappier by shortening the flight time by nine minutes. He demanded
the book be completed in three weeks, sufficient time, he reasoned, to write
the story—typically what he allotted his authors. He and a secretary assisted
Amelia with the narrative, which was divided into three distinct sections: a
brief autobiography, an account of the flight based on her flight log, and a
recap of the American aviation industry. Released in the autumn, it received
favorable reviews praising Amelia's sense of humor and evocative descriptions, although by today's standards portions of the writing would be considered pedestrian. Not that George cared about criticism. He wanted to
exploit adventure tales while they were hot, and his regimented approach to
publishing them served his purposes. Amelia dedicated the book to her hostess, Dorothy Binney Putnam. In a letter to Marian Stabler, Amelia wrote,
"My book goes to press very soon. I should like to have made it better but
time was short and I done as good as [sic] I could."[20]

   In this same letter, Amelia reported that she had seen a physician for a
pilot's license exam.[21] She held only an FAI license and agreed to be tested
for an American pilot's license, which mandated she pass a flight and physical exam. The Department of Commerce had started to license pilots and
aircraft in 1927, ending the freewheeling days when neither required certification. Amelia's Avro Avian, bearing its British registration of G-EBUG,
had recently arrived at Curtiss Field in Long Island and was issued tail
number 7083.

BETWEEN WRITING CHAPTERS, at Rye Amelia found time for parties, riding, swimming, and shopping excursions with Dorothy. There were
occasional public appearances, and in the wake of the post-*Friendship* frenzy
Amelia mulled over propositions from promoters and officials in the airline
industry but withheld committing herself. George Putnam's granddaughter,
Sally Putnam Chapman, would one day astutely observe that "had it not
been for my grandparents, Amelia would not have moved in the circles she
did. Dofry [Dorothy Putnam] invited Amelia into her world, introduced her
to a glittering array of celebrities, artists, adventurers, and socialites. To the
unsophisticated young flyer, the Putnams represented a lifestyle she had only
dreamed of. How ironic that Dorothy seemed to be Amelia's heroine, at least

for a short time."[22] Meanwhile, George seemed incapable of *not* meddling in Amelia's personal life. The two shared similar interests—books, riding, and canoeing—and were developing a closeness that Dorothy Putnam noticed and forlornly wrote of in her journal. By the end of August rumors about a love affair between Amelia and George swirled among aviators, to the chagrin of both Putnams. What Amelia thought of these rumors is unknown, but they certainly didn't stop her from traveling with George as the summer rolled to a close.

Since returning to America, Amelia had worked nonstop, but with the book completed and her schedule free of commitments, she desperately wanted to return to flying. For her next adventure, she decided to take the Avro Avian on a vagabonding vacation across the States. While she had no fixed agenda, she did have one firm short-term objective: her final destination had to be in California.

9

THE VAGABOND

AT THE END OF her transcontinental air odyssey in the autumn of 1928, Amelia Earhart would observe, "Vagabonding means change. One of its greatest charms is the excitement of moving from place to place, meeting new people, encountering unexpected situations." Harrowing mishaps in her Avro Avian had dogged her all the while. But she later explained that traveling by air was "no more arduous than a long train or automobile journey, especially if undertaken in leisurely fashion."[1] In her day many pilots, attempting to inspire the public to take up commercial flying, equated air travel with ground transportation. Indeed, in their more proselytizing moments, aviation proponents described airplanes as harbingers of peace with the ability to transform mankind, spreading what was dubbed the "winged gospel." Amelia, endowed with what she called "missionary zeal," was one of the chief proponents of this philosophy. What better means to render the gospel's aptness than to actually fly?

On August 31, 1928, the Avian lifted off from a polo field at the Westchester Biltmore Country Club at Rye, New York. Amelia, who predicted landing fields would soon join golf links and tennis courts as standard at country clubs, was at the controls, and George Putnam was her passenger.

Amelia wore goggles and a flying helmet in the open-cockpit tandem plane, which was so versatile its folding wings enabled it to fit in a garage, and so light she could lift its tail off the ground. Its wingspan reached 28 feet, its length 24 feet 3 inches. Equipped with an 84-horsepower Cirrus II engine, the Avian could achieve a cruise speed of 85 miles per hour and had a gas capacity of 35 gallons, which translated to a range of some 400 miles.[2] Packed inside the Avian were new air navigation maps and fifty pounds of baggage. In her log Amelia described the first leg of the trip: "We crossed the Hudson River, went a little south of course. Initially at 2,500, then up to 8,500 for smooth air. Headwind all the way to Sunbury. Initially went past Bellefonte (1:55 P.M.) but decided to return to mail field. Circled the valley for field, landed 2:20 P.M."[3]

After lunch, Amelia and George flew on to Rodgers Field in Pittsburgh, where disaster overtook them. Rolling out from a landing, Amelia hit an unmarked ditch, smashed the landing gear, cracked the propeller, and damaged the left lower wing. She and George escaped without injury, but the incident received newspaper coverage. Both were shaken up, but for different reasons: George, because his wife was in the dark about the excursion; Amelia, because of the potential damage to her reputation.

The press reported it was her first accident in years of flying, a disingenuous statement proffered by George, who also claimed it occurred "through no fault of hers."[4] It was the first of many instances in which he rushed to put out press releases exonerating Amelia of any fault in her accidents, which exasperated her fellow aviators. And who could blame them? He maintained her image as a model pilot while her colleagues struggled to procure financing for their planes and flights, and to drum up the necessary publicity. Her friend Bobbi Trout, an excellent pilot, later summed up the sentiment shared by many aviators: "If I had a promoter like Putnam, I could have done the things Amelia did."[5] But at least privately, Amelia was more circumspect than George. While she usually followed his lead, brushing off her accidents, she did sometimes take responsibility. About this mishap she later wrote she had not taken the precaution of overflying Rodgers Field to examine it before landing.

Parts for English Avro Avians were not easy to come by then. George had to buy a new Avian and have it flown from New York to Pittsburgh, where over two days a crew toiled to repair Amelia's plane, substituting the new parts. The two next headed to Dayton, Ohio, George's last stop on the grand tour before taking a train home. Amelia went it alone from there. Terre Haute, St. Louis, and Muskogee, Oklahoma, followed, with Amelia charming and befriending locals wherever she landed. Women clamored to have her as a house guest upon hearing that she was tired of hotels and the publicity they brought. Every night Amelia sent telegrams to her mother and to George giving them her location, a promise both had exacted before she departed.

DAYS INTO THE TOUR, Amelia's inexperience led to another near calamity. After she refueled at Fort Worth, she pointed the tiny plane's nose toward Sweetwater, but with hot air currents boiling up from the arid land below she encountered turbulence. Her air map was torn from her lap and blew out of the cockpit, leaving her lost. With sunset nearing and her gas supply diminishing, she followed a ribbon of cars on a highway to what she hoped would end at a suitable airfield. One never materialized, though, and she had no choice but to set the plane down on the main street of a small community, the oil boom town of Hobbs, New Mexico. The Avian was stored for the night, and after fried eggs, coffee, and bread at the Owl Café, Amelia plopped into bed, exhausted and sunburned.

Not surprisingly, following this incident, Amelia became an ardent advocate for sign painting: having the names of towns painted in bright colors on water towers or the roofs of buildings as an aid for pilots. She later played a role in promoting this system. At the time, getting lost didn't carry the stigma for pilots that it does today, although even now it still occurs, because not all planes are equipped with the most current electronic navigational tools. Amelia used pilotage and dead reckoning to navigate: with a map and compass she would fly from landmark to landmark, calculating groundspeed and arrival time based on the wind speed and the direction and distance between landmarks.[6]

At Hobbs the general store manager topped off the Avian's tanks before Amelia set off for Pecos, Texas, about 100 miles southwest of Hobbs. Still without a map, she used railroad tracks—the "iron compass"—and the Pecos River as navigation aids. At Pecos the Rotary Club gave her lunch, and she high-tailed it out that same afternoon for El Paso, but in transit motor problems forced her down among mesquite bushes and salt hills. Luckily she landed near a road with help readily available. The plane was rolled back to Pecos at a slow pace of ten miles an hour, with stops every three miles to let the wheel bearings cool.

Apparently a burned valve seat had caused the motor stoppage, which could have stemmed from bad fuel or a faulty valve. It was unlikely Amelia had used a chamois to strain the gas and eliminate sediment and water before refueling in Hobbs—a wise precaution at the time, especially when one was away from a home field. And she was not in the habit of performing routine maintenance on her plane, such as changing the oil and cleaning the spark plugs. Had she been, it was doubtful her numerous forced landings on the tour would have occurred. By contrast, using the exact same plane, Lady Mary Heath had made only one forced landing on her flight through Africa in 1928. Overcome by sudden sunstroke, she had managed to set the plane down in a veld, avoiding thorn bushes, and her Avian sustained only a bent undercarriage fitting, which was welded at the next stop. Lady Mary did all her maintenance, and at Cairo two airmen found her engine running "like a sewing machine" and better than when she had started out. This she attributed largely to her own diligence in performing one to three hours of routine work daily, which included doing the tappet clearances and cleaning the petrol and oil filters.[7] A year after Amelia's tour, in 1929 pilot Ruth Nichols reported making no forced landings during a 12,000-mile trip promoting aviation country clubs.

WHILE DELAYED IN PECOS five days for engine repairs, Amelia watched a mad dash of thirty-seven planes clocking in for the transcontinental National Air Races, and in honor of her presence the Town of Pecos named her local referee at the stop. Off the airfield, rattlesnake hunting and excursions to oil fields with the locals occupied her time, when she wasn't flipping through the pages of her newly published book, which George had had flown in from New York.

Armed with new maps, she set course for Arizona, where she made another forced landing, coming down at an isolated ranch near Douglas because her engine overheated. Within hours she was able to proceed to Yuma by following the Southern Pacific Railroad tracks. The sand field at Yuma presented its own problems, however, when well-meaning residents helping Amelia into takeoff position inadvertently gave the tiny plane a mighty push, sending it onto its nose.

By September 13 she was off to Glendale, California, arriving after a flight of two hours and fifteen minutes. Amelia, no doubt annoyed at what the press reported as her "half a dozen mishaps before arriving at her Western destination," avoided flying in to Mines Field in Los Angeles, which was the last stop on the National Air Races and the location for the Aeronautical Exposition. She told newsmen she was "just an amateur, a dub, flying around the country for personal amusement."[8]

AVIATION PROMOTER CLIFFORD HENDERSON thought Los Angeles a good venue to bring in throngs of spectators for the Aeronautical Exposition. Since its first air meet in 1910, the city had been kind to aviators. In 1927 Charles Lindbergh's arrival in his *Spirit* had drawn a mob of thousands to the city's Vail Field during his goodwill tour promoting commercial aviation. According to one historian, "Upon Lindbergh's arrival old men threw their hats into the air, women cried, and others shrieked, cheered, and roared until their voices were exhausted."[9] To be sure, in 1928 Amelia didn't get the same attention he received, but in 1935 hysterical fans would yell and mob her in Oakland, California, and Newark, New Jersey, when she landed after her record flights. When she visited Mines Field she was given a standing ovation, however. The exhibition showcased the latest aircraft, magnificently displayed on the field, and Amelia weaved in and out among them looking for her next machine.

With the Avian hangared at Los Angeles, Amelia flew as a passenger to San Francisco, where as a guest of the Army's 381st aero squadron she was made an honorary major and presented with the silver pilot's wings of the air service. She wore them proudly for the remainder of her life and would even sit for a portrait photograph dressed in a formal gown to which the wings were fastened, with a string of pearls gracing her neck.

NEVER ONE TO SHIRK from adventure, Amelia chose to fly home on a more northerly route. Her second leg out of Los Angeles resulted in yet another forced landing when the Avian's motor cut out near the Tintic, Utah, junction of the Union Pacific Railroad tracks she was following. Upon landing the plane nosed over on soft ground, smashing the propeller beyond repair. She was in remote country in central Utah, and a day later, on October 1, she arranged to have the Avian shipped by rail to Salt Lake City for a new propeller. (It was unclear why she didn't carry a spare propeller; often long-distance pilots lashed one to their planes.) A few days later she too boarded a train to Utah's capital, where headlines soon announced: AMELIA EARHART KEPT BUSY IN SALT LAKE; CHARMED, SHE WOULD LINGER and FLIER ENJOYS FORCED STAY.[10] George Putnam seized the sudden publicity bonanza and had her speak at three local high schools, discuss social problems before the board of the local Community Chest, and tour a settlement house.

On October 9 Amelia pointed the nose of the Avian eastward, flying over the Continental Divide to Cheyenne, and then on to Omaha and other stops without further incidents. She was the first woman to make a round-trip, solo flight across the United States. It was another rite of passage, and she had begun to learn the basics: navigation, meteorology, and the impor-tance of keeping her plane in good flying condition. She had landed on roads, grass, and sand; such diverse surfaces required different techniques for taking off and landing. Despite her many mishaps, when interviewed on her return to New York, she likened the 8,000-mile air jaunt to a pleas-ant vacation. She also added that it was her job with *Cosmopolitan* that now demanded her time.

10

OFF AND RUNNING

AMELIA'S FIRST ARTICLE FOR *Cosmopolitan* included pictures showing her fashionably dressed in a variety of outfits: a formal gown with a fur stole, a dancing frock, and sportswear for riding, tennis, and flying. Amelia looked the part of an all-American girl—pretty, confident yet slightly demure, exhibiting not a trace of brashness. Editor Ray Long introduced her to his readers, writing: "She will talk to you as her friends about her experiences in the air." In November 1928 exuberant Americans were enjoying seemingly endless prosperity and progress, and Ray Long joined the bandwagon, predicting people would soon "fly to our work…as casually as today we take taxis or drive our own motorcars."[1]

A month later, Amelia contributed to the magazine a lackluster rehash of her recent transcontinental flight. Her subsequent articles (a total of sixteen until February 1933) covered such topics as "Shall You Let Your Daughter Fly?," "Why Are Women Afraid to Fly?," and "Fly America First," among others. She also wrote occasionally for other magazines. She came to consider her editorial position at *Cosmopolitan* a chore because of the volume of correspondence. Recommend a flying school, her fans asked, or, How can we convince our parents or boyfriends of the safety of flying? Although she soon hired a secretary, her strenuous schedule of lectures and appearances allowed precious little time to respond to letters.

Upon Amelia's return from the West Coast in October, George presented her with a punishing schedule of lectures and appointments to promote the new book and solidify her position as America's foremost woman aviator. One month alone could entail thirty stops across a ten-state area. Leaving a lecture at midnight, she might drive all night, eat breakfast with reporters, and then nap a few hours before the grueling schedule started anew with her speaking at a luncheon and an evening engagement. A good week brought her an income of $2,400, as compared to the $35 weekly salary she had earned at Denison House in early 1928. At times she traveled with George; indeed, early in her career he booked himself along with Amelia to give talks on his Arctic explorations.

Sometimes Amelia flew to appointments, weather permitting, but occasionally hired pilots chauffeured her and her entourage around. British airman Bill Lancaster told Lady Mary Heath that George Putnam had hired him as a backup because Amelia was not yet experienced enough to handle larger aircraft. Bill flew but was officially known as the mechanic, George having sworn him to secrecy in his role.[2]

Audiences admired Amelia's spontaneity, sense of humor, and sincerity, and most remembered her personality rather than what she actually said. Aviator Louise Thaden, after hearing Amelia at a meeting of pilots following her 1928 Atlantic flight, remembered "she wasn't especially good looking." But once Amelia talked "a warm personality overshadowed everything else, and she became, somehow, beautiful."[3] Hungry for a heroine, audiences embraced her wholesomeness. George Putnam played a large part in coaching Amelia for her appearances, and she developed a seemingly natural rapport with all people, regardless of their age. "I deluged her with suggestions," he would later remember. He instructed her on the style of clothes to wear, to smile with her lips closed to hide the gap between her front teeth, and the proper methods of using a pointer, cards, and microphone. He advised her not to "let your voice drop at the end of sentences," and to end "matters crisply and definitely."[4] Of course George was "packaging" Amelia, but he could not have foretold how expertly she would assume the mantle placed upon her shoulders—or her relentless dedication to her new role.

Amelia appeared on stages everywhere, it seemed. There were speeches at clubs, universities, the American Red Cross, and events honoring welfare and social workers. Most important were activities celebrating pilots and the aviation industry. In December 1928 Amelia went as a guest of the government to the International Civil Aeronautics Conference, held to commemorate the Wright brothers' first flight, in 1903. The national media photographed Amelia, flanked by Orville Wright and Senator Hiram Bingham, president of the National Aeronautical Association, in front of the new Wright memorial at Kill Devil Hill. That she and George Putnam managed to position her so prominently was remarkable, considering there were 441 foreign and American delegates in attendance.[5] This type of brazen publicity undoubtedly triggered some pilots' animosity toward Amelia. In October 1928 Dorothy Putnam had reported after her dinner conversation with three internationally known aviators, "Gosh, how these three flyers loathe Amelia! It's a shame."[6]

The Putnam marriage was continuing to disintegrate, though George made attempts to hold on to Dorothy. "G. P. is determined to woo me and win me all over again and he's certainly concentrating," she noted in her journal on November 4. "He's even breaking dates with A.F.!" Whether George was truly panicked or merely postponing the inevitable breakup of his marriage is unknown. Either way, his reconciliatory gestures failed to impress Dorothy, and he continued to travel with Amelia, the both of them attending air shows and giving lectures. Whereas rumors of a Putnam divorce over Amelia had once circulated only among aviators, they now reached the public. Hilton Railey, contacted by one news agency, was "very obviously worried" about their effect, wrote Dorothy in her journal on November 22. A day later, Amelia announced to the press that she was no longer engaged to Sam Chapman. Shortly afterward, Dorothy began an affair with Frank Monroe Upton, a war hero and an acquaintance of the family.[7]

GIVEN ANY OPPORTUNITY, AMELIA campaigned to make commercial flying attractive to women travelers by lauding its safety and advocating for improvements in food and facilities at airfields, where attractive buildings were replacing hot dog stands and shacks. Universities and aeronautical shows and exhibits, with their concentrated audiences, were prime venues to air her opinions. She targeted young people, too. Addressing students at Columbia University in July 1929, she decried women's "inbred timidities," which were fostered by an "artificial difference between the sexes," citing the curricula at schools that prevented girls from learning mechanical skills.[8] Building model airplanes was the rage among boys, and to jumpstart girls' interest in the hobby she donated an Amelia Earhart trophy to be awarded to the girl earning the highest number of points in a model airplane contest. (It is difficult not to speculate what Amelia would think of women's progress in twenty-first century aviation industry. Today, eighty-one years after Amelia's speeches, when opportunities for women abound, they still number less than ten percent of the total pilot population.)

In early February 1929 Amelia's Avro Avian was one of forty planes displayed at the New York Aviation Show at Grand Central Palace. Her name figured prominently in press coverage of the event, where she and Lady Mary Heath sponsored a booth showcasing flying garments for women.[9] While in the New York area Amelia also had her first lesson flying a Ford Trimotor, a type of plane she would fly again in March. How much of the actual flying she did is unknown, and it's unlikely she performed a takeoff or landing, but she would have gotten a feel for handling the plane, which was some 10,000 pounds heavier than her Avro Avian.

Throughout March she continued to fly her Avian and other small planes, although with more mishaps and incidents. Landing at Curtiss Field on Long Island, New York, she nosed over the Avian, breaking the propeller; she was forced down in a Moth at Philadelphia while flying in an aerial caravan to Washington, D.C., to honor Ruth Nichols; and later she made an emergency landing in the Avian during a storm near Buffalo. The month ended on a high note, however, when on March 28, at Brownsville, Texas, Amelia passed the test for a Department of Commerce transport pilot's license, earning certificate #5716. The four-hour written exam covered meteorology, navigation, engines, and the department's rules and regulations, followed by a flight test. Although the license required 200 hours of solo time, instrument flying experience was not needed. Amelia was the fourth woman to receive the highly valued ticket, after Ruth Nichols, Phoebe Fairgrave Omlie, and Lady Mary Heath. Only forty American women held any type of pilot's license at that time.[10] Months later, Amelia started a new flight logbook that brought forward from a previous log a total time of 559 hours and 46 minutes.[11] At best her record keeping was suspect since she kept poor records of her flight hours, and it is unclear how she arrived at this figure.[12]

For the flight test Amelia would have used a type of plane she was comfortable with and probably flew a lightweight Avian or similar craft—she had a difficult time transitioning to larger aircraft that demanded a higher skill set. Elinor Smith, who had achieved notoriety in 1928 for her illegal flight under New York's four East River suspension bridges, would recall that in March 1929 Amelia showed up for a demonstration flight in a Bellanca, a high-performance plane she wanted to buy. Even after two flights, Elinor, a demonstration pilot, found that Amelia couldn't hold altitude or heading and "wobbled all over the sky."[13] Because of Amelia's poor performance, the designer Giuseppe Bellanca refused to sell her his plane even though she reputedly had in her pocket a check for $25,000 to cover its purchase price. Amelia would instead buy a Lockheed Vega later that year.

AMELIA MAY HAVE HAD trouble flying occasionally, but her publicity machine raced along in full gear, and in July her and George's efforts came to fruition again. She was appointed assistant to the general traffic manager at Transcontinental Air Transport (TAT), a newly formed commercial airline company also known as the Lindbergh Line. At its headquarters in New York, Amelia was tasked with flying its routes as a passenger while focusing on the needs of women travelers. Tat's officials felt women wielded considerable power in convincing the men in their lives to fly and expected Amelia's presence would be the draw they needed. Airlines would continue to try to lure women passengers over the coming years, and in her speeches and articles Amelia described their strategies and success stories. She would later write about the new enticements. United Air Line stewardesses, all of whom were registered nurses, offered to hold mothers' babies at stops, and TWA gave every woman a gardenia corsage as she deplaned.[14]

The unpressurized TAT trimotors flew at low altitudes in turbulent air. The company's combination rail-air service, costing about $300 (about the price of a basic new car), required passengers to ride trains for the nighttime portions of the journey. Air travel at night, as well as over the Allegheny

Mountains, was deemed too dangerous until the 1930s. By then technology had advanced sufficiently to permit all-air transcontinental routes.

On July 8 the movie star Mary Pickford christened a TAT Ford Trimotor at Glendale, California, where shortly afterward Charles Lindbergh started its engines to proceed eastbound on the inaugural flight. Meanwhile, in Columbus, Ohio, the westbound air service began the same day.[15] Amelia tried to appease Dorothy Putnam, who had been fretting at her lack of attention, by inviting her on the flight from Columbus; she accepted, although the two rode in separate airplanes.

At Winslow, one of the westbound stops, Charles's wife, Anne Morrow Lindbergh, again met Amelia whom she described as "very likeable and very intelligent and nice and amusing." The two women had attended a banquet several months earlier, after which Amelia had profusely thanked Anne in a letter for her "graciousness in absolving me from blame in the ridiculous 'Lady Lindy' publicity.... The title was given me in England, I believe, probably because one or the other of us wasn't a swarthy runt. You understand my dislike of the title isn't because I don't appreciate being compared to one who has abilities such as Colonel Lindbergh has, but because that comparison is quite unjustified." The Lindberghs had seen the barrage of "Lady Lindy" photos that Putnam released to the media immediately after the *Friendship*'s takeoff from Boston a year earlier, weeks before Amelia reached England. This letter represented yet another example of Amelia's adroit manipulation of circumstances, which helped to maintain her untarnished image.[16]

TAT's promoter, C. M. Keyes, also hired Eugene Vidal, a handsome ex-Army airman and West Point graduate, and former air mail pilot Paul "Dog" Collins, to join his burgeoning enterprise. Amelia's future forays into aviation would be intrinsically linked with theirs. Eugene's son, the author Gore Vidal, traveled as a boy on TAT flights and recalled: "As the passengers dined, and the plane lurched, and the smell of exhaust filled the cabin, cylindrical cardboard ice cream containers were tactfully passed around."[17] (The empty containers were provided because of the likelihood of air sickness.)

BY JUNE 1929 AMELIA had become bogged down with the administration of the Women's Air Derby, which further cut into her free time. The first cross-country race for women pilots, the derby would begin in August in California and end at the National Air Races in Cleveland, Ohio. On behalf of women entrants she had bombarded the offices of the National Aeronautical Association and the Cleveland race committee with telegrams to oppose their newly proposed rules. These rules dictated that a male navigator/mechanic accompany each entrant, and that the race to Cleveland start east of the Rockies to protect the women from the hazards of crossing the mountains. The entrants had been outraged upon hearing this. They insisted they would not enter under these restrictive conditions, and the NAA and the committee ultimately backed down.

It was the derby, as well as future record attempts, that Amelia had in mind when she was shopping for a new airplane and tested the Bellanca. She had settled instead on the Lockheed Vega, but postponed the actual purchase until July 30. That day she sold the Avro Avian and purchased a used Vega with a 225 horsepower Wright J5A Whirlwind engine. (In 1929 a new Vega, with the Wright engine, went for $14,750.)[18] The plane weighed 1,650 pounds empty, about double the Avian's weight. Besides a much faster cruising speed, the Vega was trickier to land: it required a 50 mile-per hour landing speed, about a third faster than the Avian. Lieutenant Orville Stephens flew Amelia in her Vega to California, where aviation legend Wiley Post tested the craft and declared it so out of rig and unfit to fly that Lockheed gave her another Vega in trade, registered as NC31E. The Women's Air Derby would start in weeks, leaving Amelia little time to learn how to handle the plane.

Her demanding schedule was one reason Amelia shortchanged her flight training, not allowing sufficient time to become familiar with her new plane. Her most celebrated peers—including Jacqueline Cochran, Edna Gardner Whyte, and Elinor Smith, among others—shared the opinion that Amelia simply did not have enough flying hours to warrant her making the longer flights she would embark on later. None of these three liked George Putnam, either. "He would promote these things and demand that she do them, way above her ability," said Whyte, who dubbed him a "heel." Smith claimed he had threatened to sabotage her own up-and-coming flying career when she didn't cave in to his various demands, one of which involved piloting Amelia around while pretending to be a nonflying crew member.[19]

Even though the derby race was slated to start in a few weeks and practice time was running short, Amelia was still making public appearances. In late July George cooked up a deep-sea-diving stunt for Amelia and asked his wife to join in the attempt. The first dive frightened Amelia, and the *New York Times* summed up her reaction under the headline MISS EARHART BALKS.[20] The next day she successfully dived and stayed underwater for twelve minutes. Dorothy Putnam also dived, and photographs of her fuller figure in a swimsuit were flattering, whereas Amelia looked skinny and unhealthy. George's push for this ludicrous charade cost Amelia valuable time that would have been better spent preparing for the upcoming derby.

ON A SUNDAY AFTERNOON, August 18, in Santa Monica, California, a throng of screaming spectators ringed Clover Field while dozens of newsreel planes flew overhead. Nineteen airplanes—in either the smaller sport or faster categories, determined by horsepower—were lined up in two rows to start the Women's Air Derby. Trailblazers all, the female pilots sat at the ready, awaiting takeoff. Ten drops of the red flag alerted each pilot of her turn, and upon seeing the final signal—the white and red flags coming down together—she would blast off.[21]

When her turn came, Amelia gunned the throttle of her red Lockheed Vega. The tail came up; she stepped on the right rudder to correct for torque, pushed the nose down to gain speed, and climbed away, setting course for San Bernardino, the first of eighteen stops along the way to the final destination of Cleveland, Ohio. Of all the planes entered, her Vega was the most feared competition. Not only was it fast and stable but its enclosed cockpit kept out sun, wind, and rain, thus helping to alleviate fatigue over the grinding 2,350-mile course. Hers was one of only two enclosed cockpits in the derby.

Grime and sweat would be the women's constant companions. The journey saw them flying in desert air so turbulent and violent they worried about stresses on the airframe, while battling 100-degree heat, rain squalls, and low visibility. On the ground they endured locals who drove their cars onto runways, which were often little more than dusty strips. Their planes' routine maintenance would also prove troublesome, at least until the derby was well under way and its glitches ironed out. Each town strove to outdo the others in hosting the ladies, and at each stop speeches and endless banquet dinners of rubbery chicken deprived the women of valuable sleep.

Only licensed women pilots with 100 solo flight hours, 25 of them cross country, were allowed to race, and Amelia figured that almost all those in the country who were qualified had entered. The race rules stipulated that the entrants wear parachutes and carry a three-day food supply (malted milk tablets and jerky were favored) and a gallon of water. Forced landings were expected on the inhospitable Southwestern terrain, where conditions could become life threatening.

By the time the race ended the condescending nicknames "Petticoat Pilots," "Ladybirds," and "Flying Flappers" would be discarded, the women having earned their stripes and taken another step toward encouraging lay-men to fly. The humorist Will Rogers's phrase "Powder Puff Derby" would stick, though. An aviation enthusiast, he had witnessed the start at Santa Monica and observed the women had no time for "maternal worries. They had given their lives to the carburetors."[22]

At the first stop, San Bernardino, billowing dust contributed to a number of incidents. Opal Kunz did a pancake landing in her Travel Air, damaging the gear, while Amelia overshot the runway, scattering bystanders but causing no harm to them or her Vega. The next day, cigar-chomping Florence "Pancho" Barnes followed the wrong railroad tracks and ended up lost. After landing her Travel Air she heard cries of *"Hola! Hola!"* from bystanders, and had to beat a hasty retreat out of Mexico toward Yuma, where Amelia's Vega was awaiting a new propeller from Los Angeles. Amelia had landed long, using up most of the runway, and then nosed over and bent her propeller. In an attempt to deflect blame for the crash, she would later claim the stabiliz-ers were at fault, but in reality she had landed too fast and too far down the runway. She had not realized that because of the extreme heat, she would need a longer landing roll-out. (This was the same place where, a year earlier, her Avro Avian had also nosed over when onlookers pushed the plane toward the runway.) By this time in the race, the pilots Claire Fahy and Thea Rasche had claimed sabotage, saying their machines were tampered with en route, but their claims were not substantiated.

Bobbi Trout, flying a Golden Eagle, landed just short of Yuma when her engine quit, and unfortunately she chose a deeply plowed field in Mexico in which to set down. Her wheels dug into the furrows, and her plane ended up on its back, requiring an extensive rebuild. Mechanics towed it to Yuma for repairs. Delayed three days, Bobbi, who was said to look like a man and fly like one, was determined to finish the race regardless of her standing. Her grit would earn her the admiration of both pilots and sponsors.

At Phoenix Pancho led in the heavy aircraft class, which included Amelia's Vega. The superb pilot Louise Thaden—who had earlier set women's endurance, speed, and altitude records—claimed second place in her beautiful blue and gold Travel Air, with Gladys O'Donnell's Waco third. Just south of Phoenix tragedy struck when Marvel Crosson, a skilled Alaskan bush pilot, crashed and died in an accident that was precipitated by carbon monoxide poisoning, according to Travel Air, the plane's manufacturer. Despite the calamity, which had led to criticism from several newspapers and calls to stop the race, the aviators resolved to carry on and compete in Marvel's honor.

In Pecos the next day, catastrophe struck Pancho when she landed atop a car parked on the edge of the strip, flattened its roof, and wrecked her plane's upper and lower right wings. No one was injured, but despite swearing and shouting and stomping around, Pancho was out of the race, her craft irreparably damaged. Landing behind her came the pretty actress Blanche Noyes in her crippled Travel Air, which had gotten banged up after an emergency landing to squelch a cabin fire, followed by a takeoff in mesquite brush. She patched the fabric skin with tape, had the landing gear welded, and then headed out again, still in the race.

TWENTY THOUSAND THRILLED SPECTATORS milled around the airport at Fort Worth. There Louise Thaden ranked first, while in the light aircraft class Phoebe Omlie maintained her lead in a Monocoupe, but Amelia was the star attraction. Policemen hired to contain the crowd could barely control the mob of autograph seekers surging toward her Vega when she taxied in.

Wichita, the home of Travel Air and Louise Thaden, pulled out all stops to welcome the women. Escort aircraft buzzed above the field and included a plane that was making an in-air broadcast of the ladies arriving to entertain the audience below. At 3:17 P.M. Louise flashed across the runway, then circled and landed. Still in the lead, she had resisted showing off, though she later recalled that only her tightly cinched parachute straps had kept her from jumping around the cockpit in excitement.

On the eighth day of the race, at Columbus, Louise charged ahead, followed by Gladys, Blanche, and Ruth Nichols, whose journey in a Rearwin thus far had gone without major problems. Ruth's luck ran out at Columbus. Upon landing, her plane hit a steamroller paving a portion of the runway, somersaulted, and flipped onto its back. She crawled out, unhurt, but she was no longer a contender.

The last dash occurred on Monday, August 26, a 120-mile afternoon leg into Cleveland, Ohio, the site of the National Air Races. In midday haze Louise Thaden's Travel Air dove toward the finish line in a powered descent, roaring by the Cleveland grandstand, where thirty thousand fans shouted their approval. The first to finish the Women's Air Derby, she clocked in with an elapsed flying time of 20:19:10, winning a purse of $3,600. Gladys O'Donnell took second place, and Amelia was third, trailing Louise by slightly over two hours.[23]

Amelia's inexperience in the Vega again caught up with her as she landed in front of the grandstand, with her plane bouncing hard three times, smacking up and down, and using up most of the runway. She managed to avoid an accident but emerged shaken and white-faced from the cockpit. Her overall performance in the race had not been stellar by any means, but of course she had owned the Vega less than a month.

THE NATIONAL AIR RACES of 1929, a ten-day flying circus at Cleveland, would draw a thousand aircraft and five hundred thousand spectators by its end on September 2. Charles Lindbergh, Jimmy Doolittle, and Eddie Rickenbacker, among other famous pilots, either performed or watched closed-course events and stunt displays. A key attraction was the arrival of the dirigible *Graf Zeppelin* on its way toward Germany, its home base. Capable of making Atlantic crossings in four days, dirigibles were at that time the only commercial aircraft able to fly across oceans.[24]

A day after the derby contest ended, there began closed-circuit events for women, including a 5-mile pylon competition and pursuit races. Amelia

was disqualified in the first, having missed a pylon in a turn, and she did not
perform in the others. She did try her hand at flying a 9491 glider belonging
to Wallace and R. E. Franklin, American glider manufacturers. The pilot
Frank Hawks waxed ecstatic about the machine and might have told Amelia
it flew like a toy, but the results were almost catastrophic. Amelia claimed she
could not get the glider to stop turning and flew it into the ground. She paid
the Franklins for the glider's loss.[25]

TWO YEARS EARLIER AMELIA'S correspondence with Ruth Nichols
had sparked the initial interest for organizing women pilots into an association. At Cleveland, before the pylon race, Amelia had gathered women pilots
in her hotel suite to discuss organizing such a club. The groundwork had also
in part been laid by Neva Paris during the derby: bubbling with enthusiasm
and energized by the race, Neva had gone from plane to plane at stops, telling the women of the forthcoming meeting. At the hotel the women ban-
tered back and forth, but the friendly talk ceased when Amelia proposed
that they race equally with men, in the same types of airplanes. Phoebe
Omlie, Elinor Smith, and Lady Mary Heath objected, arguing that women
could not handle these dangerous larger aircraft. In light of Elinor's often-
repeated statement that big machines were no harder to handle than those
smaller, her resistance seemed out of character, as did Mary Heath's, since
she had aspired to a career as a commercial airline pilot. True, some racing
planes were "flying coffins" because of their radical designs, but safe racing
planes existed and were popular with women and men. Amelia was fiercely
committed to equal rights for women pilots; she ultimately persuaded Mary
Heath and Phoebe Omlie, but Elinor Smith wouldn't budge from her position. Officially formed in November 1929, the organization was named the
Ninety-Nines and was chaired by Louise Thaden until 1931, at which point
she asked Amelia to become president because of her prominence.

Talented Neva Paris, who had contributed enormous energy to getting the group going, would perish after spinning in to a Georgia swamp
in January 1930. And even before the 1929 National Air Races ended, on
August 29 Lady Mary Heath crashed a Great Lakes Trainer while practicing a dead stick landing and was nearly killed. She recovered, but her severe

injuries effectively ended her aviation career, though she would fly as a private pilot. During the derby, the experienced bush pilot Marvel Crosson had died as a result of carbon monoxide poisoning. Then, as now, it was said there are old pilots and bold pilots but no old, bold pilots. The shortened life expectancy of pilots in Amelia's day poignantly bore this out.

11

FASTER

ABOUT A MONTH AFTER the Women's Air Derby, on September 3, 1929, the stock market peaked, ending a five-year tear of skyrocketing prices. Even small-time investors—clerks, maids, and cab drivers—had been buying securities on margin with borrowed money, scooping up stocks. While the economy boomed, Americans bought goods on installment plans, a new form of credit. Popular purchases included radio sets, costing about $135, and automobiles, which could cost three times that amount and more. Not everyone assumed the good times were endless. Astute investors sold at the peak, but most Americans believed stocks would increase in value and stayed in the market. As September marched on, however, stock prices began a downward slide that accelerated until panic set in and investors began screaming "sell." On Black Tuesday, October 29, the market collapsed and many lost their life savings, marking the beginning of the Great Depression.[1]

No one could have foretold the Depression's debilitating effects on the country or its extreme length. President Herbert Hoover attempted to reassure citizens that business would remain sound, but by 1933, 25 percent of the workforce would be unemployed. Amelia would have to work harder as the lecture trade and airline profits dried up; TAT faced severely reduced business and would lose almost $3 million in its first eighteen months of service despite halving its fares in January 1930.

But those events lay in the future. In November 1929 Amelia and her secretary, Nora Alstulund, were in Los Angeles with the indomitable maverick Jack Maddux and his wife, Helen, at their home on 49 Fremont Place. Maddux had owned a regional airline in California that had recently merged with TAT, forming TAT-Maddux, and Amelia was working for both its western and eastern divisions as assistant to the general traffic manager. Also visiting the Madduxes were Charles and Anne Lindbergh; Amelia would later write a flattering profile of Anne for *Cosmopolitan*.[2]

Amelia was "having a lovely time here flying a great deal," she wrote her mother. After piloting a borrowed Lockheed equipped with a Pratt & Whitney Wasp 425-horsepower engine, she boasted, "Today I think I broke the women's speed record in average time of 184.17 m.p.h."[3] However, the record was not ratified because Amelia had flown only 1 mile rather than the 3 kilometers mandated by the Fédération Aéronautique Internationale, the body responsible for approving aviation records.

That the FAI had finally agreed to recognize separate records for women can be attributed to vigorous petitioning by Lady Mary Heath, although Amelia would attempt to claim credit. Most of the FAI's male members did not want to admit women's records, but Heath was not one to be put off by the imposing organization. Finally, in 1928, her efforts had resulted in the founding of separate categories for women in altitude, speed, and endurance.[4] It is difficult to comprehend why Amelia did not credit Heath for her longstanding labors. Rather, Amelia wrote Bobbi Trout, "I have been advocating separate records for women, so that their accomplishments may be officially recognized."[5] She seemed to ignore Heath's efforts entirely and later told other pilots that she had been the chief campaigner for establishing these separate categories.

WHILE IN LOS ANGELES Amelia visited her father, who was happily married to his second wife, Helen, but in declining health. "He looks thinner than I've ever seen him, and Helen says he has no appetite at all and tires very quickly now," she wrote to her sister, Muriel. He fretted about making mortgage payments on his cabin and 5 acres in Eagle Rock, north of Los Angeles, saying he was "long on friends but short of cash."[6] She was not surprised, later writing, "I know the family failing about money."[7] Amelia paid off the $2,000 mortgage on the property and had a life tenancy freehold drawn up that would transfer to his widow upon his death, although title of the property remained in Amelia's name.

By now Amelia was also sending money and clothes to her mother and sister on a regular basis. Muriel had married Albert Morrissey, a business-man and veteran of the First World War, in June and was enduring a trying pregnancy. Amelia encouraged her mother to "stay with Pidge [Muriel]. I think she needs you and apparently Albert is no judge."[8] Muriel's long mar-riage with Albert would be fraught with difficulties, especially with regard to finances. In Albert's eyes his wife was a spendthrift who couldn't manage money; she considered him a selfish and stingy husband who deprived her and their two children of necessities. Amelia would soon help the couple pur-chase a house in Medford, Massachusetts, not far from where Albert worked in Cambridge.

Yet as Amelia's celebrity status grew, the distance between her and her family widened. Amy and Muriel were immersed in a traditional way of life revolving around family, whereas Amelia was consumed with her career and toiled long hours. Amy was hurt because she no longer had heart-to-heart talks with Amelia and would later write, "I felt the only time I had a chance to talk to her was when I was holding on to her coat tails."[9] Amy would remain preoccupied with family, whether immediate or extended, and she devoted all her energy to them since she did not hold an outside job. She was displeased that George Putnam had created such a hectic schedule for Amelia, leaving less time for her and Muriel. Further, she disapproved of the increasing intimacy between them, as Putnam was still a married man.

In mid-September 1929 Dorothy Binney Putnam and her youngest son, Junie, entrained for Reno, Nevada, where she established residence in order to obtain a divorce from George. Considering their eighteen years of marriage and two sons, Dorothy had agonized over the decision, but as she told a friend, George "doesn't need me anymore."[10] Although Frank Upton wanted to marry her, it was doubtful that alone would have convinced her to leave George. Rather, she had endured "public humiliation over George

and Amelia," as her granddaughter wrote many years later, and was determined to give her husband the freedom he apparently desired.[11] Despite
George's attempts at dissuading her from going to Reno—divorce still very
much carried a stigma then—she was convinced he did not love her. An
heiress, Dorothy didn't need George's financial support, but he expressed
concern that any future husband would take advantage of her wealth and
before consenting to the divorce insisted she create irrevocable trust funds
for their two sons. She accepted this condition, and they agreed to joint
custody of the boys, with George paying a portion of their yearly expenses
as well as a $5,000 one-time sum to Dorothy. An emotional Dorothy wrote
in her journal on December 20, "I released him just so he could marry her
[Amelia]. She's to get my husband, my house, my lovely garden—but not my
furniture!"[12]

Shortly after the divorce was granted, George made the first of at least
two marriage proposals to Amelia. Whereas Dorothy had agonized over
divorcing him, Amelia was almost terror stricken at the thought of marrying him. In 1930 she wrote to a friend, "I think I may not ever be able to see
marriage except as a cage until I am unfit to work or fly or be active—and of
course I wouldn't be desirable then."[13]

Now Amy Earhart had further reason to dislike Putnam. He was divorced
and twelve years older than Amelia, she disdainfully told Muriel. (In fact,
he was only ten years Amelia's senior.) The situation echoed painful episodes
from Amy's own life. In her later writings she would never mention her own
divorce, nor would she discuss Edwin's alcoholism or the poverty and hardships the disease brought upon the family. A proud and obdurate matriarch,
she retained a powerful capacity for denial in her continued attempts to pre-
serve the family's honor.

THE DEPRESSION HAVING BEGUN, 1930 brought an increasingly
strenuous schedule of activities for Amelia, for which she crisscrossed the
country to give speeches and lectures and to act as a judge at flying contests.
When possible she flew her own Lockheed to events; otherwise she preferred
driving her car. One month-long lecture itinerary began at Hamilton, Ohio,
on March 23, and concluded at Meadville, Pennsylvania, on April 24, a tour

that encompassed twenty-four stops, including a two-day layover at Purdue University. Before and after, there were other commitments—on April 26 she was an official guest at a mock naval warfare exhibition off the Virginia coast; on May 4 she was the only woman pilot participating in "Famous Fliers' Day" at the New York Air Show.

A day after Amelia's appearance at the air show, Englishwoman Amy Johnson departed from London for Darwin, Australia, flying alone in an open-cockpit Gipsy Moth named *Jason*. The twenty-seven-year-old slip of a girl, whose longest cross-country flight to date had been only 150 miles, battled dust storms, torrential rains, and mechanical breakdowns on the 11,000-mile odyssey. Her route transited Vienna, Bagdad, Karachi (where she was hailed as the "British Girl Lindbergh"), Rangoon, Bangkok, Singapore, and Java before she crossed the 500-mile stretch of the Timor Sea to Darwin, where she landed on May 24 to great acclaim. A licensed ground engineer, she made repairs to *Jason* en route herself or supervised others, and carried tools and spare parts, as well as a small revolver. (She didn't have reason to use the latter, fortunately, although she was once frightened by what she called "savages" who had surrounded *Jason* after she landed on an island in the Dutch East Indies.) Burnt red from sun and wearing a pith helmet, men's khaki shorts, men's socks, and oil-stained shoes, she was no fashion plate at her arrival, but Australians went wild. Congratulatory telegrams poured in from renowned aviators, including Charles and Anne Lindbergh, and awards and celebrations awaited her at home. That Amy came from a middle-class background and had struggled to finance her flight only added luster to her achievement.

Amy Johnson's epic flight might have further prompted Amelia to go after record flights herself. Competitive by nature, Amelia now set aside more time to fly. On June 25, she achieved two feminine speed records at Detroit: 281.47 kilometers per hour over a 100-kilometer course, and 275.90 kilometers per hour over a closed circuit of 100 kilometers with a 500-kilogram payload. On July 7, also at Detroit, she set another speed record over a straight 3-kilometer course of 291.55 kilometers per hour. For these officially recognized, FAI-ratified flights, she used a borrowed Lockheed Vega even though earlier in the year she had bought a new Vega of her own with a 420-horsepower Pratt & Whitney engine. Less than a month later, on

August 4, Pancho Barnes would better Amelia's speed record by piloting her Travel Mystery Ship 315.67 kilometers per hour, although for unknown reasons the flight record was never ratified.[14]

Meanwhile, new rules proposed for the 1930 Women's Air Derby had aviators in an uproar. In the interest of the women's safety, according to the committee, planes with more than 200 horsepower were barred from the race. In effect, this eliminated the country's best women aviators, who piloted powerful ships—including Amelia, Pancho Barnes, Ruth Nichols, Blanche Noyes, and Elinor Smith. (The mother of a newborn, Louise Thaden had already decided against entering.) Additionally, two army pilots and a flight surgeon were required to accompany the women's race eastward. Amelia announced she had "neither the means nor the desire to provide another plane for the race," and she and the other leading female pilots stuck to their guns and refused to enter the competition.[15] Still, the discriminatory restrictions did not block women from participating in other races, and the Pacific Women's Air Derby proceeded from Long Beach, California, to Chicago, where the National Air Races were set to begin in late August. Other women flew in the Dixie Derby, from Washington, D.C., to Chicago.

IN 1930 AMELIA LEFT her position at TAT, either owing to a dispute over the firings of her friends Eugene Vidal and Paul Collins or simply as part of a general housecleaning at the airline, which was suffering financially. Vidal expressed no remorse at being fired from TAT and was confident he had the business acumen and ready market to run a new airline. Nicholas and Charles Townsend Ludington, brothers who were wealthy businessmen, agreed to invest in his idea, a regular New York–Philadelphia–Washington service that would fly "every hour on the hour," then a revolutionary concept. The New York–Washington round trip would be $23, and tickets would be sold in railway terminals.[16] (The airline used the Newark terminal because there were no commercial airports in the metropolitan New York area at the time.) As general manager of the Ludington Line, Vidal appointed Amelia vice president in charge of public relations and traffic management, and in September 1930 the airline began regular service, using ten-passenger Stinson trimotors.

These were still the early years of commercial aviation, a nascent industry that few people yet took seriously. Eugene Vidal would later relate anecdotes of the airline's startup days: Passengers afraid of flying would bring alcohol aboard and would throw the empty bottles out the window, where the glass would shatter against the propellers and puncture the fuselage. (The line finally redesigned the windows not to open.) As for weather forecasts, at the start of the day's New York—Washington run, recalled Vidal, they sent the "very best pilot. After he landed, if he reported the weather to be all right, then we sent out the later scheduled departures; if not, they stayed on the ground." And one time passengers ended up back at the same airport they'd left a few hours earlier, after a dispatcher in Philadelphia put Washington-bound passengers on the New York-bound plane by mistake.[17]

Despite being "terribly occupied with the infant airline," Amelia was obligated to fly west after receiving an urgent wire from her father's doctor in California. Seriously ill, suffering with inoperable stomach cancer, Edwin was nearing death and wanted Amelia by his side. Describing the scene to her mother, Amelia later wrote that "he didn't want to go....He was an aristocrat as he went—all the weaknesses gone, with little boy's brown puzzled eyes." While there she paid his "100 debts," reassured him he had just won a legal case (in fact he had not), and faked telegrams to him from her mother and sister. Despite the hardships Edwin had caused his family, she still adored him.[18]

Shortly after Edwin died in September, Amelia seriously damaged her Lockheed Vega while landing at the Hampton Roads Naval Air Station at Norfolk, Virginia. The plane nosed over and went on its back, its fuselage breaking. She blamed the crash on her over-application of brakes. She suffered a wound to the scalp and her passenger in the rear cabin a broken finger, but wearing a turban over the bandage, she kept a speaking engagement that night at the Norfolk-Portsmouth Traffic Club. However, she would be without an airplane for nearly a year until Lockheed rebuilt the Vega with another fuselage and a 450-horsepower Pratt & Whitney Wasp C engine.

The stress of her father's death and the Vega accident, plus a heavy workload—articles to write, promotion for the Ludington Line, and speeches—along with her family's continued financial problems, began to wear on Amelia. Where earlier in the year she had written her mother not to worry about accepting money from her, she expressed frustration in a letter dated October 13: "In sending your check last month, I forgot to tell you that the money is for you. I know how easy it is for you to give it away to Pidge and the Balises [Amelia's aunt's family]. However I am not working to support either. Little things are all right but I don't want any large proportion to get out of your hands—borrowed or given."[19] Despite Amelia's instructions, Amy would continue to dole out her daughter's hard-earned money to whomever she wanted.

Again George proposed to Amelia, in the fall of 1930, shortly after he had joined the publishers Brewer and Warren as vice president. This time she accepted. Amelia had expressed reservations in the past, which some of her friends shared: during a lunch with Amelia, Elinor Smith told her she would rather see her married to Genghis Khan. Bobbi Trout later reasoned that "Amelia gave in to G. P. and married him because he was a darn good promoter, and after all, the promotion that he did would bring in money. That was hard to get during the Depression and she was smart enough to know that."[20] His love for her might have exceeded hers for him, although many of her friends were convinced she reciprocated his feelings. Her close friend Jacqueline Cochran wrote, "She was nuts about him. It was her attitude. Her face would light up when he'd telephone or the way she'd look at him." For her own part, Cochran couldn't understand Amelia's attraction for George, who she said was the "dullest person I've ever been around."[21]

Marrying Putnam ranked among Amelia's smarter career decisions. Lonely yet ambitious, she probably felt the partnership would enable her to accomplish more record flights and maintain her role as the eminent spokesperson for women in aviation. With only three guests present, the couple wed at George's mother's house at Noank, Connecticut, on February 7, 1931. The thirty-three-year-old bride wore a brown suit with a crepe blouse and brown lizard shoes, an unremarkable outfit for a momentous occasion. What was remarkable, however, was the letter she handed to George before the ceremony, which read in part: "In our life together I shall not hold you to any medieval code of faithfulness to me, nor shall I consider myself bound to you similarly.... I must exact a cruel promise, and this is that you will let me go in a year if we find no happiness together."[22] After reading the letter, George smiled and nodded before taking her hand; he later deemed it "brutal in its frankness but beautiful in its honesty."[23] Amelia borrowed a wedding ring for the ceremony, but she never wore one thereafter. She and George elected not to go on a honeymoon; Monday morning found them both at their respective offices. In a letter to her mother dated February 22, Amelia merely wrote, "I am much happier than I expected I could ever be in that state. I believe the whole thing was for the best."[24]

12

THE AUTOGIRO

AFTER THE FIRST WORLD WAR a young Spanish engineer named Juan de la Cierva had designed a bomber for a military competition, and its woeful first flight changed the course of his career. During a low-level turn it stalled and then crashed, and though the pilot was unhurt, the disaster drove Cierva to resolve the problem of the stall. He set to the task and in the 1920s invented the autogiro, an aircraft that would not stall and therefore would not go into a spin.[1] It took off and landed almost vertically, with the ability to make short hops into and out of small fields, lawns, and country club grounds, and thus held great appeal to both aviators and the public. Some observers compared an autogiro in motion to a wasp or flying windmill: it was equipped with an engine in front, short, stubby wings, and rotor blades mounted above the open cockpit. Today we might consider it a cross between an airplane and a helicopter, although both of these require more training and skill to fly. The autogiro was safer than airplanes, although landing one was tricky, especially in crosswinds. Pilots remarked that while the machine might get damaged in a crash, they would walk away from the wreckage.[2]

In 1928 Harold F. Pitcairn acquired the American rights to the autogiro, and at his factory in Willow Grove, near Philadelphia, he continued to refine its design. Pitcairn's model was priced at a hefty $15,000, some $4,000 more than an airplane of similar size and power. A brilliant promoter, he cooked up unusual schemes to publicize the craft and made certain to secure extensive press coverage, aided by voluminous copy and photographs churned out by his advertising agency. For his development of the machine and contributions to American aviation technology, the National Aeronautic Association awarded him the prestigious Collier Trophy for 1930.

THE AUTOGIRO FASCINATED AMELIA, who was grounded until the Detroit Aircraft Corporation finished rebuilding the Vega she had crashed in the fall of 1930. A pilot without an aircraft is no pilot at all, and eager to get back in the air as well as the limelight, she recognized an opportunity in the new aircraft. In December 1930 she became the first woman to fly an autogiro, at Willow Grove. Four months later, on April 8, 1931, she set an unofficial altitude record in the Pitcairn autogiro, reaching 18,415 feet and making the front page of newspapers across the nation. While she claimed that she made the flight for one reason only—because Pitcairn had asked her to determine the craft's ceiling (or absolute altitude)—she maintained "there was no idea of seeking a record" but admitted that an NAA official observer had been on site and a sealed barograph was put in place, both of which were required to verify a record.[3]

George Putnam and Harold Pitcairn were cut from the same cloth, always on the lookout for a publicity bonanza. Two weeks after Amelia's altitude record, Pitcairn's machine, the PCA-2, was demonstrated before President Herbert Hoover on the grounds of the White House. Pitcairn also offered complimentary rides to journalists, who would then go tout his autogiro's revolutionary characteristics in newspaper columns.[4]

Meanwhile, during the year Amelia was flying the autogiro, Brewer, Warren & Putnam released a book coauthored by the machine's inventor: *Wings of Tomorrow: The Story of the Autogiro*, by Juan de la Cierva and Don Rose.

ALL OF THIS PRESS coverage caught the attention of the Beech-Nut Packing Company, eager to promote its chewing gum and cash in on the headlines. George Putnam stepped in to negotiate a deal between Amelia and the company, which agreed to provide her with an autogiro whose fuselage was emblazoned with the Beech-Nut logo. In return Amelia would pilot the "flying billboard" while setting a record for the first transcontinental flight in an autogiro, all while promoting Beech-Nut's product.

Unknown to her, though, a professional pilot named Johnny Miller, whose talents extended to aerobatics and test flying, had also ordered a PCA-2 and planned a similar flight. Awaiting their crafts, the two met at the Willow Grove factory, where Amelia, Miller later claimed, told the Pitcairn company pilots she "was not interested in all the aerodynamics and short landing procedures"; she "just wanted to fly it across the continent and then fly around the country."[5] She was simply after the record. In contrast to Amelia's apparently haphazard approach to training, Miller had spent hours learning about the autogiro, which included practicing more than a hundred takeoffs and landings.

With mechanic Eddie de Vaught and 100 pounds of spare parts and tools aboard, Amelia launched from Newark for the Pacific Coast on May 28. The PCA-2, equipped with a 330-horsepower Wright engine, cruised at about 80 miles per hour, so flying into a 25-mile-per-hour headwind, it traveled at the same rate as a car. The trip was tiring, requiring a stop every two hours to refuel because the inefficient craft could only hold a limited amount of gas, and the flying was hands-on, meaning Amelia had to be actively handling the flight controls at all times. Pictures taken from the jaunt show her dressed in a shirt and tie, jacket, and jodhpurs, her face lined from fatigue. At stops she handed out sticks of gum, demonstrated the craft, and patiently answered questions thrown at her by pilots as well as kids and their parents. She kept smiling in the face of inane comments, such as one from an elderly lady who thought it would be a cute machine in which to chauffeur her husband about. Amelia and Eddie reached Oakland, California, on June 6, having traveled the northern route through Wyoming and Colorado without any mechanical incidents along the way.

Upon her arrival in Oakland, Amelia and George Putnam were stunned to find she had been upstaged: Johnny Miller had flown solo across the country in his autogiro and landed in San Diego a week earlier. Furious that his wife had lost her bid for a record, George decreed she would fly her autogiro back to the East Coast, in the hopes of capturing a round-trip record. Thus began a series of misadventures for Amelia.

Her first accident in the autogiro, when she crashed before a crowd at Abilene, Texas, on June 12, made national headlines. During a takeoff she forced the craft off the ground before it was ready to fly, and it dropped thirty feet, hitting two cars, damaging its propeller and rotor, and endangering spectators. Putnam rushed out a press release that exonerated Amelia and blamed the accident on a "small whirlwind which passed under the plane and reduced the air pressure."[6] Amelia was quick to say she hadn't been careless. But within weeks the aeronautic branch of the Department of Commerce would strongly disagree, finding her "guilty of carelessness and poor judgment" and officially reprimanding her, despite her claim that she had exercised her "best judgment" in handling the crash.[7] Amelia and Eddie headed eastward after another autogiro was dispatched to Texas, and she concluded the 76-stop campaign in Newark on June 22.[8]

Meanwhile, Amelia's rival, Johnny Miller, ended up back at the Pitcairn factory having had no accidents or mechanical problems during his round-trip transcontinental flight. When factory mechanics looked over his autogiro after his June 30 landing, they determined all it needed was an oil change. For the next several years Johnny would tour the country in his beloved craft, demonstrating it at air shows, including the National Air Races. He was "in the money," as he later said, sometimes earning $1,000 for each roll on top of a loop, a complex maneuver that proved to pilots the essential sturdiness of the machine. Johnny went on to become a legendary airman who was still flying in his nineties.[9]

Amelia finished up her autogiro escapades with two more crashes in 1931. During the summer she flew locally and landed on a fence at Camden, New Jersey, and reportedly said she would not fly another again.[10] Despite her claim, she was lured into flying for Beech-Nut as part of a new advertising campaign, perhaps drawn by the money. ("Here I am jumping through hoops just like the little white horses of the circus," she wrote to a friend.)[11] Then, in September at the Michigan State Fair Grounds, she failed to level off while landing and the machine dropped 20 feet. The craft sustained serious damage, ending up with a demolished landing gear, a bent wing, and twisted rotors, but Amelia was unhurt. Her husband, along for the tour, fared worse.

George suffered three cracked ribs and a sprained ankle after running to the accident site and tripping over a guy wire. A few hours later Amelia set off to another engagement in Saginaw, flying a borrowed machine.[12]

A month before the Michigan crash, *Cosmopolitan* published Amelia's article titled "Your Next Garage May House an Autogiro," a puff piece lauding the craft's usefulness for commuting and getaway vacations to country retreats. Although during the fall she made a third autogiro tour in the South, without incident, there is no record of her flying one after 1931. This concluded Amelia's short career with the autogiro, as more pressing demands took up her time. In between the Beech-Nut campaigns, she had done lecture tours, and late in the year started work on a new book, later released by Brewer, Warren & Putnam as *The Fun of It*. Exhausted from the grind of lecturing and flying for hire, she determined the following year would allow her more freedom. Her Lockheed Vega was finally rebuilt, its inspection certificate signed off on September 17, 1931, and her head was ablaze with ideas for new record attempts.

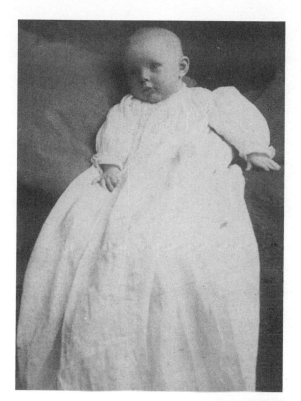

Baby picture of Amelia Earhart wearing white christening gown, c.1897. National Air and Space Museum, Smithsonian Institution (SI 82-8676).

Amelia Earhart as a nurse's aide in Canada. Photo courtesy of Kansas State Historical Society.

Crew of Friendship *upon their arrival at Southampton, England, following their trans-Atlantic flight, c. June 18, 1928. Left to right stand two unidentified people, Lou Gordon (mechanic), Amelia Earhart (passenger), Wilmer Stultz (pilot) and the Mayor of Southampton. National Air and Space Museum, Smithsonian Institution (SI 2002-3007).*

Eugene Vidal. Courtesy of the Library of Congress, Harris & Ewing Collection.

Amelia Earhart walking with her husband, George Putnam. Putnam is wearing a suit and tie and carrying his hat; Earhart is wearing trousers, long-sleeved white shirt and scarf. Buildings, possibly hangars, appear in the background. National Air and Space Museum, Smithsonian Institution (SI 82-8669).

One-half right rear view of Pitcairn PCA-2 Autogiro (r/n NC 10780), operated for the Beech-Nut Gum company, sitting on the ground. Amelia Earhart stands beside the aircraft in flight clothes, and factory smokestacks are visible in the background. National Air and Space Museum, Smithsonian Institution (SI 85-3357).

Left to right: Paul Mantz, Amelia Earhart, Harry Manning, and Fred Noonan posed in front of Earhart's Lockheed 10E Electra (A/C No. NR16020) prior to taking off from Oakland, CA for Honolulu, HI, March 18, 1937. Original, photograph autographed by Earhart, Manning, and Noonan. National Air and Space Museum, Smithsonian Institution (SI 2009-31377).

Amelia Earhart stands on the wing of her Lockheed 10E Electra as she heads for the cockpit before her take-off to Paramaribo, Dutch Guyana, from Caripito Airport, Caripito, Venezuela, June 3, 1937. National Air and Space Museum, Smithsonian Institution (SI 2003-11320).

13

SECOND CROSSING

IN SOME WAYS Amelia Earhart profited from not having her own airplane to fly during 1931 because she learned from the mistakes and triumphs of other well-known pilots. One was Ruth Nichols, who had begun a flight across the Atlantic. With much fanfare and advance press, Ruth departed in her Lockheed Vega from New York for Paris in June 1931, but during a landing en route at St. John's, New Brunswick, she overran the runway, crashed, and seriously injured her back, which required her to wear a cast for months. It was a banner year for other aviators, though. Wiley Post and navigator Harold Gatty flew a Vega around the world in slightly over eight days; Clyde Pangborn and Hugh Herndon Jr. barreled nonstop over the Pacific in their Bellanca; flying a Lockheed Sirius, Charles and Anne Lindbergh surveyed air paths from New York to Alaska and Japan; and numerous other successful flights made headlines.

All of these flights reinforced Amelia's burning desire to firmly establish her reputation as an aviator. She wanted vindication, and only a stellar flight, a first for women, could erase the impression that she had been no more than a "sheep" or a "sack of potatoes" on the *Friendship* flight in 1928. She decided she would fly solo across the Atlantic, a "flight merely for the fun of it," as she described it, which would prove to her and to "anyone else interested, that a woman with adequate experience could do it."[1]

The mishaps of her friendly rival Ruth Nichols may have influenced Amelia to prepare carefully. Ruth had probably been rushed by the hoopla preceding her attempted flight to collect on the publicity and cash contract promised her by Paramount News. It seems she had also not thoroughly evaluated the layout of the short runway at tiny St. John's airport, and apparently other aviators questioned her preparedness. In Ruth's memoir, *Wings for Life*, she described meeting the Lindberghs in early 1931 with her adviser, Clarence Chamberlin, during which Charles Lindbergh warned of the dangers of a crossing and urged her to carry an emergency radio set. He had not been convinced she would succeed.

A year later, in 1932, Ruth was gearing up to make another transatlantic attempt. There was also talk of Elinor Smith shoving off across the pond if her mysterious backer—"Mrs. Question Mark"—came forward with more funds.[2] George Putnam realized that Amelia's status and reputation as America's best-known woman pilot would be jeopardized, or possibly lost forever, if any woman made the solo transatlantic flight first. Besides, income generated from Amelia's stunts replenished the family's coffers, and the economy remained devastated by the Great Depression. It was a once-in-a-lifetime opportunity that George and Amelia could not let pass by.

According to George, Amelia broached the subject of a solo transatlantic flight to him in the winter of 1932 over buttermilk and breakfast at their home in Rye. This bit of lore that he propagated made for a good tale, but he knew of her plans well before then, having freed up her schedule to allow for what would be the zenith of her career. She would maintain a course of speaking engagements until departing, however.

What experience Amelia had gained during her previous flights would culminate in this attempt, but she sorely lacked the skills needed for flying by instruments alone. Her previous flights had been made in good weather, under conditions allowing visual navigation. She hadn't practiced navigating in storms and fog. And she had little experience with interpreting weather by reading plotted charts of isobars, fronts, and high- and low-pressure systems, all of which was crucial information to pilots. She relied on the flight planning and weather expertise of professionals.

The weather window for transatlantic hops was short—and it was already spring. George had decreed her departure would take place on May 20, 1932, the fifth anniversary of Charles Lindbergh's flight from New York to Paris. Amelia would no doubt have recalled that bad weather had thwarted the *Friendship*'s departure in 1928, on the first anniversary of Charles's flight. Nonetheless, Amelia was impatient and there was a push to launch on this new date.

Yet again George recruited Dr. Kimball of the United States Weather Bureau in New York, who had so ably performed for his team in 1928. The meteorologist was surely pleased by the coverage of the flight that appeared in the *New York Times*. One article, under the headline OCEAN FLIGHTS OF MIXED VALUE: WHILE CONTRIBUTING LITTLE TO THE SCIENCE OF AERONAUTICS, THEY HAVE LED TO BETTER CHARTING OF ATLANTIC WEATHER,[3] pointed out Kimball's assistance to Amelia. Working quietly behind the scenes, Kimball and his colleagues rarely received the recognition they deserved.

It was imperative that Amelia find an expert in long-distance flying right away to prepare her and her Vega for the crossing. Over a game of croquet one sunny April afternoon in Rye, Amelia told the Norwegian flyer Bernt Balchen of her wish to fly the Atlantic solo and requested his help. Bernt, famous for his Polar flights with Richard Byrd, promised to get her and the Vega ready. Still, she had doubts. She told the taciturn, blue-eyed Norwegian that if he had reservations about her or the Vega at any time during the training, he should say so and she would cancel her plans without holding him in any way responsible. To maintain secrecy, she chartered her Vega to Bernt, who was known to be planning an Antarctic expedition with Lincoln Ellsworth. The smokescreen worked, freeing Amelia from advance ballyhoo and expectations of the press and public, who didn't realize she was training for a distance flight, and it allowed her time to study instrument flying under Bernt's tutelage. Because Bernt didn't believe she had the stamina for an ocean flight departing New York, he decided he would fly her to Harbour Grace, Newfoundland, from where she would fly solo.

Bernt brought on board mechanic Eddie Gorski and transferred Amelia's crimson, gold-striped Vega to Teterboro Airport in New Jersey, near the Hudson River, just across from New York. To increase the Vega's range to 3,200 miles—which required 420 gallons of fuel—the fuselage was strengthened and extra fuel tanks were housed in the wings. Another tank went in the cabin, which was now cleared of seats. Instructing her how to best work the fuel system, enabling even distribution of weight as each tank emptied, was Major Edwin Aldrin, father of future Apollo 11 astronaut Buzz Aldrin.

The new instruments installed in the Vega included a drift indicator and an aperiodic compass, along with a directional gyro that required frequent resetting to readings on the magnetic or aperiodic compasses. Neither Amelia nor George ever mentioned whether the Vega was equipped with an artificial horizon, an instrument that shows whether a plane is climbing or diving, the direction of turn, and its bank angle. By 1931, use of the artificial horizon was becoming standard in blind flying, and it is improbable that anyone would have undertaken a hazardous transatlantic flight without it. The Vega would also have had a turn and bank indicator in its panel—another necessity.[4] Rounding out the Vega's new equipment was a supercharged Pratt & Whitney Wasp engine with 500 horsepower.

Amelia decided against carrying a radio set. She was not, nor ever would be, proficient in Morse code or in using a telegraph key, which were needed to communicate at the time. Elinor Smith later reported that Amelia was the object of much criticism in aviation circles because she refused to take along a radio set. Nor would Amelia carry a life raft or other survival equipment.

IN MID-MAY AMELIA HAD lunch with Ruth Nichols at her home in Rye, where they discussed problems inherent in ocean flying. Ruth figured she was planning a flight, possibly over the south Atlantic, but Amelia didn't let on. During all this time, only George, Bernt, Eddie, and Amelia's cousin Lucy Challiss—who was staying at the Putnams' home—were privy to the secret flight. During the lunch Amelia also expounded on her philosophy of long-distance flights: "I don't bother to go into all the possible accidents that might happen. I just don't think about crackups."[5]

Despite what Amelia told Ruth, she did in fact take several precautionary measures and was clearly unsure she would survive the transatlantic flight. In April Amelia had a new will drawn up appointing her husband the executor and trustee of her estate. (Signed with her legal name, Amelia Earhart Putnam, the will was dated April 5.) In May she sent her friend Louise Thaden a two-page letter of directives—to be performed should she not live: "As Vice President of the Ninety Nines, you will succeed to the Presidency if anything happens to me. To make your job easier—in case—I am listing what you will find in the club files and making a few suggestions for future conduct of its affairs." The letter went on to detail Amelia's dealings with members and her hopes for the club's future.[6]

Newsreel footage of Amelia shot just before her takeoff further indicated her unease. Her high-pitched voice wavered and she lacked her customary poise: "I *think* I am ready for a transatlantic hop. I've chosen to use a plane with which I am familiar, having flown it at least three years. I *think* I couldn't have undertaken this trip unless I had confidence in the plane, the engine, and perhaps my own experience."[7] The risky crossing had been flown solo only once—by Lindbergh, from New York to Paris—and many other pioneering pilots had been lost, never to be seen again.

ON MAY 19 DOC Kimball at the weather bureau notified George of fair skies all the way to Harbour Grace. Amelia dashed home to Rye, changing into her flying costume of jodhpurs and a shirt, over which she would don a heavy brown flight suit. Again, as in 1928, she carried no personal baggage; a toothbrush was her only accessory. She did not possess a passport, nor in fact did she have governmental approval for the flight.[8]

With Amelia and Eddie as passengers, Bernt flew the first lap from Teterboro Airport to St. John's, New Brunswick, where the three stayed overnight. By this time George had leaked her plans to the press, and in St. John's newsmen pressed Amelia for details. She stood firm, saying she would not give out her destination until reaching Harbour Grace, although newspapers nationwide speculated it was Paris. Comparing her proposed flight to Lindbergh's, optimistic journalists predicted she could reach Paris in fifteen hours, taking into account her faster plane (its Wasp engine had more than twice the horsepower of his Whirlwind) along with its better instruments and modern, more complete weather reports.

Following a four-hour hop, the trio arrived in Harbour Grace on May 20. While Amelia napped at a hotel, Bernt and Eddie topped off the tanks to their full capacity and stowed aboard a thermos of soup and three cans of tomato juice—but no can opener. Amelia would end up using an ice pick to puncture the cans' lids during the flight.

Bernt pored over weather reports prepared by Kimball and wired to him by George Putnam, but the decision to leave rested solely with Amelia. That day, a low-pressure system with heavy cloud cover lingered over the eastern Atlantic but was expected to move north out of her flight path. Forecasts for the following day called for northwestern or westerly winds, low clouds with good visibility below, and light showers. Despite the uncertain weather, Amelia was in a hurry to launch, just as she had been four years earlier, in Trepassey, when her impatience had spurred the argument with Bill Stultz. Although Amelia was determined to take off, it's possible the next day would have brought more favorable weather.[9] She later told newsmen that the weather reports from both sides of the ocean had been 100 percent wrong; two days later, Bernt stated he had advised her to postpone departing because low temperatures aloft might contribute to icing.

The final mechanical checks were completed by Bernt Balchen before Amelia arrived at the airport, where they reviewed the course and weather forecasts. Bernt recalled her uncertain demeanor before takeoff: "She looks at me with a small lonely smile and says, 'Do you think I can make it?' and I grin back: 'You bet.' "[10] Amelia's Vega roared off the runway at 7:20 in the evening, then climbed and circled before flying over Conception Bay. Skies were clear and sunset was at least two hours away. Bernt, Eddie, and the airport manager stood atop a cliff watching the red plane disappear over the horizon toward Europe.

Amelia still had not said where she was headed, be it Ireland, Paris, or Rome, as some supposed. A *New York Times* headline the next day read: MRS. PUTNAM FLIES ALONE FOR PARIS ON 'LINDBERGH DAY,' and announced she was due at her destination that morning.[11] Meanwhile, officials and spectators had begun to gather at Le Bourget in Paris to greet her. At the weather bureau in New York, George told reporters his wife "intended, if the plane were in good condition, to continue to France after soaring over Ireland."[12]

Leaving Newfoundland, Amelia climbed to 12,000 feet, spotting three small icebergs below. She was on course, tracking the great circle route toward Valencia Island at the southwestern tip of Ireland, her first intended landfall. Two hours later the moon rose and patches of scattered clouds fused below her into solid overcast covering the ocean. The next two hours of the flight went well, with no mechanical problems or storms, until she saw ahead of her a towering cloud mass, much too high to climb over. Barreling into the cloud, her Vega was tossed about through turbulent air like a tiny wood chip.

She encountered the first of several technical issues that would plague her throughout the flight when her altimeter failed, its pointers swinging around its face erratically. This was the first altimeter malfunction she had ever experienced; without the instrument, critical for blind flying, she would not know her height above water or land. Only visual cues could confirm her proximity to either.

She then saw flames spewing from the Vega's engine exhaust manifold. A cracked weld in the manifold had begun to burn through, which could become a fire hazard to the plane. She weighed the risks of returning to Harbour Grace and landing at night with a heavy load of fuel—if she could find the unlit airport—but despite the failures of the exhaust manifold and altimeter she elected to continue on. She reasoned she could be more than halfway across the Atlantic in the time it would take her to get back to Newfoundland.

Even worse was to come. The storms went on unabated, despite the weather bureau's prediction that they would be temporary. All through the long night bad weather persisted, bringing the scourge of all aviators: ice. An accumulation of ice weighs down an aircraft, changes the shape of the wings, and can adversely affect the engine's operation. Amelia had seen icing choke the *Friendship*'s carburetor over the Atlantic in 1928, and she knew its hazards.

Seeing a layer of slush forming on her windshield, Amelia climbed to a higher stratum hoping to escape its effects. That being unsuccessful, she had no choice but to descend to warmer air, which put her skimming over churning whitecaps in the darkness, dangerously close to water.[13] The smallest lapse of attention would have submerged the plane in the waves. Again she climbed, but again ice began to form. She was forced to fly near the water until the wretched night ended. Her flight log aboard captured the horrors of the experience and revealed a secondary reason she skimmed the waves:

13 HOURS ON THE WAY. IF ANYONE FINDS THE WRECK KNOW THAT THE NON SUCCESS WAS CAUSED BY MY GETTING LOST IN A STORM FOR AN HOUR AND THEN THE EXHAUST MANIFOLD RE-SOLDERED AT ST. JOHN BLEW OUT. HAVE CRAWLED NEAR THE WATER FOR HOURS DREADING FIRES.[14]

Amelia and her team had never disclosed that the manifold had been re-welded at St. John's, which leaves one to question the plane's mechanical fitness for the journey. Who signed off on the repair? Was it a hack job to get her on the way quickly? An expert repair or the installation of a new manifold could have prevented the problem. Newspapers had reported the manifold fitting, a new one, had not shown the "least sign of trouble...on the way to Harbour Grace."[15]

At dawn Amelia found the Vega between two cloud layers, the top at approximately 20,000, the other scattered around 1,000 feet above the water. Around this time she reached up to turn the valve for a reserve fuel tank, only to have gasoline drip onto her shoulder. This fuel leak was the final straw for Amelia. She now worried that the manifold would ignite fumes from the gasoline. She abandoned any thoughts of flying on and determined to land as soon as possible.

She did not know her position, but below, the waves indicated a strong wind from the northwest. She turned north to correct, thinking the wind had pushed her south off course. Then she noticed a small fishing vessel, which she thought was about 100 miles off the coast. After the Vega circled it three times, the little boat tooted its whistle and let off a small smoke bomb, confirming the sighting. At least everyone would know she had made it that far.

Although Amelia later claimed she arrived near Valencia Island, the Vega made landfall farther north, at County Donegal, on the northwestern tip of Ireland. Had she continued on this errant northerly course she might have come upon Scotland or flown farther over the ocean, missing land entirely.

In any event, she was 200 miles off course, a significant deviation from her plotted route.

Looking down at lush green countryside, Amelia spotted a winding railroad track. She expected the tracks would lead to a town and an airfield, as was typical in the States. Finding neither, she opted to land in a pasture. After checking it for wandering livestock (another bane to pilots), she swooped down to land at Culmore, near Londonderry in Northern Ireland.

Her face streaked with oil, she climbed out of the plane to ask an approaching farmer, "Where am I?"

"In Gallagher's pasture," he replied in a lilting Irish accent. "Have you come far?"

"From America," she said.

The farmer would recall that night that "when she spoke with a woman's voice, I would like to have fell through the earth."[16]

In 14 hours 54 minutes, Amelia Earhart had flown 2,026 miles, landing at 1:45 P.M. local time.[17] She alighted with 100 gallons of unused fuel (on which the Irish government levied an import tax). Even if her plane had not had mechanical problems, it's doubtful she could have reached Paris, since the winds at Le Bourget had turned unexpectedly strong from the southwest. Parisians were disappointed to learn she would not be landing there. Despite falling short of her destination, Amelia was ecstatic at having made the transatlantic crossing alone, the first by a woman and a feat that eclipsed those of any woman pilot in the world.

14

CELEBRITY

ALTOGETHER AMELIA EARHART'S solo transatlantic flight was an achievement of which she had every reason to be proud. She was the first woman to fly the Atlantic solo and the only person to fly it twice, and she established an unofficial record for the longest nonstop distance flown by a woman.[1] Her Atlantic crossing also broke a speed record set in 1919 by Englishmen John Alcock and Arthur Whitten Brown, but her Lockheed Vega, fitted with the latest technology, hardly warranted comparison to the primitive Vicker Vimy bomber the men had flown thirteen years earlier.

While Amelia's flight had not contributed to the scientific advancement of aviation, as she herself admitted, it instilled in the public more confidence in the reliability of engines and airframes. All such endeavors affirmed the probability of future commercial transoceanic flights. The airlines were seeking to conquer the oceans, the newest frontier. To carry passengers, they would first use flying boats because landplanes were then incapable of carrying sufficient payloads. Weighing up to 41 tons and equipped with luxurious amenities, these were seaplanes with hulls that allowed them to land on water.[2]

Amelia's flight also buoyed the spirits of women worldwide and was hailed as a victory for feminism, as indeed it was. Her feat had increased the "prestige of her sex," noted an article in the *New York Times*.[3] Looking back on her era, we today can find it difficult to comprehend the rampant discrimination women then faced. Many professions excluded them. Universities and technical institutions did not admit women into engineering, medical, or law programs, nor were bar associations open to them. Hospital privileges were denied to women physicians. Even in teaching, a profession in which women dominated, they earned only half the salaries paid to men and lost their jobs if they married. The majority of working women had low-paying jobs: clerks, cooks, and maids.

Amelia brushed off the "feminist" label, but there were few women more committed to the cause than she, and both in her flights and in the way she lived her life she demonstrated that women were men's equals. She deftly used humor to temper the image of feminists as strident. "Feminine resentment at all the 'catty things' men say about women drivers and women pilots" was the impulse behind her transatlantic flight, she said to the *Boston Herald* in 1932.[4] Several months after making this statement, she would join the National Woman's party in calling on President Hoover to support legislation granting equal rights to women.

AFTER AMELIA LANDED at Culmore, she was driven to nearby Londonderry, where she placed a call to George at the Hotel Seymour in Manhattan. No ships had reported seeing her plane, no one had word from her, and George had been up all night frantically pacing his suite awaiting news, along with Hilton Railey, who manned the telephones. Among the first calls George made were to Amelia's sister and mother; the latter quipped that any landing on land was a success. Around the globe teletype machines began clattering with news of her landing. Within a day Amelia was deluged with congratulatory cables, including telegrams from President Hoover, heads of state, aviators, and friends. Her plane secured for the night in Culmore, she slept at a nearby country estate.

The following morning cameramen staged and shot a reenactment of her landing, which George had arranged to be included in a newsreel shown in America shortly afterward. In a plane chartered by Paramount News, Amelia was then flown to Hanworth airfield, near London, where

American ambassador Andrew Mellon and other officials awaited her. At the rain-soaked airfield Amelia posed for pictures, bandied with reporters and gave interviews, and watched a fistfight erupt between a cameraman and a reporter vying for coverage. Despite saying she was not tired, her adrenaline-spiked excitement had dissipated, and the photographs showed her to be fatigued with a drawn face. Still, she made a transatlantic radio broadcast before arriving at the American embassy, where she gave another round of interviews after dinner, wearing a borrowed pink dress. The next day she shopped for a new wardrobe at Selfridges on Oxford Street, where her Vega, having been flown to London by another pilot, would be displayed until it was shipped home.

Unlike her 1928 trip to London, when Hilton Railey ran interference, Amelia had no one to help manage the arriving avalanche of invitations. Overwhelmed, she turned to George to provide assistance—and to share in her glory. George soon set sail to Europe on the S.S. *Olympic,* even though he was busy lining up a position as chairman of the editorial board of Paramount Studios in Los Angeles, at the same time that he was arranging Amelia's post-flight appearances in New York and Boston.

There was some criticism of Amelia's solo flight in the press the day she landed. Read the *New York Post*: "We think it an almost entirely silly and useless performance. About all she has proved is that well-known phenomenon of nature that a girl can't jump quite as far as a boy can."[5] The *New York World-Telegram* announced, "Amelia Earhart has given us a magnificent display of useless courage."[6] Britain's C. G. Grey, editor of *The Aeroplane*, lay another barb, writing that her 1932 flight in a modern airplane simply proved "a woman is capable of doing what a mere man did in 1919, but in three hours less than the man's time."[7]

On the other hand, the *Boston Sunday Globe* and the *Los Angeles Times* heaped fulsome praise on Amelia's achievement, comparing her flight to Charles Lindbergh's 1927 crossing. The first printed a map, labeled "Two Flights Just Five Years Apart," comparing portions of their routes; the second posited, "But for a leaky gasoline gauge she might have duplicated the five-year-old feat of Colonel Lindbergh and landed the plane in Paris, according to her original plan."[8] These were exaggerations, to say the least. Even if Amelia had landed in Paris she could not have duplicated Lindbergh's

3,600-mile flight, since he launched alone from New York. In contrast, Harbour Grace was about 1,900 miles from the tip of Ireland, so Lindbergh's flight was 1,700 miles longer than hers. Nonetheless, by staging the flight on the fifth anniversary of Lindbergh's, Amelia and George had invited these comparisons, which reputable national newspapers rushed to embrace.

In Putnam's autobiography, he describes himself as a hustler since childhood—but Amelia clearly was not. Yet through some combination of ambition and reticence, she allowed herself to be pulled into George's publicity stunts; she let newspapers exaggerate her accomplishments and reprint his press releases that exculpated her from blame for her own accidents. George continued to be her stepping stone to fame and a better life, and while she would retain an untarnished public persona throughout her life—and even after—his reputation would eventually suffer.

UNTIL GEORGE ARRIVED in Europe, Amelia sorted through the relentless onslaught of invitations alone before selecting which ones demanded her participation. She attended air meets, luncheons, and dinners, and was received by the Prince of Wales at Buckingham Palace, with whom she later danced at a charity ball in a shimmering dress described by one reporter as "Atlantic green."[9] At a reception at the Royal Aero Club she also met other notables, including the aviators Lady Mary Bailey, Winifred Spooner, and Amy Johnson. Over time these grueling appearances, accompanied by obligatory speeches, strained her voice, leaving her only able to whisper. Other commitments pressed, too. She dashed off a final chapter briefly describing the Atlantic flight for *The Fun of It* and cabled it to Brewer, Warren & Putnam for the book's imminent release.

In early June George arrived at Cherbourg, France, and Amelia was there to meet him on board C. R. Fairey's yacht *Evadne*. She greeted him with a smile, standing in a doorway, and said "Hi!"—a perfunctory welcome that said everything and nothing, as if her flight had been a mere local jaunt. They went to join Fairey's party for breakfast and soon after entrained for Paris.

At the Gare St. Lazare station a boisterous crowd was on hand to cheer Amelia, shouting *Vive Miss Lindy,* a cry she would hear throughout her visit in Paris. She was awarded the Cross of the Knight of the Legion of Honor (she was called the "reflection of Lindbergh" at this ceremony) and a gold medal from the Aero Club of France. She called upon the mother of Charles Nungesser, who perished on a transatlantic flight in 1927, and laid flowers on the Tomb of the Unknown Soldier and on the Monument to the Escadrille Lafayette. George, familiar with Paris and European customs, was a marvelous help to his wife, whose face glowed from the admiration continually bestowed on her. He, on the other hand, was red-eyed and teary with hay fever, caused by the enormous bouquets of flowers banking their hotel suite.

Leaving Paris, Amelia and George were flown to Rome for a conference of aviators, all of whom were men, their chests laden with medals. While in Rome she was received by the Pope and by Prime Minister Benito Mussolini. From there she and George proceeded to Brussels, where King Leopold presented her with the Cross of the Order of Leopold. On June 15 the couple boarded the *Île de France* for New York, with Amelia's disassembled Vega on board.

The attention continued upon her return to the United States. Thousands of spectators cheered her arrival in a tickertape parade down Broadway, reminiscent of that given Lindbergh, and on a much larger scale than the *Friendship*'s crew had received in 1928. There was a dinner at the White House, and on June 22 the National Geographic Society awarded her its Special Gold Medal, the first woman to be so honored. Another award followed when the United States Senate voted to confer upon her the Distinguished Flying Cross, which had previously been bestowed on men only. She was also the first woman to receive honorary membership in the National Aeronautic Association. She would also be awarded the coveted Harmon International Aviatrix Trophy for the year 1932.

THE CELEBRATIONS FINALLY BEHIND her, Amelia returned to flying her Vega, which had been reassembled and inspected after its voyage. She had in mind a feminine nonstop transcontinental record but only told the press she was heading west to Los Angeles to attend the summer games of the Tenth Olympiad. In reality she wanted to start the flight from the West

Coast to take advantage of prevailing westerly winds—tailwinds that could boost groundspeed and shorten the flight time. On July 1 she flew George and his son David to Los Angeles in the Vega.

Nine days later she made an attempt for the record. She took off from Los Angeles, but a fuel feed problem forced her to stop at Columbus, Ohio, for slightly over an hour. She landed at Newark, New Jersey, with an elapsed time of 19 hours 14 minutes—a woman's record, but it was not nonstop. Disappointed, Amelia claimed she wasn't attempting a record and made the flight solely to practice navigation. Two years earlier Frank Hawks had blasted across the country in 12 hours 25 minutes. Amelia felt challenged to make another attempt soon.

Amelia returned to Rocknoll, her home in Rye, New York, while George remained in Los Angeles for his job with Paramount. She loved the rambling, slate-roofed house atop a hill, with its sloping lawn and gardens filled with a profusion of flowers. The property was her sanctuary away from crowds, a refuge and meeting place for her many friends (not all of whom were pilots), and relatives. At times members of the Ninety-Nines congregated there, leading George, who joked that he had to "establish machinery for masculine self-protection," to form a club for their husbands.[10] He named it the Forty-Nine Point Five Club (also known as the 49 ½-ers) and it remains active to this day.

Amelia's home at Rye also became a retreat for Eugene Vidal, her former boss at the Ludington Line, who had become estranged from his wife, Nina. The daughter of Tennessee senator Thomas Gore, Nina was a beautiful, high-strung socialite reputedly more interested in partying than in nurturing her son, Gore. She did not share her husband's passion for aviation. By the summer of 1932 Vidal was a frequent visitor to Rocknoll as was young Gore, who was sure Amelia was in love with his father. Whatever the nature of her feelings, there was no question that Amelia was devoted to him, given her loyalty and the help she would later provide to further his career as director of the Bureau of Air Commerce. Little Gore adored Amelia and wanted her to marry his father. Years later, when an interviewer asked Gore if the two had had an affair, he replied: "She had more than that. I said to him, 'Why didn't you marry her?' . . . He said, 'I have never really wanted to marry another boy.' And she was like a boy."[11] Despite Gore's allegations, this author has found no evidence one way or the other to substantiate an affair between Amelia and Eugene.

After flying to the West Coast with Eugene and her cousin Lucy Challiss, whom Amelia claimed was the only aviation fan in her family, Amelia rejoined George and David in Los Angeles, where they had been enjoying local sporting events when not hobnobbing with athletes, movie stars, and other celebrities. Meanwhile, the *Oakland Tribune* announced that Amelia would sponsor a trophy race for women pilots at the National Air Races in Cleveland during the week of August 27 and would award an Essex Terraplane automobile to the woman who came in first.[12] She decided against participating in any of the races in Cleveland, although she would drop in to visit. The hiatus in Los Angeles had refreshed Amelia, and another nonstop record flight attempt loomed.

Amelia launched the afternoon of August 26 from Los Angeles, her Vega stashed with tomato juice, soup, and water, and flew over the Sierras toward Albuquerque. From there she flew a federal airway, the same used by commercial airliners. The Vega sped over St. Louis and points eastward, swooping in to land at Newark just before noon on the twenty-seventh, a 2,626-mile flight that established two records. The first woman to make a nonstop flight across the country, she had also set a woman's world distance record, ratified by the FAI shortly after. But she shaved only nine minutes from her flight time of a month earlier and attributed that to adverse cross-winds. Additionally, thunderstorms on her route to Kansas had forced her to follow the federal airways instead of flying a direct course. The punishing flight, the longest she had made, left her short tempered when a small crowd swarmed around her in Newark. "Don't come near me. You know what I feel like," she exclaimed before recovering her usual gracious manner.[13] Four days after her landing James Haizlip smashed the transcontinental record with a time of just over 10 hours, a little more than half Amelia's.

The course planner for both pilots' flights had been Commander Clarence S. Williams, a navigation wizard Amelia regularly employed. For his work on the August flight she paid him $53.05, writing him that "her last attempt was certainly the hardest." She also commented that she hoped to do a "better job" sometime.[14]

EVERY MONTH AMELIA sent her mother $100, a sum sufficient to provide for a small family, yet it was never enough.[15] Amy continued to dole out her allowance to Muriel and other family members, ignoring Amelia's instructions to budget the money carefully. Amelia also sent Amy and Muriel stylish clothing, and gave Amy money explicitly for her vacations and medical bills. Amelia paid half the expenses to maintain the mansion at Rye, and both she and George added to a joint account for other costs, including lavish entertaining and the salaries of their retinue—secretaries, servants, gardeners, and other employees. On top of this, she paid to keep an airplane and to fly, which required an outlay for hangar rental, inspections, mechanical jobs, parts, gasoline, and oil—to name just a few of the ongoing costs. The Putnams may have projected an image of wealth, but they sustained it only through constant diligence. Today we would call them workaholics.

Seeing money slip through Amy's hands exasperated Amelia. She not only dealt with an irresponsible mother and sister, she had to reconcile financial messes created by other family members. When her aunt Margaret Balis died in early 1932, it was discovered that she had borrowed $2,000 from a trust fund established for her mentally handicapped brother Theodore. There was no money to repay the loan, and he needed financial support. Amelia said no one could have treated him worse than his own family and had her lawyer negotiate an agreement in which she would loan money to a new trust set up in his name.

Amelia resumed lecturing in the fall of 1932, visiting Chicago and other Midwestern cities. She next planned a tour to New England with George along for moral support because, for unknown reasons, she did not like the territory. Earlier Amy implied she might want to accompany her but then hesitated. Not sure of her mother's plans, Amelia wrote, "You said maybe it was just as well that you didn't go so there would be no chance of your disgracing me or words to that effect."[16] In any event, Amy stayed with Muriel, perhaps declining the offer after hearing George would accompany her daughter.

Amelia's nineteen-stop lecture itinerary began in Brooklyn, New York, on November 10 and concluded at Toronto, Canada, on December 13, with an interim appearance at her father's alma mater, Thiel College, in Greenville, Pennsylvania, where she was awarded the honorary degree of Doctor of Science. She gushed in a letter to her mother: "I met several people who were in Dad's class and others who knew him. I found his record for scholarship, i.e., age of graduation has never been equaled. Everyone remembered Dad as so handsome and bright."[17]

In this same letter Amelia revealed she had sold her Lockheed Vega to the Franklin Institute Museum in Philadelphia, although she refrained from disclosing that the sale netted her $7,500. The airframe worn, the plane outdated, she kept only the motor, which was later installed in her newer Vega, registered as NR 965Y. After a few weeks at home, she would begin yet another round of lectures on the West Coast. Her stellar year of accomplishments ended, she would become even more famous as her circle of influential friends widened

15

THE TREADMILL

IN THE SUMMER OF 1932 Franklin Delano Roosevelt, then governor of New York, chartered an airplane to transport him to Chicago, where at the Democratic National Convention he accepted the party's nomination as presidential candidate. Roosevelt, a former assistant secretary of the navy, was a charismatic, handsome politician—a visionary in many respects. An aviation enthusiast, he was the first candidate to fly to a convention, a fact surely noted by Amelia Earhart. And in an age in which women's opinions outside their family circles were not solicited—much less taken seriously—Roosevelt admired strong, independent women, who in turn trusted him and became loyal followers. As president, he appointed the first woman to the Cabinet: Frances Perkins, United States Secretary of Labor. His wife, First Lady Eleanor Roosevelt, was a popular, respected figure in her own right and supportive of Amelia's ventures.

Had the fates cast a different role for Eleanor Roosevelt, she might have lived as adventurous a life as Amelia did. She was smitten with Amelia's daring flights and bravery and actually considered taking flying lessons until her husband forbade the idea. The two women first met in the fall of 1932 when Eleanor invited the Putnams to Hyde Park for an informal dinner that preceded Amelia's lecture at Poughkeepsie, New York. The two women found they were kindred spirits and became friends, with Amelia and her husband being occasional guests at the White House. President Roosevelt would later be instrumental in helping Amelia with several aspects of her world flight.

Amelia's hectic schedule went on unabated during the beginning of 1933. At a banquet in January the Romanian government awarded her and Charles Lindbergh medals for their aeronautical achievements. Eight days later, she and George threw a small dinner party at Rye to honor Auguste Piccard, the famous Swiss balloonist. Of American aviators, Piccard most admired Amelia and Lindbergh, and consequently Charles and his wife also attended. To the Putnams' mortification, a day later the press reported in detail Charles's conversations with Piccard, leaked by another dinner guest. Immediately George sent a letter of apology to the Lindberghs on Amelia's behalf. In her reply, Anne Lindbergh consoled Amelia, asking her not to think any more of it, and also thanked her for spending a recent wonderful evening with her grandmother and aunt in Cleveland.

Following the January events, Amelia proceeded to California and began a lecture tour, which she later described to her mother as "much more intensive than I had planned because the management [George] kept trying to squeeze in more and in these times I thought I might as well do as much and get as much as I could." Concluding this letter was a plaintive request that Amy not give away money from the check she enclosed, "if the giving means fostering dependence and lack of responsibility."[1] That was another reference to Muriel, who depended on her mother's generosity—or rather, Amelia's—as well as Amy's help with housework and childcare.

Besides lecturing, Amelia was heard on radio broadcasts, a popular vehicle for celebrities and certainly the most far-reaching media at that time. One such airing occurred on February 24, when Edwin C. Hill, a well-known radio commentator, interviewed Amelia for "The Inside Story" on WABC in New York. That same day First Lady Eleanor Roosevelt discussed "The Woman as a Wage Earner" on WEAF. During the gloom of the Depression, Americans would huddle around the family radio set, a prized possession and sometimes their only source of entertainment. President Roosevelt took radio's social significance to a new level, with his famous fireside chats pulling in listeners across the country.

ON APRIL 20 THE Putnams were guests for dinner and an overnight stay at the White House. In a masterful publicity move arranged by George, after dinner Amelia and Eleanor Roosevelt, who wore long evening gowns and white gloves, went for a ride in an Eastern Air Transport Condor. After Amelia introduced Eleanor to the pilot, he handed over the flight controls to the First Lady. Thrilled with the ride in the star-speckled night sky, she said, "It was like being on top of the world!"[2] In Amelia's speech addressing the Daughters of the American Revolution the next day she remarked on the fine example set by Mrs. Roosevelt, who, she said, "flies and enjoys it."[3]

By this time Amelia was using her speeches as platforms to foster her beliefs. She stumped for commercial aviation, equal rights for women, and pacifism, and it was the latter that sparked the most ire. To the audience of three thousand DAR members hanging on to her every word, Amelia said she and they did not "see eye to eye. You are very much interested in the national defense through the army and navy." Amelia then dropped a bombshell, proposing women should be drafted in war, and added that members of organizations advocating armaments should themselves be willing to bear weapons. "I feel that such would be as patriotic a move as any because by such a means war might be ended." The audience gasped but recovered to politely applaud.[4] In general, she did not see the importance of national defense, and a few months earlier had proposed funds for such be instead given for unemployment relief.

Amelia did not have expertise in this area beyond her few months serving as a nurse's aide during the First World War. She was exhibiting the celebrity's familiar tendency to give voice to opinions even when on precarious ground, fobbing off her sometimes naïve opinions on the public. In discussing the careers of women pilots, she complained that females did not receive the "free" training given men: most professional pilots at the time had been trained in the military.[5] One wonders, though, how she would have responded had the military branches opened opportunities to women flyers in 1933. Nonetheless, she claimed that hostilities would end if women had to carry weapons and fight in wars; that the elderly should be drafted first since they start war; and that women should partake in "dirty work and real fighting instead of dressing up and parading down the streets."[6] This last point was indeed a slap in the face to the nurses and other women who had helped before, during, and after the First World War, including those who had sold Liberty bonds and performed volunteer work for the Red Cross. Other women had driven ambulances along the European front, and they too had suffered wounds from the trench warfare.

DURING THE FIRST WEEK of May, Amelia resigned as vice president of the National Aeronautic Association and left the group because she opposed its plans to turn over its monthly magazine to a private agency, and to initiate a membership campaign. She spent most of May and June at Rocknoll, a leisurely break interrupted only by a few appearances and pleasure excursions. Her Vega was in flying condition, and though she seldom used it for other than occasional trips, in June it was called into immediate action. Cliff Henderson, director of the National Air Races, invited her and Ruth Nichols to compete in the 1933 Bendix Race, the first time women flyers were allowed to participate. Amelia scrambled to prepare for the famous cross-country air race, considered then perhaps the ultimate test of flying skills. To soften the impact of the two-week notice he gave the ladies (the men had months to prepare), Cliff offered a special award of $2,000 to the winning woman pilot and a consolation prize of $1,000 to the other.

The Bendix was an all-out race for speed, in conditions similar to those a pilot faced in everyday travel by airplane, with varying terrain and weather. It was not a handicapped race, nor were limitations placed on the engine power of the entries or the route chosen by pilots. The dash began in New York and terminated in Los Angeles. The colorful Roscoe Turner, later renowned for flying with his pet lion Gilmore, won the event, and his time of 11 hours 30 minutes became an east-west record. One contender crashed his Gee Bee on takeoff after refueling at Indianapolis and died from his injuries the next day; another withdrew. En route Amelia dealt with nauseating gas fumes leaking into the cockpit, a loose hatch cover, and motor troubles, which required an overnight stop for repairs. She landed in Los Angeles a day behind her male competitors, all of whom had flown more powerful ships. Ruth, flying a borrowed Lockheed Orion, arrived a day after Amelia. Despite her poor showing, Amelia took home the promised $2,000 purse, and the flight was a good practice run, a shakedown for her next project: another nonstop transcontinental record attempt.

After taking off from Los Angeles, Amelia landed at Newark Airport on July 8. She had cut her previous time by nearly two hours, but problems dogged her on the 17 hour 17 minute flight, which was not a record because it was not nonstop. Another loosened hatch cover forced her to land at Amarillo, Texas—after she flew 75 miles holding it down—a delay that cost more than two hours as well as the nonstop record. She refueled at Columbus, Ohio, and took off in rain and low visibility to Newark, where three hundred spectators and George cheered her landing. In greasy white coveralls, her hand sprained from holding the latch cover, Amelia apologized for her appearance. It would be her last major flight until 1935.

THE MONTH OF JULY heralded great achievements for aviators. Wiley Post flew alone in a Lockheed Vega, the *Winnie Mae*, around the world in less than eight days, the first *solo* circumnavigating flight. The Vega was equipped with new instruments, including a Sperry Automatic Pilot and a direction-finding radio to assist with navigation. An estimated fifty thousand people greeted him when he landed back in New York on July 22. In mid-July General Italo Balbo's fleet of Savoia-Marchetti S-55X flying boats arrived from Rome over Lake Michigan to Chicago, the site of the "Century of Progress" World's Fair. As the twenty-four huge ships swooped in to land, stunned onlookers stood amazed at the demonstration of Italy's air power. Amelia had met Balbo in Rome a year earlier after her 1932 ocean flight. She too visited the Chicago fair, posing for photos in a hot air balloon.

Also in July, the long-distance flyers Jim Mollison and his wife, Amy Johnson, each famous for their solo record flights, made a joint east-to-west crossing over the Atlantic. Launching from Wales, they flew the hard way, against prevailing winds. Twenty-four hours out, Amy's flight log reported making landfall at Newfoundland, and she wrote "economizing petrol to try

to make N.Y."[7] Amy urged Jim to refuel at Boston but he insisted on pro-
ceeding nonstop to New York. Close to the Bridgeport, Connecticut, airport,
some 50 miles from New York, their twin-engine De Havilland Dragon sput-
tered dry, out of fuel. Exhausted, Jim landed downwind at night in marshy
ground. The plane flipped onto its back, wrecked beyond repair. Both he
and Amy were injured and briefly hospitalized, and it was then that George
Putnam stepped in.

He showed up at the Plaza Hotel the day they checked in and on behalf
of Amelia invited them for a weekend at Rocknoll. Unknown to all concerned then, it would include a luncheon with President Roosevelt and his
wife at Hyde Park. Jim Mollison returned to England to outfit another
airplane, but Amy stayed on, basking in the warm reception she received
from the Americans. Given her allure and friendliness, it was no surprise she
appealed to most everyone she met. She looked upon Amelia, who would
become enormously influential on her, as a big sister and thought her an
ideal heroine.

Amy returned to the Plaza, which became her headquarters. She wrote
her father:

> I am constantly in touch with Amelia and her husband and am well in with the
> White House and the Government at Washington (or I think so—anyhow one eve-
> ning they sent a couple of men to see me specially on trying to get women interested
> in using the airlines)... On Friday I am motoring to Boston with Amelia... She
> is the first woman Vice President of an airline, which is being opened at Boston,
> so we are going together for the inauguration.[8]

The new airline, a subsidiary of the Boston & Maine Railroad, operated five
daily flights between Boston and Portland, Maine, priced at $9.50 round
trip, and two daily between Boston and Bangor, at $23 round trip, with
additional stops on some routes. The president of the new carrier, named
the Boston-Maine Airways, was Paul Collins, Amelia's colleague from the
Ludington Line, which Eastern Air Transport had acquired after it failed
to receive an air mail contract. The fledgling airline had in service trimotor
Stinsons, the very same used on the Ludington. To furnish and operate the
planes, the principal stockholders, who included George Putnam, formed a
holding company named National Airways, Inc.

Amelia toiled for months to breathe life into the little airline and sell seats. On the inaugural flight thousands turned out to cheer her at Bangor. The following summer she would promote the line again, and a crowd of ten thousand turned out to glimpse her at another event in Bangor. Under George's aegis, the marketing was extraordinary and innovative. Influential people were invited to personally meet Amelia at the airport; women were offered free rides or asked to visit her at formal teas; local clubs hosted festivities honoring her and the new airline. By 1934 service had been added to Montreal and Burlington, Vermont.

Paul Collins was eager to replace the airline's Stinsons with the Lockheed Model 10 Electra, a new twin-engine ten passenger plane. Northwest Airways also wanted the plane for its northern transcontinental route, and on May 26, 1934, two days after taking delivery of the first of five Electras it acquired that year, the airline would inaugurate service from Chicago to Seattle. Amelia was involved in advising Northwest on the purchase. She was also acquainted with the route, flying as an observer on a Northwest survey flight to Seattle in a Ford Trimotor, in January 1933. In March 1933 she wrote Northwest vice president Croil Hunter, "Concerning specifications for the twin-engine Lockheed, Paul Collins expressed himself as satisfied with details of construction, motors, gears, sound-proofing, instruments and their arrangement, as well as with all 'gadgets.'"[9] Amelia may not have been qualified to delve into the technical aspects of the plane, but Northwest was more interested in her political influence—specifically, her friendship with Eugene Vidal. Croil Hunter thought it likely Vidal would be selected director of aeronautics at the Department of Commerce, and the airline hoped for government support for improvements along its proposed route.

IN SEPTEMBER AMELIA begged off on accompanying George on a business trip to Europe, dreading the wasted weeks it would take for the voyage there and back. George sailed alone, and in his absence, her mother consented to visit Rocknoll, in what was her first stay there despite Amelia's countless invitations. Amy had become partially deaf, and she used a hearing aid and to some extent could read lips. The luxury of the household and camaraderie of the guests must have appealed to her after the weariness of

Muriel Morrissey's home and money woes. Yet the cost of maintaining the house had begun to wear on the Putnams' finances, and Amelia told Amy they planned to rent out Rocknoll and live at the Hotel Seymour during the winter.

As Croil Hunter predicted, in September President Roosevelt appointed Eugene Vidal director of the aeronautics branch of the Department of Commerce, a position he had been angling for since the president took office.[10] Amelia and George had both lobbied for Vidal's selection, as had Eleanor Roosevelt. On December 18 the cover of *Time* magazine featured Gene, plum exposure that even George had not managed to get for his wife. A month after Vidal's new position had been announced, George wrote Hunter at Northwest: "I was talking about you over the weekend. Gene Vidal was with me. As you noted, he has landed where we said he would land.... There are interesting things that can be done, and some things that cannot be accomplished unless they are gone at it in the right way. Perhaps A. E. will talk to you a bit."[11] Amelia championed Vidal whenever possible, and his eminence in turn boosted her standing in aviation circles. He sought her advice and she sought his.

Whether their relationship evolved into a romance is unknown, but it is not out of the question. In Vidal's wallet he carried only three photographs: one of Amelia, one of his son, Gore, and one of an elderly woman beloved by the little boy. Within a year of Vidal's appointment as director, Amelia sent him a 7 x 9 photograph signed, "To Gene Vidal whose greatest fault in aviation is thinking too far ahead of the industry."[12] If George thought Gene and Amelia were lovers, he didn't begrudge him, for the two men remained good friends, and he later relied on Gene to assist Amelia with her world flight arrangements.

Gene Vidal was a natural-born flyer who probably loved aviation more than he ever loved any woman. Flying took priority over everything else in his life, whether he was inventing a new plane or discussing policy with pilots. But most of all, he loved to fly, and furthermore, he wanted everyone else to have the opportunity to do so. One of Gene's revolutionary ideas was a $700 mass-produced "poor man's airplane" made of metal. He couldn't find a company to manufacture it at a suitable price, however, since the bids he received were all above $1,500. Plus the public didn't share his romantic dream of taking to the skies en masse. His proposition that the government fund its development with a $500,000 grant from the Public Works Administration—a New Deal agency formed to battle unemployment—was not taken up. Still, Charles Lindbergh and other pilots expressed a keen interest in his various airplane designs.

IN FEBRUARY 1933 Anne Lindbergh wrote Amelia describing her idea for a shop in Macy's or another department store that would feature clothes for women pilots. She suggested crushable hats, all-purpose shoes, and convertible dresses and suits, as well as lightweight baggage. In December R. H. Macy & Co. announced that Amelia Earhart would design and launch a line of women's sports clothes. Whether Anne's proposal was the impetus for Amelia's new enterprise is unknown but it may have played a part. The collection, drawing on Amelia's experience in flying and sports, and incorporating aviation paraphernalia such as parachute silk for fabric or wing nuts for buttons, was to be housed in a special section called the Amelia Earhart Shop. Other shops in large cities, including Marshall Fields in Chicago, would carry the line, too. Amelia thus became the first celebrity designer. Sewn into each garment was an eye-catching label that featured her signature in black, with a thin red line through it connected to a little red plane in the right corner.

The entire enterprise exhausted Amelia. She had not gotten off to a good start. She was physically tired when it began, having just ended a 7,000-mile lecture tour in her Franklin car, dashing from one site to another with scarcely time to sleep. Having to deal with fashion designers flitting in and out of her suite at the Hotel Seymour and choosing fabrics was not the sort of work to which she aspired. At the same time, George was drumming up business, and reporters seeking interviews were a regular fixture at the hotel.

Some of the newspaper advertisements touting her new collection depicted a brown tweed topcoat with a removable lining for $44.75, a brown tweed suit for $54.75, and a felt hat named "Solo Flight" for $7.50.[13] There were less mundane ensembles featuring more palatable and innovative designs, but the line was overall conservative and expensive, and it never caught on. As elegant and well dressed as Amelia had become under George's tutelage, she was unable to transfer her personal style to the collection. Still, although the idea flopped, it is possible it would have prospered had it been introduced in a booming economy.

IN EARLY 1934 there emerged a furor in the aviation industry when President Roosevelt canceled all private airmail contracts, a decision that came out of a Senate committee chaired by Hugo Black, a Democratic senator. Black charged that the former Republican postmaster had colluded with airlines in awarding mail contracts. In retaliation against the airlines, the president ordered the mail to be flown by army pilots, not commercial carriers. Eugene Vidal opposed this arrangement, saying the army airmen did not have the planes or instrument flying skills to do so. Within weeks he was proven right, as army pilots began dying in plane wrecks on mail routes. By April 1934 the airlines resumed flying the mail, albeit under slightly changed names, as only new carriers were allowed to apply for the contracts. (For example, Eastern Air Transport became Eastern Airlines.)

In March, shortly after the airmail fiasco began, Amelia was called before a committee in Washington, D.C., to testify on the matter, and her statements did not endear her to key players in the aviation industry. She did not favor government airmail subsidies, asserting that "further subsidizing will throttle aviation." Airlines must "stand on their own feet," she added, and strict regulation might kill aviation before "it gets a chance to grow."[14] In contrast to Charles Lindbergh and Eastern's Captain Eddie Rickenbacker, who both proposed an independent agency overseeing the industry, she suggested a Department of Transportation to coordinate air, rail, and bus travel. It must be remembered that she was at the time vice president of an airline subsidized by the Boston & Maine Railroad. She wanted a combined agency, while the movers and shakers at conventional airlines wanted one agency dedicated to aviation only.

The Civil Aeronautics Act of 1938 created the Civil Aeronautics Board to oversee all aspects of the airline business, a type of structure that Amelia Earhart had adamantly opposed. Senator Harry Truman dismissed her comments about throttling aviation as "ridiculous," but several of her statements proved prescient. As it turned out, the CAB discouraged competition and did not allow any new, major scheduled airlines to emerge for forty years.[15]

In July Amelia and George reveled in a three-week vacation, their longest together since marrying three and a half years earlier, at the Double Dee Ranch at Sunshine, Wyoming. They drove Amelia's Franklin car there and back, on the return stopping at Atchison, Kansas, to visit family friends. The ranch, owned by cowboy Carl Dunrud, a longtime friend of George's who had accompanied him on the Baffin Land expedition, offered fly fishing excursions and trail rides. With Carl and two hands, the Putnams rode into the mountains for a two-week spell, their packing horses loaded with camping gear and food. Amelia loved the splendor of the mountains, the tranquility of the scenery, and the escape from the pressures of public life. She even filed a land claim near Dunrud's ranch and arranged for work to begin on a log cabin, planning to go back every summer, but an illness and her preparations for a forthcoming flight would prevent her return.

In the summer of 1934 Cliff Henderson laid down a new rule forbidding women pilots to participate in the National Air Races at Cleveland. The races were too dangerous for the ladies, he said, citing the death of Florence Klingensmith in a 1933 Gee Bee accident as having influenced his decision. (He seemed to conveniently forget the male flyers who had died flying this demon of an aircraft.) Amelia had been scheduled to attend the races and to fly actress Mary Pickford in from Chicago to officiate at the opening ceremonies, but on hearing Henderson's announcement she refused to participate. Other noted women pilots joined Amelia's protest and also declined to attend.

By then Amelia was preparing for a flight from Hawaii to California, a course no one had yet flown solo, and she soon headed to the West Coast. "I make a record and then I lecture on it," she had said in 1933. "That's where the money comes from. Until it's time to make another record."[16] Six years after her first Atlantic crossing, she knew the drill well to assure headlines and lecture bookings.

16

ALOHA

IN EARLY NOVEMBER 1934 Amelia arrived in Los Angeles to once again delight in its temperate climate and relaxing standard of living. Fourteen years earlier she had begun flying here, buzzing around grass fields in her yellow Kinner Airster. At the time she hadn't even considered making aviation her life's work—a preposterous thought when thousands of war veterans were seeking any sort of position in the field, whether barnstorming or giving passenger rides. She was restricted, too, by societal norms and her family's expectations for her: a genteel woman would not take up a harebrained, frivolous hobby like flying, much less make it a career.

Soon after the war, the skies around Los Angeles had begun swarming with flyers stunting for the movie studios nearby. Among the most famous was Paul Mantz, a debonair, good-looking ex-army pilot, who offered studios an alternative to members of the entrenched Motion Picture Pilots Association union. In 1931 he opened United Air Services at the Burbank airport with a complete line of aeronautical services for the film industry. To airmen and celebrities he declared, "Think of it as a Hollywood Air Force." Throughout his long career he rightfully proclaimed, "I'm not a stunt pilot. I'm a precision pilot."[1] Although six years Amelia Earhart's junior, Paul's technique, flying skills, and knowledge of the aviation industry far exceeded hers.

Knowing his reputation, Amelia sought him out to be the technical adviser overseeing all aspects of her proposed flight from Hawaii to California, some 2,400 miles over water. It was the beginning of what would become a close business and personal relationship. By some reports, Paul was "infatuated" with Amelia.[2] Shortly after her November arrival she rented a house in North Hollywood, near Toluca Lake, close to Paul and his wife, Myrtle. Amelia invited her mother for an extended visit while George, still in New York at the Hotel Seymour, planned to arrive before the holidays.

On November 27 George called his wife with shocking news. A raging fire, started when a houseman inadvertently left a heater on under an empty boiler, had swept through the mansion at Rye. The damage was estimated at $75,000. Although the house was insured, many of its contents included priceless, irreplaceable mementoes, and their loss deeply affected Amelia and George. (Thanks to George's foresight, Amelia's collection of medals and trophies was unharmed, stored in a New York bank vault.) The following year Rocknoll was rebuilt, but Amelia's affection for the new house didn't match what she'd had for the original. Losing it reinforced her desire to make Los Angeles her permanent home.

ON NOVEMBER 22 news broke that new two-way radio equipment certified for overseas flight had been installed in Amelia's Vega.[3] To reporters George insisted his wife was on a lecture tour and had no ocean journeys planned. For more than a month, Amelia and George attempted to divert attention away from the planned flight, but with little success. In fact, Amelia went on denying her plans even after she, George, the Mantzes, and Ernie Tissot, her mechanic, arrived in Hawaii aboard the *Lurline*, with the Vega lashed to the aft tennis deck.

Flying the Pacific solo was not a novel idea; Bobbi Trout and Ruth Nichols had earlier hoped to be the first, but financing for their attempts fell through. But there was widespread hostility to the idea in the press and within the aviation industry because of the dangers it entailed. On December 4, 1934, aviator Charles Ulm and his two-man crew were lost at sea while flying from Oakland, California, to Honolulu. "We are just going into the water," Ulm radioed before ditching in the vicinity of the islands. His last transmission was a feeble series of Morse code dots and dashes: "Come and pick us up." Despite a twenty-seven-day search for Ulm and his crew, a costly venture involving Army and Navy planes, submarines, and destroyers, they were never heard from again. Last to give up on the search was the U.S. Coast Guard cutter *Itasca,* which would later figure prominently in one of Amelia's flights. In an article about the accident, published on December 30, Clarence Williams, Amelia's navigation adviser, surmised that a 40-mile-an-hour wind from the south-southeast had pushed the plane north of course. Most likely Ulm had not corrected soon enough to compensate for drift and had overshot the islands; Williams noted grimly, "The ocean knows the answer."[4]

A storm of controversy awaited Amelia in Hawaii, with the Honolulu *Star Bulletin* claiming authorities should bar the flight. A week earlier, a member of the National Aeronautic Association had also tried to put a stop to it. Vociferous critics clamored that her pointless stunt flight could result in a million-dollar taxpayer-funded search if she were forced down at sea. And why, they asked, was the Army allowing her the use of Wheeler Field, along with its radio experts and mechanics? Amelia and George refused to bend, however, and in Honolulu Amelia issued a statement saying she was vacationing and was undecided about her plans.

Months earlier, however, George had struck a $10,000 deal for Amelia with the Pan-Pacific Press Bureau, whose clients, the Hawaiian sugar and allied interests, were battling what they considered unfair sugar tariffs. They actively sought celebrity endorsements to affirm Hawaii as "an integral part of the United States" and thus "entitled to quota parity with American continental producers."[5] (The Territory of Hawaii would not achieve statehood until 1959.) To prepare for the flight Amelia had already been given an advance of $5,000, with the balance to be paid her before takeoff.

But by now her sponsors, fearful of adverse publicity, sought to cancel their financial support and hastily called a private meeting with Amelia in Honolulu. There she criticized their cowardice, telling them aviation was her business. She had kept her part of the bargain and had already issued statements saying Hawaii was ready for statehood. She ultimately prevailed, and the sponsors backed down. In the meantime George was denying reports that he had made a deal with the Press Bureau.

Over two weeks, Mantz and Tissot got Amelia's Vega ready for its odyssey. While waiting, Amelia rode in an outrigger with Duke Kahanamoku, the great swimmer and surfer; planted a banyan tree in Hilo, a customary practice for celebrities; and sunbathed on Waikiki beach. On January 6 she wrote her mother, "We have been very fortunate in being guests of Chris Holmes, a wealthy cultivated 'playboy' friend of Paul's." She praised the attentive staff of Japanese servants and wondered whether she and George would ever be "satisfied with only one or two servants again after so many here."[6] Still, the barrage of criticism weighed heavily on her, and it would contribute to her fatigue on the upcoming flight.

ON THE AFTERNOON OF January 11 a light rain drizzled onto Wheeler Field, where Amelia's Vega stood ready for launch. On the advice of a navy meteorologist, Amelia had opted to slip out between two weather systems, although the U.S. Weather Bureau had recommended she wait. There would be no formal goodbye, or "aloha," for she said this was a test flight, and it would continue on to the mainland only if the takeoff went well.

Amelia eased into the warmed-up cockpit and checked the instrument panel while an anxious assembly of two hundred stood by. Looking far down the strip, she caught sight of three fire engines and an ambulance, posted there should an accident occur during the precarious takeoff. Weeks earlier, Paul Mantz had equipped the plane for a possible ditching, and aboard it were a rubber raft and a Very pistol to shoot distress signals. Over Amelia's fur-lined flight suit she wore an inflatable rubber vest, and attached to her belt were a hatchet and knife.

At 4:45 Amelia applied full throttle, and the Vega, loaded with 520 gallons of gasoline and weighing 6,000 pounds, lumbered down the muddy field. She glanced out at her mechanic running alongside, a cigarette dangling from the corner of his mouth, his face ashen. Paul Mantz was swearing and screaming for her to get the tail up; George Putnam, wiping his brow, told a nearby reporter, "I'd rather have a baby."[7] Amelia held the course as the Vega sloshed through muck, then skillfully lifted off and banked toward Diamond Head while climbing to 6,000 feet.

Amelia's navigation charts, meticulously prepared by Clarence Williams, called for fourteen changes in compass course, to be made about every hour. Williams had plotted great circle courses to San Francisco and Los Angeles, which also noted the position of ships along steamship lanes. He also provided information for Department of Commerce airway radio beams reaching westward from Oakland and Los Angeles.

She flew high over the Pacific through a star-studded night. "They seemed to rise from the sea and hang outside my cockpit window, near enough to touch, until hours later they slipped away into the dawn," she recalled.[8] Around midnight, 900 miles from Honolulu, the Matson ship *Maliko* sighted the plane's flashing lights, sending its position to shore stations. Midway, the Navy tanker *Ramapo* reported seeing the Vega as well.

During the entire flight Amelia gave no position reports. While she kept to a schedule of transmitting at a quarter to and a quarter past the hour, she usually gave her altitude, made a few observations about visibility and cloud cover, or simply said "Everything OK" or "All is Well."[9] This was useless information for anyone wanting to know her whereabouts.

Frustrated, Clarence Williams waited at Burbank to greet her, unsure if she would land at Los Angeles or Oakland. It is unclear whether Amelia knew, either, and in all probability did not decide until nearing the mainland. Williams's charts had forecast a flight lasting about sixteen hours to either location. Amelia and George had discussed the possibility of her flying through to Salt Lake City or Washington, D.C., to establish a women's distance record, and Williams had charted these cities also.

All through the flight Amelia received continuous broadcasts from commercial stations, by special arrangement. A few hours into the flight George's voice boomed into the cockpit; later, she listened to a broadcast of the San Francisco Symphony Orchestra. Hers was the first civilian long-distance flight made with two-way radio telephone. Although airlines used radio telephone equipment, its cost was prohibitive to most civilian pilots. Morse code remained the most dependable and reliable form of communication.

Amelia flew between 6,000 and 8,000 feet above the water to take advantage of forecast tailwinds. At dawn the clouds below her became solid overcast, and hours would pass before she spotted patches of blue sea sparkling beneath the Vega. She watched a break in the cloud cover expand, then sighted a steamer below—the *President Pierce*—and dove toward it. After circling it at 150 feet she lined up on its wake, confirming she was on course, according to Williams's charts. She radioed station KPO for the ship's position, which was 250 miles out from San Francisco. From there on she flew low, at about 1,500 feet. A half hour after KPO transmitted, she was reported by another ship to be flying off course in fog.

Though no one knew her terminal destination, a mob of well-wishers was gathering at Oakland airport to meet her. In the meantime, four Coast Guard ships were deployed off Golden Gate to provide her aid if needed. The sailors and naval officers standing watch "wondered why she buzzed along so blithely without ever reporting her position."[10] She was overdue, at least an hour late, and there were concerns for her safety. Later, she claimed to have throttled back the last few hours to conserve fuel, slowing her progress. Yet when the Vega landed its tanks held enough gasoline for three hours more of flying.

Eighteen hours and 16 minutes after leaving Hawaii, Amelia's red Vega streaked straight in to Oakland airport and landed. A horde of three thousand screamed her name and stampeded toward her, thrusting bouquets of American roses her way. After popping from the cockpit, she combed her tousled hair and smiled at the crowd. Mechanics grabbed on to a wing and quickly pushed the Vega into a hangar to protect it from souvenir hunters, slamming the big doors shut and securing Amelia from the mob. Tired and dirty, she most wanted a bath, but consented to a brief interview and a physician's examination at George's request. As tired as she was, she harbored hopes of flying east within a day. She would fly the Vega to Los Angeles the following day, but storms along the eastward route would keep her temporarily confined to the West Coast.

Amelia's 2,408-mile journey, the first Pacific solo flight by a man or a woman, confirmed her status as a genuine heroine. It also made her the first aviator to solo over both the Atlantic and Pacific. However, the flight did not qualify as a women's distance record. Of course, had she reached Salt Lake City or farther east as originally planned, she would have bested her previous record of 2,447.84 statute miles (her nonstop flight from Los Angeles to Newark, New Jersey). Though an extraordinary achievement, she downplayed the flight's usefulness and said it served no purpose. She complained too about her slow speed, which averaged 133 miles per hour. She blamed her late arrival on headwinds, trouble working the new compass, and the need to reduce power to conserve fuel.[11]

A day after landing, Amelia recapped her flight in the *New York Times*. She ended the article telling about the ambition she and her husband had had "to visit the alluring southwest corner of the United States that is Hawaii."[12] Critics continued to attack the flight and its role as propaganda, but the magnitude of her achievement eventually silenced them. Congratulations poured in from all over the world, and the requests for lectures were again staggering. At a gala dinner held in her honor a week later in Oakland, the host read President Roosevelt's message hailing her feat. The First Lady, having become even more enamored with Amelia, extended an open-ended invitation for her to stay at the White House.

Amelia's friend Louise Thaden took her to task for the flight, however. From Arkansas she wrote on January 12: "Congratulations again! But darn your hide, I could spank your pants!... I was scared to death. Dimmit, you're worth more alive than dead, and what profit fame when you are not here to reap the benefits...?"[13]

17

MEXICO

AFTER THE PACIFIC FLIGHT, Amelia's lecture bookings skyrocketed, as they often did after such feats. Two strenuous lecture tours, in February and March, had been scheduled following the flight. "AE is rolling around the Middle West in her Franklin lecturing every night, heaven help her, and is expected back the 26th," George wrote Amy Earhart on February 11.[1] While later recapping Amelia's engagements to Paul Mantz, George reported that his wife "spoke 136 times in 1935 before audiences totaling 80,000, a straight, flying-is-safe and pleasant sermon."[2]

In March 1935 the Mexican government invited Amelia to fly to its capital city, a goodwill flight to coincide with its current campaign to draw more American tourists. Her recent Hawaiian expedition had sparked significant interest in the islands, and Mexican officials hoped to repeat this success with their country. Intrigued, Amelia told George, "I had never been invited before. I just went to Ireland."[3] The flight to Mexico City would add to her records, and she planned to add yet another with a return hop to Newark, New Jersey. Amelia's would not be the first goodwill flight to Mexico: In late 1927 Dwight Morrow, the American ambassador to Mexico, had asked Charles Lindbergh to make just such a flight to Mexico City. Departing

Washington, D.C., in his *Spirit of St. Louis*, Lindbergh had flown nonstop for 27 hours 15 minutes, and at the luxurious embassy he had met his future wife, Anne Morrow, Dwight's daughter, on vacation from college.

Although Amelia's Vega was mechanically fit for the flights, financing the trip presented a conundrum. In stepped the president of Mexico, Lázaro Cárdenas, to lend a hand by decreeing the government would issue an airmail stamp commemorating Amelia's flight. (Not a new issue, it was an overprinting on an existing stamp.) Few people were so honored during their lifetime, and it was a measure of either George's shrewdness and bargaining power, or Mexico's desperation to have Amelia visit. Soon George flew to Mexico to supervise printing of a total of 780 red stamps on which were superimposed AMELIA EARHART VUELO DE BUENA VOLUNTAD MEXICO 1935 (Amelia Earhart Goodwill Flight Mexico 1935).

Not long after, philatelists were enraged after learning the circumstances of the very limited issue. George kept 240 of the 300 stamps remaining after 480 went to the Universal Postal Union at Berne. Of course, the unusually high percentage he held left less available to collectors, who threatened to boycott the issue. Ordinarily worth twenty centavos—less than one U.S. cent—they sold as high as $100 each and thereafter increased in value. (In 1963 the United States Post Office issued an airmail stamp of Amelia depicting her standing in front of the Lockheed Electra. Fifty-seven million were ordered for the initial printing.) Collectors also prized mail, or "covers," that Amelia took on her flights, the sale of which helped pay her expenses. From Los Angeles she planned to carry fifty canceled autographed covers to be canceled again in Mexico City. There she would take aboard thirty-five more autographed covers, then have all eighty-five canceled at Newark.

Apparently George may have overstepped his bounds in Mexico. Weeks earlier he had resigned from Paramount Pictures without giving a reason and was now devoting most of his time to his wife's career. At loose ends, he was concocting ever more outlandish schemes. While in Mexico he proposed an ambitious campaign, which led *Newsweek* magazine to report, "The expenses he quoted stunned officials. One of them gasped: 'There isn't that much money in Mexico.'"[4]

But the magazine also lashed out in other ways. "Advertisers have met the expenses of a number of Miss Earhart's daring flights," it noted—before pointing to the autogiro Beech-Nut tour, the $10,000 backing of the Hawaiian flight, and the goodwill flight to Mexico.[5] Had George Putnam been less blatant about promoting his wife's flights and had his temperament been a dash more diplomatic, most assuredly there would have been less controversy.

There was another factor at play here, however, and no one realized this more keenly than Amelia and George: The interest in aviation exploits was peaking; the public, preoccupied with making financial ends meet and sated with aviators' trumped-up feats, was tiring of record flights. The golden era of exploration was coming to a close. The aviation industry was maturing into its commercial phase, focusing on phenomenal growth in passenger traffic, and the opportunities for George and Amelia to garner publicity and make money were declining.

TWO HOURS BEFORE MIDNIGHT on April 19 Amelia launched her Vega from Burbank, California, to Mexico City, about 1,700 miles away. She first planned to fly a direct compass course, using headings plotted by Clarence Williams, but at the last minute discarded his charts. She figured the weather along the coast would be better. Aboard the plane, the same she used for the Hawaii flight, was a new Lear radio compass, which she tested on behalf of the Department of Commerce. For this experiment she earned a salary of $1.00.

During the first portion of the flight moonlight relieved the loneliness of Amelia's journey as she followed the Pacific coast, cruising at 10,000 feet. South of Mazatlán she pointed the nose of the Vega eastward and flew a compass course toward Mexico City, some 600 miles distant, but lost track of where she was after passing Guadalajara. Just then a speck of dirt in her eye blurred her vision, making chart reading impossible, she would later claim, though she might have been lost. Rather than fly on, she elected to land. She circled a dry lake bed, checking it over, then set down. Only minutes later, fifty cowboys and their womenfolk rushed to her aid, and none seemed surprised to behold a female flyer—having recognized her from newsreels, they knew exactly who she was. Looking at her chart, one vaquero pointed to their location—60 miles from Mexico City.

A half hour later Amelia was officially welcomed in Mexico City, where a crowd of ten thousand stampeded toward the Vega when it touched down, 13 hours 30 minutes after leaving Burbank. Disappointed at not having made a nonstop flight, Amelia would promise to make another attempt. No sooner had she landed, though, than a new problem reared its head: runways at nearby civilian airports could not handle the Vega's takeoff when it was fully loaded with fuel, which would be necessary to make Newark. They were too short. Mexico City is approximately 7,300 feet above sea level, a high altitude that results in less lift and mandates a longer takeoff run. (In contrast, the altitude of Burbank is approximately 780 feet above sea level; and Newark, 20 feet.) So Mexico's military officials ordered soldiers to level off a dry lake bed and fashion a three-mile-long runway, which would turn out to be little more than a dirt strip. Out came the troops' pickaxes and shovels, and in a short time the lake bed's hummocks disappeared. This sort of extraordinary aid given by military personnel would not have been extended to many other aviators. Meanwhile, Pan American Airways also gave her assistance, providing hangar storage and its top mechanics to overhaul the Vega.

While waiting for runway improvements and better flying weather, Amelia and George were entertained royally in Mexico City. There were banquets, bullfights, visits to scenic spots, a private audience with President Lázaro Cárdenas at the National Palace, and a luncheon with Diego Rivera and Frida Kahlo. George then returned to New York by commercial airliner to prepare for his wife's arrival in Newark and to telephone Dr. James Kimball's weather forecasts to her.

On May 9 Amelia blasted out of Mexico City on a nonstop route to the Newark Airport in New Jersey after an early morning takeoff. The 2,100-mile course laid out for Amelia went from Mexico City then over Tampico, Mexico, then across the Gulf of Mexico, and over New Orleans and Mobile, Alabama. From there she would fly over Washington, D.C., before landing at Newark Airport. Her rebellious streak had surfaced after aviator Wiley Post had warned against flying the 700-mile stretch over the Gulf, a riskier route that would shave only an hour off her total flight time. "I couldn't believe my ears," she later wrote about his advice for what she called her "simple little flight."[6] She ignored his warning, but it would turn out to be an imprudent decision, and later she foreswore ever again flying over water in a single-engine plane.

The Vega roared down the Mexican dirt strip at six in the morning, gobbling up a mile of runway before Amelia lifted it aloft and climbed slowly to 10,000 feet. To the south lay snow-capped Popocatépetl, its slope glistening from the rising sun's rays. When she reached the Gulf, she was forced to fly between cloud layers, with headwinds impeding her speed, but the skies later cleared and tailwinds pushed her onward. She used her radio to communicate with weather stations and airports en route, and the radio compass enabled her to home in on commercial broadcasting stations, a great labor saver that confirmed her navigation.

Upon hearing of her progress along the route, excited radio listeners began to gather at airports, eager to see the Vega flash by, as if they themselves were flying and part of the adventure. Nowhere was this more evident than at the Hoover Airport in Washington, D.C., where a large crowd had gathered after hearing she had passed through the Carolinas. There the Vega swooped down, its red and green navigation lights blinking, while Bureau of Air Commerce Director, Eugene Vidal, radioed Amelia to say, "You've done a splendid job, so come down." She waved off the invitation, transmitting, "I am going on through."[7]

An hour and 23 minutes later the Vega zoomed over the Newark Airport, circled as the flood lights flashed on, and finished with a perfect landing—14 hours 8 minutes after takeoff. Amelia's record flight was the first nonstop from Mexico City to the New York area, as well as the fastest. "That's a flier!" said Paul Collins after seeing her landing at the airport, while Doc Kimball proudly said, "Such people are good for us all."[8] The throng of three thousand yelling fans went wild, breaking through security lines and running toward the red plane. The police hastily formed a secondary cordon, but that too fell. After Amelia opened the hatch and climbed down, one burly policeman grabbed onto her left leg, another on to her right arm, resulting in a tug of war before she was freed from their grip. An infuriated George Putnam, waiting at a hangar, let loose with his famous temper and fumed at the inept crowd control. Meanwhile, Amelia, whose calm stood in contrast to George's volatility, simply smiled at the bystanders milling about. She was remarkably fit after the ordeal, claiming to be not at all tired. The navigation tools aboard her Vega had played a big role in alleviating fatigue.

Two days later, Eugene Vidal wired Amelia:

ON BEHALF OF THE BUREAU OF AIR COMMERCE I EXTEND SINCEREST CON-GRATULATIONS FOR AN ACCOMPLISHMENT OF AIRMANSHIP THAT IS WORTHY OF THE MOST EXPERIENCED PILOT IN THE WORLD. YOUR FLIGHT YESTERDAY FROM MEXICO CITY TO NEWARK AND YOUR PAST ACHIEVEMENTS IN THE AIR STAND AS UNIMPEACHABLE TESTIMONY OF YOUR COMPLETE KNOWLEDGE OF AIRCRAFT OPERATION AND CROSS COUNTRY NAVIGATION. WE SHALL LOOK FORWARD WITH PLEASURE TO RECEIPT OF YOUR REPORT ON THE PERFOR-MANCE OF THE RADIO COMPASS AND THE AIDS TO AIR NAVIGATION ON THE COMMERCE DEPARTMENT AIRWAYS WHICH YOU EMPLOYED.[9]

Amelia, for her part, again told reporters the flight had served no purpose. It is interesting to note the heartfelt praise Vidal accorded Amelia Earhart, comparing her feat to one worthy of the "most experienced pilot in the world." While it is true that her 1935 flights were among the crowning glories of her career, there were other pilots who flew more often and rigorously and who attained even greater accomplishments. Amelia's experience paled beside theirs, as she was only too well aware. Despite being the most famous woman pilot in America, she flew far fewer hours than other renowned female pilots of the time did. When requesting Vidal's assistance in renewing her transport license in November 1935, she asked that he record her total time as 1,600 flight hours; in early 1929 her log book carried forward 559 hours, suggesting that she had logged only 1,041 hours since then—not a substantial amount, by any means.

"She had very, very few hours of flying," the aviator Edna Gardner Whyte would later recall about Amelia, with whom she was friends, and a fellow member in the Ninety-Nines. Whyte, a legendary racing pilot and lifelong flight instructor who became licensed in 1929, claimed Amelia would have benefited from instructing others to fly and from racing, both of which would have built considerably more hours. As Whyte pointed out, Amelia was not included in a 1938 issue of *Look* magazine listing top women pilots in the world because of her scant flight hours. On the other hand, Whyte, a former Navy nurse who endured financial hardships to fly, had by then logged 2,800 hours. Nonetheless, she most remembered Amelia as a "very beautiful woman, inside and out. She was sincerely interested in promoting women and aviation." In contrast, Whyte harbored few good memories of George Putnam and felt he pushed Amelia to make long-distance flights that she was not qualified to undertake because of her inexperience.[10]

A PUBLICITY BLITZKRIEG BEGAN the day after Amelia landed at the Newark Airport, as accolades for "The Queen of the Air" burst forth in major newspapers. An editorial in the *New York Herald Tribune* lauded Amelia's "modesty and courage" and reflected, "The country could not have a better ambassador-at-large."[11] The *New York Times* rang in shortly after, comparing hers to "a brilliant and successful flight [that] lends confidence to those who travel the airways."[12] Another honor came her way when she was asked to serve as the first woman referee at the Indianapolis 500, the Memorial Day automobile race, on May 30.

On June 2 the press announced Amelia's appointment as a faculty member and career consultant for women students at Purdue University, a coeducational college of 6,000 students at Lafayette, Indiana. Amelia had met Dr. Edward C. Elliott, president of the university, in the fall of 1934 at the Waldorf Astoria. She had been one of several presenters, including First Lady Eleanor Roosevelt and New York mayor Fiorello LaGuardia, at the Conference on Current Problems sponsored by the *New York Herald Tribune*. Elliott had listened raptly as Amelia talked about the future of aeronautics and the hardships women encountered in the industry. His conservative appearance—business suit, stiff collar, and hair parted in the middle—belied his visionary approach to teaching. He was in the vanguard when it came to educating women and believed they should be given solid career training. To this end, he was instrumental in creating Purdue's first residence building for women, South Hall, which opened in 1934. Aviation also figured prominently at the college, and in 1930 land had been donated to build the Purdue University Airport, the first university-owned airport in the United States. In the same year, Purdue became the first university to offer college credit for flight training.

Elliott, awestruck by Amelia's speech, philosophy, and flight career, had offered her a position teaching at Purdue. She was thrilled to accept because it dovetailed with her interests in promoting quality technical education for women. For a month's work on the campus each year, she would earn $2,000 annually. Almost a year passed before the details were finally ironed out, and it was agreed that Amelia would start her new job in autumn 1935.

WITHIN A MONTH AFTER her flight to Newark, Amelia made her first parachute jump from a 115-foot training tower in New Jersey. Then, after visiting her hometown of Atchison, Kansas, where she rode in a flowered airplane float in a mile-long parade held in her honor, she wound up a lecture tour whose last stops took place in California. There the Pasadena Community Playhouse advertised her speech on June 23 as "Adventures in Flying," an "Informal Talk on the Trans-Pacific and Mexican Flights by America's Foremost Woman Flyer." Ticket prices ranged from 50¢ to $1.25. On the flier was printed praise from Will Rogers: "A night or so ago I went to listen to Amelia Earhart tell of her Trans-Pacific flight...her personality equals her flying skill. Don't miss it."[13]

Rogers would not have another opportunity to compliment Amelia. He and the celebrated aviator Wiley Post died in a plane crash near Barrow, Alaska, that summer. The plane had stalled on takeoff; experts believed the mismatched combination of Orion fuselage, Sirius wings, and floats instead of wheels on Post's plane may have contributed to the accident. The deaths shook people across the aviation world, and none more so than Amelia. She wrote an obituary for Post that was soon published in the *Forum and Century*; the following year, she and key aviators flew over Rogers's mausoleum dropping flowers.

Within days after the lecture at Pasadena, Amelia was hospitalized for an operation on her nose to treat the recurrent sinus infections that had plagued her for years. While recuperating near Los Angeles she developed an inflammation of the membrane surrounding her lungs. Bedridden, with her ribs bound, she was ill ten days. She and George called off their vacation to the Double Dee Ranch in Wyoming, and Amelia would never have a chance to holiday there again. However, in late July she and George bought a small house on Valley Spring Lane in North Hollywood. To her mother, Amy, who had returned to Muriel in Medford, she wrote gleefully of her surprise when George and the realtor sealed the purchase.

Weeks after her operation Amelia signed a partnership agreement with Paul Mantz, leasing her Vega for use in charter services and opening a new Earhart-Mantz Flying School at Union Air Terminal in Burbank. With the National Air Races scheduled in August, the two decided to enter the Bendix Trophy race to Cleveland, with the goal of placing fifth for $500, enough to recoup their expenses. A coin toss determined that they would take Amelia's aging Vega. While Paul and Al Menasco, an engine builder and friend, played gin rummy in the Vega's cabin, Amelia piloted the ship eastward from Burbank to Cleveland. Just as she hoped, she flashed fifth across the finish line. A torrent of women's protests had been directed at organizer Clifford Henderson because of his discriminatory edict a year earlier. But the 1935 National Air Races featured women pilots competing in a cross-country derby as well as in a closed-course contest at Cleveland for the "Amelia Earhart Trophy" and a purse donated by Amelia.

Even as Amelia's fame continued to grow, other female pilots went on setting new records. On September 12 Laura Ingalls flew from Los Angeles to New York nonstop in 13 hours 34 minutes, establishing a new transcontinental record for women. The petite Ingalls, a former actress, had been hard on Amelia's heels for some time. Two months earlier she had set a new east-west transcontinental record for women; the previous year she had flown 17,000 miles over South and Central America, for which she was awarded the American Harmon Trophy for women pilots in 1934.[14] Newer and faster than Amelia's Vega, Ingalls's 550-horsepower Lockheed Orion was also better equipped, with a radio compass and a Sperry Gyropilot.

Also in 1935, the stunning New Zealander Jean Batten—probably the world's greatest female long-distance flyer and navigator at the time—blazed more records. And these were not women's records, but world records for pilots of either sex. In a Percival Gull 6 she flew solo from England to South America, making the 1,900-mile South Atlantic crossing in 13 hours 15 minutes. Amelia was quoted as saying simply that her flights were an inspiration to all women. (In recognition of Batten's outstanding flights, the Fédération Aéronautique Internationale would bestow on her the Gold Air Medal in

1936, its most prestigious award. She would be the first woman so honored.[15] Amelia would never receive this award.)

Amelia, on the basis of her Pacific flight, shared with Jean Batten the prized 1935 International Harmon Trophy for women pilots, which she had also won in 1932 for her solo Atlantic flight. Despite this new honor—and despite the fact that Amelia had won the American Harmon Trophy that same year—George Putnam was disappointed that Amelia had to share the award. He felt his wife's accomplishments had been unnecessarily eclipsed. Amelia, however, only became more ambitious and focused on setting more flight records and flying new planes. During an interview in late 1935, she remarked, "I'd like to find a tree on which new airplanes grow. I'd certainly shake myself down a good one."[16]

18

THE FLYING LABORATORY

AMELIA'S NEW DREAM MACHINE was a Lockheed Electra, a twin-engine airplane capable of cruising at 200 miles per hour, with state-of-the-art equipment. Only a twin-engine craft would serve. While cruising in the Vega across the Gulf of Mexico in 1935, she had sworn never again to make a transoceanic flight in a single-engine plane. The Electra opened up limitless possibilities, including long-range overwater flights around the world. In it America's most famous woman pilot could shore up her number one status, which had become tenuous since other female flyers had begun usurping her records.

Amelia and George, however, were in no position to purchase an Electra. They simply could not afford to hand over the $50,000 the plane cost, plus the estimated $30,000 it would take to equip it. Fortunately, Amelia's association with Purdue University paid off handsomely. Her new position consulting women students required she spend most of November 1935 at Purdue, where during a dinner party at the president's home she had the good fortune of gaining a benefactor for a new plane, which George would dub a "flying laboratory." Fellow guest David Ross, an alumnus and trustee of the Purdue Board, offered to donate $50,000 toward its purchase. Soon after, Amelia received promises for another $30,000 in cash and equipment, donated by Vincent Bendix, J. K. Lilly, and manufacturers Western Electric and Goodyear, among others. Collectively, the gifts formed what was initially called the Purdue Research Foundation, and later the Amelia Earhart Fund for Aeronautical Research, with the stated purpose to purchase a plane for "pioneering in aviation education and technical experimentation."[1] Amelia would own the plane outright.

Although Amelia claimed she first intended to fly the Electra for a year for research purposes and then plan a long flight, what she called "circumstances" subsequently intervened.[2] She would not clarify what they were, but it seems clear the Putnams needed the financial bonanza another epic flight would bring. Waiting a year or more to reap a payback was inconceivable.

After considering her options, Amelia chose to make a global flight around the equator, some 27,000 miles, since no one had flown this route— man or woman. The public and press had become less easy to impress with aviation stunts, and many destinations were old hat. Before his death in a floatplane crash, Wiley Post had pioneered stratospheric flight in the jet stream. Commercial carriers such as Britain's Imperial Airways and KLM Royal Dutch Airlines flew scheduled runs in many areas of the world. The "chosen instrument" of the United States, Pan American Airways was flying to South America, and its Clipper service linked San Francisco to Macao with stops at Midway, Wake, Guam, and Manila. A Clipper plane would soon survey an air path to New Zealand as well.

While no one had traversed Amelia's exact route, parts of her planned course had been flown. Sir Charles Kingsford-Smith had pioneered a South Pacific route, and British and French pilots had long ago trail blazed other new airways. Hers would not be the first circumnavigating flight, either, although it would be the first to circle the globe at the equator. In 1924 the U.S. Army Air Service had made a 26,345-mile, globe-girdling journey in 175 days; and in the early 1930s Wiley Post twice flew a 15,500-mile course around the world, at the shorter, northern latitudes.

To deflect anticipated criticism of Amelia's proposed flight, George Putnam co-opted the term "flying laboratory," a label originally coined for one of Charles Lindbergh's survey flights. Putnam's opportunistic use of the term was hardly out of character—but leading aviators would later blast it as farfetched. Major Alford Williams, an aeronautical expert known for his syndicated column in national newspapers, cut to the chase: "Amelia Earhart's 'Flying Laboratory' is the latest and most distressing racket that has been given to a trusting and enthusiastic pilot. There's nothing in that 'Flying Laboratory' beyond duplicates of the controls and apparatus to be found on board every major airline transport." He concluded that no one ever sat at the controls of the Electra "who knew enough about the technical side of aviation to obtain a job on a first-class airline."[3]

HAVING SECURED THE PURDUE fund's financial backing, George Putnam sprang into action. He appointed Paul Mantz as Amelia's agent to help procure a new Electra and serve as technical adviser for the flight, at a salary of $100 a day. Both Mantz and Putnam were headstrong, and the two would frequently argue over details about the forthcoming flight. Renowned for his egotism, Mantz himself could be a difficult flight instructor and had a tendency to patronize Amelia. "Listen to Papa," he often told her while explaining flying procedures.

Mantz later said he regretted Amelia's decision to buy an Electra, since he thought a seaplane would be safer for a world flight. George had priced a Sikorsky S-43 flying boat at $110,000 but never seriously considered buying it, because Amelia insisted on an Electra. She had first learned of the Electra's performance while visiting Lockheed in 1933 for Northwest Airways, and it's likely she had decided on owning one then.

Production of Amelia's Electra 10E began at Lockheed in March 1936 "for a customer confidentially named Livingston," a short-lived ruse hatched by Putnam to prevent leaks to the press.[4] She would take delivery of it on July 24, her thirty-ninth birthday. Two 550-horsepower Pratt & Whitney Wasp S3H-1 engines would power the aircraft, which also had constant-speed Hamilton Standard propellers installed. It would feature an all-metal external surface, retractable landing gear, and flaps. It had a wingspan of 55 feet, an overall length of 38 feet 7 inches, and a height of 10 feet. The aluminum-surfaced Electra gleamed beautifully, which delighted Amelia.

However, Paul Mantz wanted the rudders and wing borders painted red or orange to aid in rescue if it were forced down, while George Putnam urged the use of Purdue's colors, old gold and black. In the end, Amelia won out, and it was not painted at all.[5]

The machine would also include a navigator's station in the aft cabin, with a table on which to spread charts, and a chronometer in rubber mounts fitted beside it. An aperiodic compass, altimeter, airspeed indicator, and several other instruments were also installed at the station. Amelia controlled the Sperry Gyropilot and deicing equipment from the cockpit.

In the coming year the plane would undergo extensive modifications to its fuel system and radio equipment. Six fuel tanks were installed in the fuselage, along with additional tanks in each wing, which raised the craft's capacity to 1,150 gallons. Amelia could operate the cross-feed fuel system with one master valve in the floor of the cockpit. When fully loaded with fuel the plane exceeded the gross weight of a normal 10E by more than 50 percent.[6] At the time this sort of excess weight was not unusual in record attempts because heavy fuel loads were needed to travel long distances, but it resulted in precarious takeoffs.

Amelia's radio equipment bears the most scrutiny because it figured so profoundly in what would be her last flight. The Electra included a Western Electric 13A 50-watt transmitter equipped for operating on a "daytime" frequency of 6,210 kilocycles (what we now call kilohertz); a "nighttime" frequency of 3,105 kilocycles; and a 500-kilocycle frequency intended as an emergency transmitting channel.[7] Transmission required either the use of a handheld microphone, or Morse code with a telegraph key. The first method, radiotelephone, was just coming into vogue; Morse code was by far the most frequently used and most reliable means of communication at the time, but Amelia was not adept at using it. Transmissions would be received on new Bendix aircraft radio equipment, an RA-1 receiver, covering from 200 to 10,000 kilocycles in five bands. A Bendix radio direction-finder loop, which could take bearings from frequencies between 200 to 1,430 kilocycles and was turned from inside the cockpit, would be installed on top of the plane just in front of the cockpit overhead latch. Direction-finding radio navigation was fairly new—and was not commonly used except by commercial carriers. Amelia had no experience with it, though its use could be crucial in locating a small island, because a fix with celestial navigation was not as accurate. With the direction-finder loop antenna, she would be able to take radio bearings on a radio beacon or a ship's transmitter. The navigator could also work the transmitter and listen to the receiver at his aft station.[8]

Also installed was a 250-foot trailing wire antenna, which was weighted on the end and wound onto an electrically driven reel in the Electra's tail. Low frequencies, such as the 500-kilocycle channel, require long antennas and communicate in code only. When the Electra transmitted on 500 kilocycles, ships and shore stations could get a fix on its transmissions and relay that information back to the plane.

MEANWHILE, AMELIA'S PERSONAL LIFE was somewhat tumultuous.

Her sister, Muriel Morrissey, had been lurching from one financial crisis to another. The Morrisseys' house, purchased with Amelia's money, had been foreclosed on, although Amelia and George stepped in with more funds to tide the family over. Muriel's domestic squabbles with her husband escalated throughout 1936, and she was considering a divorce. Naturally Amelia worried about her mother's living in this depressing environment, and in June treated her mother and young cousin Nancy Balis to two months abroad in France, England, and Scotland. War clouds were growing in Europe as Hitler's and Mussolini's military reach extended, but Amy and Nancy returned safely after an uneventful trip. Overwhelmed with work commitments, Amelia asked George to meet Amy and Nancy on their return to New York. More and more, he assumed a traditional wife's role—running errands, handling household details, and corresponding with Amy Earhart.

In early March George had written Mrs. Earhart with particulars of Myrtle Mantz's bitter divorce suit against Paul, in which she alleged adultery and extreme cruelty on his part. Hot tempered and jealous, Myrtle had once shot a .32-caliber Smith & Wesson pistol at her husband, but missed. Paul recalled that once the shock and tension of the attack had passed he "jumped out of bed...took the gun away and slapped her face."[9] Named a correspondent in the suit, Amelia found her name splashed across newspapers, as rumors surfaced of a love affair between her and Paul. Amelia brushed these off, as did George, but the notoriety cannot have pleased them. A little more than a year later the popular radio commentator Walter Winchell fueled another rumor when he claimed that Amelia would divorce George Putnam to marry not Paul Mantz but instead "an aviation inventor."[10] It is possible Winchell was referring to Eugene Vidal.

As the year progressed Amelia's new house at 10042 Valley Spring Lane in North Hollywood engaged more and more of her time. The house had originally been a small bungalow, but over time the Putnams added dens, a master bedroom, a guest room, and staff quarters. With George often in New York on business, Amelia supervised its modifications and found dealing with architects and contractors to be a pleasurable diversion. She had also paid $3,000 toward back taxes and assessments on her late father's property in order to gain clear title. The new airplane and the new house in sunny California were sources of great joy to Amelia. She decided she wanted her mother to share in this happiness and the next year would invite Amy to move in to the house. George would write Amy about the suite awaiting her, particularly its bathroom, which he described as a "Roman dream of elegance."[11]

AMELIA HAD RETURNED TO the lecture circuit in 1936 as well. A thirty-stop tour began after she left Purdue, and she followed that with another round of nineteen appearances that ended in California on February 17. By the end of 1936, she would deliver nearly 150 lectures during the year, at $300 per speech, which alone amounted to an annual income of $45,000.[12] She also netted fees from consulting at Purdue, writing articles, appearing on radio programs, and other miscellaneous bookings, all of which made her, by far, the top-earning woman pilot at the time. George had also arranged a franchise of Amelia Earhart luggage. Meanwhile, her female colleagues scrambled to find financing for their flights.[13]

On April 19 Purdue University officially announced its "fund for purchase of a 'flying laboratory' in which Amelia Earhart...will hop here and there around the world."[14] Four weeks later, on May 14, the press reported that she was planning a solo flight around the world, which she would vehemently deny throughout the year.[15] But during an overnight visit to the White House that same day, Amelia and George told Mrs. Roosevelt of Amelia's plans for the flight, stressing confidentiality. A month later, George followed up on a discussion that had occurred that night. Writing to the First Lady in June, he asked "to avail ourselves of the help you so kindly offered when we last saw you. Our wish is to be put in touch with the proper person in the State Department whose aid can be enlisted in connection with A.E.'s proposed world flight."[16] At Mrs. Roosevelt's request, the State Department agreed to help procure the countless permissions and clearances from foreign governments of every country Amelia would fly over or visit. Civil servants, their salaries paid by taxpayers, handled the labor-intensive minutiae, though George paid incidental expenses, for telegrams and postage.

George later tapped his friend Vicomte Jacques de Sibour, a pilot whom Amelia had met after her transatlantic flight in 1932, as adviser for the flight's international routes. The London representative for Standard Oil Aviation Products, Sibour arranged to have caches of fuel and oil, as well as spare parts, shipped to various destinations along the proposed path. With all these preparations under way, Amelia planned to begin the flight on March 15 of the following year, 1937.

Unknown to George and Amelia, on May 13, 1936, President Roosevelt signed an executive order annexing the American equatorial islands: Howland, Baker, and Jarvis. After the First World War, Japan received the Marshall, Caroline, and Marianas islands in the Pacific as mandates from the League of Nations, making it advisable for the United States to strengthen its presence in the area. At that time, administration of the three desolate bits of coral sand in the South Pacific was transferred from the Bureau of Air Commerce to the Department of Interior. Before this transfer, and apparently without any connection to Amelia's plans, BAC director Eugene Vidal had made the building of an emergency landing strip on the islands a pet project because there were no airports along this South Pacific route. The Interior Department named Richard B. Black, a civil engineer and former explorer, as the new administrator of the equatorial islands. Although Vidal was no longer associated with the project, it was he who later suggested the islands' potential availability to his good friend Amelia.

ON AUGUST 2 AMELIA made her first takeoff in the Electra, at the airport in Burbank. Paul Mantz, who had begun flying the new ship a few weeks earlier, would ride Amelia hard as he drilled her in the techniques for flying the big plane so unlike her Vega. Lockheed's test pilot Elmer McLeod also trained her during the initial phase, and Ruckins "Bo" McKneeley was hired as her full-time mechanic.

In contrast to the Vega's cockpit, which seemed almost primitive by 1936, the Electra's had more than a hundred dials and gadgets that Amelia had to either "look at or twiddle."[17] She had had difficulty transitioning to the Vega from smaller planes and now faced a formidable task learning to fly the more sophisticated Electra. Amelia bemoaned the complexity of modern planes, stating that "too often in the attainment of speed other considerations have been sacrificed," at the same time she was writing about the Electra.[18]

Paul Mantz, not at all satisfied with Amelia's progress after the first month, urged her to log more hours. Amelia opted to fly in the prestigious Bendix Trophy Race for a shakedown and familiarization flight, and in late August she, Bo, and Mantz flew to Floyd Bennett Field, in New York, where the westward race would begin. On September 5 Amelia and copilot Helen Richey, an excellent aviator and former airline pilot, landed in Los Angeles, placing fifth overall and winning $500 despite problems en route with the fuel system, cockpit hatch, and cabin door. Louise Thaden and Blanche Noyes came in first in a new Beech C17R Staggerwing, winning $7,000 and earning the honor of having been the first women to ever place first. Laura Ingalls swooped in to place second in her Lockheed Orion. Male pilots and race organizers were stunned that women had performed so well.

Amelia's first flight in the Electra without another, more qualified copilot was to Purdue in late September, with George and Bo McKneely as passengers. Installation of the radio equipment began in Ohio the following month, but the new Bendix receiver and loop would not be fitted and tested adequately until February of the next year.

In autumn of 1936 Amelia was at work campaigning for President Roosevelt in his re-election bid, stumping at her lecture stops. However, after hearing Roosevelt had reorganized the Bureau of Air Commerce and fired Eugene Vidal and his two assistants, she sent a scorching telegram to the White House pleading that Vidal be reinstated. It is unclear whether her telegram alone had saved Vidal's position, but the president did not restructure the bureau, Vidal returned to his job, and Amelia continued her efforts on behalf of Roosevelt's re-election.

In November Amelia had to deal again with the White House. Under George, the flight planning had become a logistical nightmare, with the route unconfirmed and questions arising about exactly how Amelia was to refuel on a long leg over the Pacific. The proposed route proceeded westward from San Francisco to refuel in Honolulu, another 3,900 miles to Tokyo, and then onward around the rest of the world. Airports for land planes had not been built over the Pacific Ocean route. In a letter dated November 10, Amelia wrote President Roosevelt, "I want to reduce as much as possible the hazard of the takeoff at Honolulu with the excessive overload. With that in view, I am discussing with the Navy a possible *refueling in the air over Midway Island*" (emphasis in the original letter).[19] From Midway she planned to fly to Tokyo, then head back toward the equator. The president agreed to assist Amelia, and the next week the chief of naval operations received a memorandum confirming his support and asking the Navy to help Amelia.

What concerned those knowledgeable about the aerial refueling technique was Amelia's ability to handle the approach, complex docking, and detachment from a tanker. The Navy declined to pay for her training, so she agreed to bear the expense. Even if she did acquire the skills needed, though, who would spell her on the long over water hop, which entailed some 24 hours of nonstop flying? Paul Mantz disapproved of the entire idea. At this point Eugene Vidal suggested Amelia use a mid-Pacific island airport to refuel rather than attempt a hazardous midair refueling on the way to Tokyo. The Department of the Interior put into motion a chain of events to build an airport on Howland Island, a tiny bit of coral sand and scrub in the middle of the Pacific. (Its earlier plan to build on Jarvis Island had been canceled to better accommodate Amelia's planned route.) With an elevation of only 18 feet, Howland Island was a mile and a half long and a half-mile wide. Designated a Works Progress Administration (WPA) project, the construction was slated to start in early January and was estimated to take three months.

Another roadblock appeared in January when the runway project ran afoul of bureaucracy. The WPA funds could be released only with clearance from the Treasury Department, and Amelia was once again compelled to appeal directly to the White House for help in getting the go-ahead. She tele-grammed President Roosevelt concerning the "appropriation in amount [of] three thousand dollars which covers all costs other than those borne by me for this mid Pacific pioneer landing field which [will be] permanently useful and valuable aeronautically and nationally."[20] Four days later, on January 11, 1937, Roosevelt approved the Howland Island airport project.

It's clear that without the help of President Roosevelt and Eugene Vidal Amelia could not have made her takeoff deadline. And perhaps without their assistance she would not have made the flight at all. With the ongoing logis-tical problems and her hurried flight training, it was astonishing that she and George did not reschedule the proposed March 15 takeoff. The rush, the shortcuts, and the swiftly changing plans all made the flight that more dan-gerous. Yet the effort to keep the takeoff date went on, even though Amelia had not formally announced it to the press.

The announcement came on February 12, 1937, at the Hotel Barclay in New York at a press conference arranged by George. It failed to result in the hoped-for front-page coverage, appearing on page 25 of the *New York Times*, although her "hometown" newspapers in Boston covered it more extensively. The announced route, chosen to take advantage of the prevailing easterly trade winds just south of the equator, would originate in Oakland and include stops at Honolulu, Howland Island, New Guinea, Australia, India, and East Africa before crossing the Sahara Desert to Dakar, in French West Africa, and continuing to Natal, Brazil. After reaching Brazil she would follow established commercial air routes to her starting point in the United States.

To emphasize the scientific aspects of the "flying laboratory," Amelia told reporters gathered at the packed conference that her flight would test long-distance pilots' responses to fatigue, food, and efficiency, and she stated its main objective was to "establish the feasibility of circling the globe by commercial air transport."[21] (One wonders how international pilots reacted upon reading her journey would prove the "feasibility" of routes they were already flying.) Amelia withheld announcing the planned takeoff date of March 15 until several weeks later, February 21.

When asked why she wanted to make the global flight, Amelia simply replied, "Because I want to."[22] Nearing age forty, she had matured beyond making flights for "fun." And as in her previous ventures, she felt her achievements might encourage women to become more independent.

For a navigator, Amelia had planned to use Captain Harry Manning, the merchant marine officer of the United State Lines who had befriended her as she sailed home after the *Friendship* flight in 1928. He intended to take a three-month leave of absence from his job and accompany her as far as Australia, where she would continue alone. Manning, a private pilot, was proficient with a telegraph key and Morse code and was skilled in using radio direction-finding equipment. Furthermore, he had received extensive instruction in the Electra's radio equipment—certainly more than Amelia had. But as able a seagoing navigator as Manning was, he was not trained as an aerial navigator. This potential problem was addressed only weeks before Amelia's planned departure, when Paul Mantz insisted another navigator be brought on board.

George found a solution in Frederick J. Noonan, a gaunt, tall aerial navigator formerly employed by Pan American and now looking for work. The forty-three-year-old Noonan was a veteran of numerous Pan Am Clipper crossings and was highly respected among his peers. He was rumored to have been fired from the airline for a drinking problem, though he had in fact resigned because of the line's practice of overworking its crews. There was no question he was a heavy drinker, however, and his coworkers' testimony bore this out. Noonan, who was undergoing a divorce and career change, hoped to open a navigation school, and he embraced the opportunity to join the flight and benefit from its publicity. Unfortunately, unlike Harry Manning, he was not proficient in Morse code or radio work. It was determined he would leave Amelia after landing at Howland Island and take a Coast Guard cutter going back to Honolulu because his skills would be most useful in locating the island.

Amelia again turned to Clarence S. Williams to prepare extensive charts with precise compass headings and flight times. The U.S. Weather Bureau in Oakland also aided by assembling a small notebook of historic weather observations—precipitation, temperatures, and winds—along the route for the months of April and May. In February 1937 Lockheed's Clarence "Kelly" Johnson, the Electra's designer and a flight engineer, helped Amelia in calculating how to get the maximum mileage out of the plane by leaning the fuel mixture. The two spent many hours flying the Electra with various power settings and different weights, and Kelly taught Amelia to use a Cambridge analyzer instrument to get the most miles per gallon. He considered Amelia to be a good pilot who was "very sensible, very studious, and paid attention to what she was told."[23]

George, meanwhile, continued to work on flight preparations, which involved the remunerations that would result from a successful flight. He was already booking a post-flight lecture tour for Amelia at $500 per appearance and had arranged the printing of six thousand special covers for stamp collectors to be carried on Amelia's plane. He appointed Gimbel Brothers, the New York department store, to act as the sole agent for their purchase. The covers were priced at $2.50, or $5.00 for those bearing Amelia's autograph.

In addition, he sold the exclusive rights for Amelia's flight story to the *New York Herald Tribune*, though the deal very nearly died when its editor and owner, Helen Reid, insisted Amelia talk to absolutely no one but her newspaper's representatives. One of Reid's editors cabled George that Amelia was "not to say a word" to other newspapers until her stories were written and dispatched. George rightly asserted that this was ridiculous and offered to refund the advance monies he had received. Reid backed down. George did agree to her request that, when possible, Amelia would provide a "gastronomic record," sending back hotel menus from her various stops and commenting on what she ate.[24]

As if Amelia wasn't busy enough, she now faced a pressing problem: she needed to obtain an instrument rating, without which she could not proceed on the proposed flight. In the past Eugene Vidal had helped her sidestep bureaucratic obstacles such as this, but he had resigned from the Bureau of Air Commerce in late February. According to *Time* magazine, he was "tired and exasperated" and had been the "butt of incessant attacks" since the bureau's creation.[25] In any event, he could no longer advise and assist Amelia in an official capacity.

The three-part examination for the instrument rating consisted of a written test, a demonstration of proficiency with radio navigation aids, and a flight performed solely with reference to instruments. To expedite the process, the registration branch allowed Amelia to skip the first two parts of the test. With the windshield covered in the Electra, the examiner watched her perform a one-hour flight check of her ability to fly entirely on instruments. She passed—the confirmation was cabled to the Branch on March 11—and was signed off for the world flight.

AFTER A SERIES OF flight tests in early March, Amelia announced a revised launch date of March 14, but rain and overcast skies delayed the departure until three days later. On March 17 the rain stopped, and in late afternoon the sun shone intermittently through gray clouds at the Oakland airfield, where three thousand spectators stood by to await the takeoff. Amelia wore slacks, a plaid shirt, and a loosely knotted scarf, along with a leather jacket. She waved at friends standing near the runway and climbed aboard the plane. In the Electra's rear cabin compartment were Manning and Noonan. Paul Mantz, who planned to leave the flight in Honolulu, sat in the cockpit with Amelia. They agreed to perform the takeoff together, Paul handling the throttles and retractable landing gear, and Amelia manning the other controls. When she released the brakes, the heavy craft, loaded with 947 gallons of fuel, gained speed as it splashed through puddles before lifting off, its takeoff run shortened by a brisk headwind. Amelia circled the field and headed toward the Golden Gate Bridge.[26] The world flight was finally under way.

19

LUKE FIELD

FOR THE MOST PART, the flight from Oakland to Honolulu went well, with the four-person crew working together effectively. Amelia piloted during the 2,410-mile journey, though Paul Mantz spelled her for ten minutes each hour. An hour after they departed Oakland, a Sikorsky Pan American Clipper soared into view, winging its way on a 7,000-mile pioneer trail to New Zealand. On her previous oceanic flights Amelia had never seen another aircraft. She snapped two photographs of the lumbering flying boat before her faster Electra outpaced it.

En route Fred and Harry proved they were up to the daunting task of navigating to Howland Island. In the aft cabin Manning was working the radios, communicating with Pan Am and shore stations. As it became night Noonan took star sights with the bubble octant, keeping Amelia updated on their position. The Electra, meanwhile, barreled through a clear, dark sky, the moon shining on its cowling, with puffs of white clouds lying interspersed below. Hours into the flight, Manning advised Amelia to throttle down to avoid reaching Honolulu before dawn. With Manning and Noonan so far aft, communication with the cockpit required them to either climb a catwalk above the fuselage fuel tanks or pass forward a short bamboo fishing pole to which messages were clipped.

The trip was not without troubles, however. Manning burned out a generator while transmitting a long 500-kilocycle signal for direction-finding purposes. This problem could have influenced Amelia's subsequent radio transmissions on the world flight. To avoid any future problems with overloading the electrical system, she would keep her transmissions so short that radio direction-finding equipment would not work effectively.

During the flight's last six hours the starboard propeller became stuck at a fixed angle of pitch. Engineers at Wheeler Field would surmise that icing en route may have affected lubricants in the propellers' hubs, but they deemed it more likely that the hubs had been nearly dry since leaving Oakland. The propellers would be repaired before the next takeoff.

In the early morning the Electra's crew sighted Diamond Head and prepared to land at Wheeler Field. As Paul Mantz banked tightly to check the wind sock, Amelia yelled: "Don't! Don't!" As he would later remember, "She was very fatigued and kind of exuberant. She calmed down when I made a normal approach pattern and we landed."[1] The newspaper reporters on hand reported her as tired and saying she felt that the flight was longer than her 1935 solo hop from Honolulu to Oakland, which was actually three hours longer. According to a subsequent biographer, Amelia claimed Paul had made a "hard" landing at Honolulu—but witnesses said otherwise.[2] In fact, the *Boston Post* reported she "set her plane down in a perfect landing," although Paul had landed the plane, of course.[3] His landings at Wheeler and later at Luke Field did not damage the plane's landing gear and cannot have caused the near disaster that would soon take place, in Honolulu.

THE FIRST LEG of the flight established a new east-west crossing record of 15 hours 47 minutes. The plane landed on March 18, 1937, at 5:45 A.M. with four hours of fuel remaining and was taxied into a squadron hangar, where it underwent routine maintenance and inspection under the direction of military officers and a Pratt & Whitney representative. At all times in Hawaii it was under the guard of military police. Paul, Amelia, Fred, and Harry were whisked off for a breakfast of fresh scrambled eggs and then taken to the lavish Waikiki Beach home of Christian and Mona Holmes to rest. (The Holmeses were friends of Paul whom Amelia had stayed with while waiting to take off for California in January 1935.) Back in Washington, D.C., on the same day, Eugene Vidal boasted to newspaper correspondents about Amelia's prowess as a long-distance pilot. "Sure, she'll make it." He also reiterated Howland Island's importance as a "stepping stone" for future Pacific flights.[4]

As work on the Electra continued, Amelia enjoyed the Holmeses' luxurious accommodations, while Paul returned to Wheeler Field in the early afternoon. Both propellers were removed for disassembly and inspection and transported for reconditioning to the Hawaiian Air Depot at Luke Field. As further testimony to the extraordinary aid extended to Amelia by the armed forces, servicemen worked for most of the night to repair and deliver the propellers back to Wheeler for reinstallation on the Electra, at no cost to Amelia. There they prepared the plane for an early morning takeoff, with a mere three hours of rest, only to have no one from Earhart's group appear until midmorning. Meanwhile, by prior arrangement, military ships were positioned to provide aid en route to Amelia. The minesweeper *Quail* was halfway between Honolulu and Howland Island, the cutter *Shoshone* lay offshore near Howland, and the *Ontario* was midpoint between there and Lae, New Guinea, the third projected stop on the flight.

Everything on the Electra seemed to be in order. For forty-five minutes Paul test-piloted the craft, accompanied by his fiancée, Terry Minor, and Christian Holmes. Before leaving Wheeler, Paul indicated he might land at nearby Luke Field, a shared Army-Navy airport on Pearl Harbor's Ford Island, to perform an instrument check and evaluate its 3,000-foot concrete runway. After setting down at Luke, he informed the commanding officer that the Electra's engines and propellers worked excellently and affirmed Amelia's decision to use its concrete runway to take off for the next leg, as its surface was preferable to the clay at Wheeler. This was the first notice the Army had of a change in runway plans. Paul and Amelia had agreed that she would launch soon, provided the weather was favorable. Paul then ordered the plane's fueling at Luke.

What was expected to be a routine job evolved into a raucous argument between the Standard Oil Company's man and Mantz when sediment appeared in a chamois strainer as the fuel was put in the plane's tanks. Paul refused to load this bad gasoline and pulled strings to have the Air Corps sell him 590 gallons of high-octane fuel. The plan was for the Electra to carry a total of 900 gallons on the next hop, some 1,800 miles to Howland Island.

Shortly after the fueling, Paul told the field's officers that Amelia, Manning, and Noonan would make a dawn takeoff. The following day's weather forecasts portended well for the flight. A moderate rain fell throughout most of the night but stopped before dawn.

By 4:30 A.M. Amelia and her party had arrived at Luke Field. By 5:00 Paul had completed a walk-around inspection of the Electra, checking the flight controls, tires, struts, and all exterior items. Moving into the cockpit, he did a run-up of the engines. While he finished up, Amelia reviewed the weather forecasts and course headings. Upon Paul's signal that all was ready, she walked across the apron and climbed a wing to enter the cockpit through the overhead hatch. Manning and Noonan were sitting in the rear cabin compartment.

Daylight was advancing and flying conditions were good, with scattered clouds at 3,000 feet, a southerly wind of only 2 miles per hour, and adequate surface visibility. Amelia asked to have the floodlights lit to study the runway and decided to briefly postpone the takeoff until closer to daylight. As more natural light bathed the field Amelia readied the Electra for its taxi to the runway's end. After she started the engines, the wheel chocks were removed and the four-ton craft lumbered down the runway, followed by the Luke Field fire truck. As another precaution Air Depot men were stationed at 200-foot intervals off the west side of the runway. From the eastern sky golden rays emerged. It was 5:40 A.M., but sufficient light enabled reporters and servicemen standing watch to observe the run.

On reaching the runway's end Amelia turned the Electra to face southwest for the takeoff and made a final check of the engine gauges and instruments. She moved the throttles to full power, and the plane began to gain speed. Confident of a successful liftoff, she figured in another ten seconds the heavy Electra would be airborne.

Suddenly the Electra's right wing dipped. Then the plane spun left, still accelerating, in an uncontrollable ground loop. It was now tilted with its right wing low, and its entire weight was supported by the right wheel. Then the right landing gear collapsed, followed by the left. The wounded craft slid on its belly with a horrific sound of grinding metal and a shower of sparks and came to rest heading 200 degrees off its original takeoff path. Gasoline began spurting from the drain wells, drenching the runway, and Amelia cut the ignition switches to prevent a fire. Miraculously, there was none, and the fire truck reached the scene within minutes.

Pale and shaken, Amelia opened the plane's hatch. "Something went wrong. It seems as if I hit a wet spot," she cried.[5] Other than Manning's suffering a sore wrist, none of the occupants was injured. The plane was in bad shape, however. The wreck had damaged the right wing and engine nacelle, the underside of the left engine nacelle, and the bottom of the fuselage. Both propellers were twisted like pretzels. The right rudder and stabilizer were bent, and the landing gear was demolished.

AMELIA AND GEORGE FIRST blamed the accident on a wet runway and blowout of the right tire, which newspapers reported the following day.[6] However, the plane's tire tracks indicated the blown tire was a result, not a cause, of the ground loop. Veteran pilots interviewed by the Honolulu *Star Bulletin* a day later "agreed that no structural failure was responsible for the crash" and were certain that a "tire blow-out and subsequent crushing of the landing gear was a result, and not the cause, of the accident."[7]

Amelia would later describe the accident as follows: "Suddenly the plane pulled to my right. I reduced the power on the opposite engine and succeeded in swinging from the right to the left. For a moment I thought I would be able to gain control and straighten the course. But, alas, the load was so heavy, once it started an arc there was nothing to do but let the plane ground loop as easily as possible."[8] She would also later write that perhaps the landing gear's right shock absorber had given way, but again, this appeared to be a result, not a causal factor.

Amelia had tried to correct the right turn by throttling back on the left engine, but she did not apply the rudder to keep the plane straight on the runway, which is standard procedure. "Never jockey the throttles," Paul Mantz had often stressed to Amelia. "Hold her straight with the rudder and push everything to the firewall, smoothly."[9]

But why she did not abort the takeoff is even more puzzling. If she had immediately applied full left rudder to stop the right turn and pulled both throttles to a closed position, the plane would have coasted to a stop; or she could have judiciously applied the brakes, and she would not have crashed.[10]

It is unlikely the fuel load contributed to the accident. Previously Amelia had made takeoffs with more fuel than had been loaded in the plane at Luke Field. Moreover, by attributing the accident to the plane's weight, Amelia was setting herself up for much more serious problems when, during her next flight, she left behind useful equipment for fear of overloading the Electra.

IMMEDIATELY AFTER THE CRASH soldiers from the Hawaiian Air Depot roped off the Electra. They proceeded to work all day in heavy rain to salvage the wreckage, preparing for it to be shipped to the mainland for repairs. Mechanics found the pitch of the propellers to be identical and the oleo leg air valves in good condition. The next day a Department of Commerce inspector arrived to investigate the crash, but the branch did not levy a fine against Amelia for failing to officially report the accident. It is unclear whether she was required to pay for the damage the Electra had caused to the Luke Field runway.

Within a week, military officers in Hawaii convened for an official investigation of the crash. Their report concluded that the Army had accorded Amelia complete assistance for her flight, and conditions at Luke Field had in no way contributed to the accident. It is worth asking what became of the newsreel footage of Amelia Earhart's Luke Field accident. Cameras caught the Electra as it taxied to takeoff position, and this footage remains available today,[11] yet the footage of the actual takeoff has never been found. Whether it was lost, suppressed, or even destroyed remains unclear.

The civilian response to Amelia's takeoff was muted, and generally newspapers reported the blown tire theory. But newspaper columnist and aeronautical specialist Major Alford Williams laid the blame squarely on Amelia's shoulders: "She lost control of the plane during a takeoff on the concrete runway on a standard Army airdrome, and wrecked the 'Flying Laboratory.' And there again the public got a garbled story and a cleverly contrived explanation...plus a heroic story about cutting the ignition switches and saving the lives of her crew. That ship got away from her on the takeoff—that's the low down."[12] In addition, a short piece titled "Mourning Becomes Electra," which appeared in *Time* magazine on March 29, scathingly criticized the accident as well as the flight attempt.[13]

Williams believed the Bureau of Air Commerce would not grant Amelia permission to make another flight attempt, but it did. Even before leaving the accident scene she declared she would make another attempt at the world flight, and George wholeheartedly backed her with a telephone call and telegram. She believed the accident tarnished her reputation as America's best-known woman pilot and felt compelled to redeem herself. At noon the day of the accident, the beleaguered Earhart party boarded the steamer *Malolo* for Los Angeles, and before they departed Amelia had a message transmitted to the cutter *Shoshone* at Howland Island saying she would "try again, and next time hopes to be less of a nuisance."[14]

AMELIA ARRIVED HOME in Los Angeles on March 25, refreshed from the voyage, and informed the press the forthcoming flight's route might need to be changed. "I have not lost confidence in my ship," she added, making the claim that it was "carrying too much gasoline" at Honolulu.[15]

It has been said that George pushed his wife into making the second flight attempt, but despite his initial encouragement of her, his correspondence and actions indicate otherwise. To his friend Helen Reid at the *Herald Tribune* he wrote, "As to me, I've urged her to do just what she wants to. I'd like it if she quit. But she won't. So my job is clear—to help her all I can."[16]

George's devotion to Amelia during this period is all the more poignant in light of later events. His letters to Amelia after the accident were sprinkled with endearments. "I love you very much and would rather play & work with you than with anyone.... Comb that out of your carefully tousled hair."[17]

In another letter he wrote, "I wish this flight wasn't hanging over us. You know I agree...with your ambition & will abet it. And 98 percent I know you'll get away with it. *But* we both recognize its hazards—and I love you dearly—and I don't want you to run risks." George closed by describing the happy times they would have together after the trip, adding that they would still have them "should you for any reason decide to quit."[18]

HIS RESERVATIONS NOTWITHSTANDING, scrounging up money for the second attempt became George's all-consuming chore, and to this end he marshaled all his resources. The Electra had not been insured because at the time planes were considered too risky to underwrite. Their personal funds depleted, George estimated he required $30,000 from benefactors to cover expenses. He and Amelia were charged $4,100 to transport the plane to Burbank, which included $1,086.10 billed by the Hawaiian Air Deport for salvage work; plus sailing fares on the *Malolo* for Amelia and her crew; and flying an engineer back to London from Karachi, where he had been stationed to overhaul Amelia's plane. In addition Lockheed estimated structural repairs at $14,000.

For the second attempt millionaire businessman Floyd Odlum, whose wife, aviator Jacqueline Cochran, was a close friend of Amelia's, made a donation of $10,000, and Victor Bendix and others also contributed. In April Amelia signed a contract with Harcourt, Brace and Company for a book that would carry the title *World Flight*, with the publisher's advance on royalties applied to cover the flight's expenses. Before departing she would draft the first five chapters, a summary of her flying career through 1935. Once the second flight was under way, she would send notes en route. (The book was posthumously released as *Last Flight*, with her sparse dispatches rewritten and arranged by Putnam into an entertaining narrative.) The Putnams also mortgaged their California house. "Friends helped generously, but even so, to keep going I more-or-less mortgaged the future," she wrote in the spring of 1937. "Without regret, however, for what are futures for?"[19] She had also mortgaged her husband's future, but he did not complain about the debts saddling him.

To realize the financial benefits from a successful world flight, Amelia planned to begin the second attempt as soon as the Electra was repaired, probably in May. She and George maintained secrecy about the proposed takeoff to all but a few people, hoping to avoid the hullabaloo that advance press could create. Meanwhile, countless preparations started anew and included obtaining permissions and clearances from foreign countries, which the State Department handled again, and new charts to be prepared by Clarence Williams. Working at his usual frenetic pace, George masterminded the details for the flight. Yet again, Jacques de Sibour helped with permits and ensured the availability of gas and oil along the route.

Rescheduling the flight entailed new considerations about the route's direction. After consulting meteorologists, Amelia decided to reverse the original course and fly eastward to avoid storms late in the flight. She also might have wanted to avoid another takeoff at Honolulu early in the flight. Now, the longest and most crucial leg of the flight—from Lae, New Guinea, to Howland Island, a mere speck in the ocean—would be flown *against* prevailing winds, which would slow the plane down. The long oceanic hops eastward to the mainland would also bring the same unfavorable winds.

On April 8 Amelia and Paul Mantz signed a note whereby she agreed to pay him $1,000 to "drop around at Lockheed to oversee work on ship twice a day until completed provided he is not out of town or on a picture. In these cases he will make up time."[20] Several weeks later Amelia and Paul appeared together as guests of honor and speakers at the University Club of Los Angeles. The speaking fee helped to replenish Amelia's coffers a bit, and Paul benefited from the publicity.

Lockheed's employees worked hard to repair the Electra's damage and modify it to Amelia's requirements. Added were a cabin hatch, structural stiffeners, and stronger landing gear collars, oleo struts, and tires.[21] The engines, sent out for overhaul, were found to need fewer repairs than originally feared. Meanwhile, George hired radioman Joseph Gurr to test the plane's radios and also repair the antennas under the fuselage, since components for the trailing wire had been destroyed in the crash. Amelia chose not to have a trailing antenna reinstalled: without Harry Manning among the crew, she reasoned that she and Noonan, who did not know Morse code well enough to use it, would not need it. Accordingly, Gurr redesigned the antennas, moving the antenna mast on top of the plane forward to lengthen the top antenna and transferring the transmitter's output tuned through the loading coil to this new longer antenna. He believed the new antenna would increase the amount of radio energy emitted on the 500-kilocycle frequency, thereby improving the signal strength and range.

After Gurr explained the changes to Amelia, he offered to review the operation of the radio direction-finder loop with her. Seeing her hesitate, he realized she did not know how to work the loop. (The radio receiver with a loop antenna was used as a direction finder to find the general direction of a radio range station. When correctly tuned, Amelia would hear a signal from an operating transmitter and would rotate the antenna from inside the cockpit until the signal became weaker and faded to a minimum. By directing the plane so the signal remained at a minimum she could home into a station.) She had used it briefly only once, under the supervision of her crew while flying to Honolulu. In the very short time allotted to him—Amelia had to rush off to another appointment—he helped her practice using the loop. The short training session ended with Gurr instructing Amelia which frequencies worked best with the radio direction finder. This hurried training ended all too soon. Had the radio proficient Manning gone along on the second flight, it might have ended differently.

Although Manning had told Amelia he could not sign on for the second attempt because his leave of absence ended, years later he said her stubbornness had disconcerted him: "Amelia Earhart was something of a prima donna. She gave the impression of being humble and shy; but she really had an ego, and could be as tough as nails when the occasion required it. I got very fed up with her bull-headedness several times. That's why she brought Noonan into the picture—in the event that I were to give up on the flight. AE herself was not a good navigator; and Noonan was a happy-go-lucky Irishman."[22]

On April 4, Fred Noonan, while celebrating his birthday with his new bride, crashed head-on with another car near Oakland and was cited for driving in the wrong lane of traffic. It was his second automobile accident within several months. Reporting the second accident, newspapers identified him as "Amelia Earhart's navigator." To Amelia he had sworn sobriety, but his recent accidents brought into question whether he had really abstained.

Several of Amelia's colleagues attempted to dissuade her from making the second world flight attempt. Jacqueline Cochran, whose desert ranch in California Amelia frequented, could not understand Amelia's unpreparedness for the journey or her sense of urgency. Before her own record flights, Jackie had rested and focused on the task ahead, whereas Amelia was distracted and did not give sufficient time to fundamental details. After she described the Luke Field takeoff crash to Jackie and her houseguests at the ranch, Amelia said, "Aren't you going to ask me, 'Are you going to try it again?'" Jackie replied, "I hope you don't." She believed Amelia too physically frail to make the trip and expressed grave concerns about the navigation. As Jackie recalled, "I told her she wasn't going to see that damned island [Howland]." She warned Amelia, "I wish you wouldn't go off and commit suicide because that's exactly what you're going to do."[23]

Louise Thaden couldn't comprehend Amelia's reason for the proposed flight, either, and tried to nail it down after seeing her in early 1937. "Why stick your neck out...?" she asked Amelia. "You don't need to do anything more. You're tops now and if you *never* do anything you always will be." Amelia responded, "I've worked hard and I deserve *one* fling during my lifetime."[24]

THE ONGOING DOMESTIC TRIBULATIONS of Amelia's family eased considerably following Amelia's return to Los Angeles. Amy Earhart was comfortably quartered in the Putnams' Hollywood house, attended to by servants. Still, she had not reconciled herself to liking George and denigrated him whenever possible. Amy's caustic comments didn't ruffle him, yet there were times when Amelia had to banish her mother to her room to keep peace at the dinner table. Despite George's reputation for callousness, he was tolerant with children and the elderly, and demonstrated remarkable patience with Amy in the coming years. His attitude was all the more notable given Amy's tendency to surround herself with people who shared her low opinion of him. Muriel, in contrast, held George in high esteem and years later remarked on the kindnesses and financial aid he had extended to Amy. By the spring of 1937 her marital crisis had abated; she had not taken advantage of Amelia's offer in January to hire a divorce lawyer. Muriel remained married to Alfred Morrissey until his death.

IN LATE APRIL AMELIA raised additional funds for the flight by speaking before five hundred members of the Gimbels Stamp Club in New York to sell more covers. In May she was in the public eye again when a portrait of her graced the cover of *McCall's* magazine, bearing the words AMERICA'S GREAT WOMEN—AMELIA EARHART, WHO SPANNED AN OCEAN AND WON A WORLD. A sketch of the Electra appeared below her picture.[25]

Upon returning to Los Angeles Amelia announced her flight would commence before June 1. The date was further narrowed down on May 15. That day, the managing director of the St. Louis Air Show, speaking on behalf of Paul Mantz, who would compete there at month's end, reported that Amelia would take off from the West Coast the next Saturday on her second attempt to fly around the world.[26] On May 19 Lockheed delivered the rebuilt Electra to Amelia. She thought it unnecessary to test fly the plane other than taking a one-day trip to Oakland. She decided on a hasty departure, reasoning that the transcontinental journey eastward would serve as a shakedown flight and thus did not officially announce that she had begun the circumnavigating flight. George and mechanic Bo McKneeley would accompany her and Fred Noonan to Miami.

In the midafternoon of May 21, 1937, the Electra soared aloft from Union Air Terminal at Burbank, California, to begin Amelia Earhart's second world flight attempt.

THE LAST FLIGHT

ON MAY 23, 1937, Amelia and her crew arrived in Miami, Florida, after stopping at Tucson and New Orleans. This transcontinental shakedown flight was not an auspicious start to Amelia's planned globe-girdling journey. At the airport in Tucson a fire had broken out in one of the Electra's engines, and the repairs had necessitated an overnight stop. While traveling to Miami Amelia found the plane's Sperry autopilot needed adjustment, and the radio transmitter malfunctioned. Nor did her arrival in Miami bode well. She mistakenly landed at Eastern Air Lines' terminal—the wrong airport. Right away she took off for Miami Municipal, where she dropped the plane in, smacking it down hard on the runway. It was an embarrassing arrival—she told newsmen it was the hardest landing she had made in the Electra—but Pan American Airlines' mechanics certified there was no damage.

Not until May 30 did Amelia announce the start of her second world flight attempt and the proposed route. She planned to travel from Miami to Brazil, cross the ocean to Dakar, and then fly across Africa to stops in India, Singapore, Australia, and New Guinea, among others, before island-hopping across the Pacific back to the States. The news of her second try was relegated to the back pages of most newspapers, which were instead headlining strikes

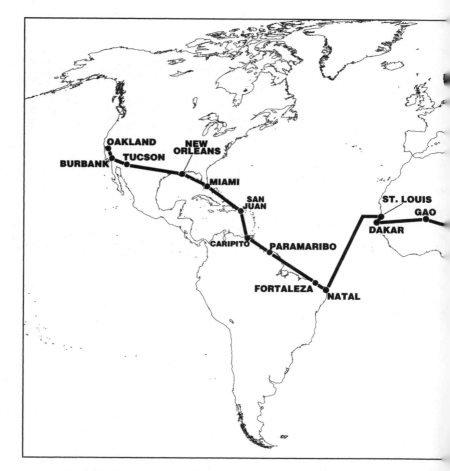

Map of Amelia Earhart's last flight

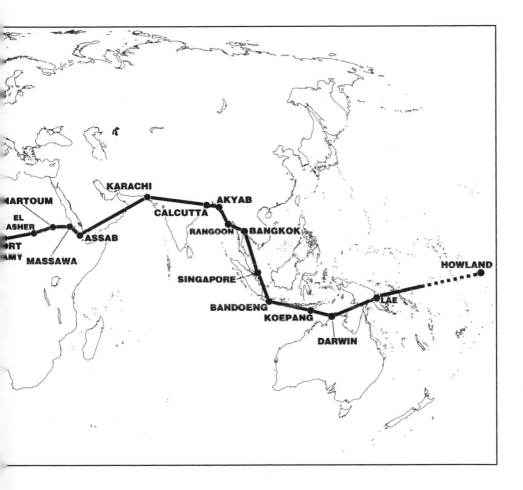

and riots from domestic labor unrest and international events. Amelia also did a turnabout on the entire reason for making the flight. Where previously its stated impetus was scientific, she now claimed she was making it purely for fun. Apparently the harsh criticism she had received after the Luke Field crash had caused her to rephrase the rationale for the global expedition.

Last Flight included quotations from an interview Amelia supposedly conducted in Miami with *Herald Tribune* syndicate reporter Carl Allen. However, in a later telegram Allen confirmed that the interview from which the statements were taken had been held at Oakland before the first flight attempt, in March 1937. Amelia had asked him not to release the interview until she completed the flight. Allen was a good friend, and during the interview she told him, "I have a feeling that there is just about one more good flight left in my system and I hope this trip around the world is it. Anyway, when I have finished this job, I mean to give up long-distance stunt flying." A number of reasons prompted her decision, Allen said. George urged her to "give up hazardous flight attempts," and she added, "I'm getting old and want to make way for the younger generation before I'm feeble, too."[1] Allen would dispatch his interview to the press on July 3, 1937.

During the next week or so in Miami, Pan Am mechanics prepared the Electra for its next hop, to San Juan, Puerto Rico. Technicians again modified the radio antennas, adjusted the autopilot rudder control unit, and checked the radio direction-finder. A short test flight indicated there were still problems with the radio receiver, but Amelia again declined an offer to have a trailing wire antenna installed for the 500-kilocycle equipment because neither she nor Noonan were proficient in Morse code.

As it turned out, Joseph Gurr's attempt in Burbank to modify the plane's antenna proved ineffective. Amelia would be relying on voice radio telephone to communicate, so she removed the Morse key from the Electra and let it be known she would communicate on voice using 6210 kilocycles and 3105 kilocycles. Through a tragic miscommunication, radio operators on the Coast Guard cutter *Itasca*, which would soon be positioned off Howland Island, were unaware that Amelia was limited to radio telephone communication. Therefore, in this most dangerous flight of her career, there would be no point person coordinating the many crucial communication details. Even while Amelia was en route, Commander Warner K. Thompson, *Itasca*'s captain, was still trying to nail down the Electra's frequencies and radio schedule.

ABOUT EIGHT HOURS AFTER lifting off from Miami on June 1, Amelia and Fred set down at the Isla Grande Airport, in Puerto Rico. Fred's expert navigation and Amelia's successful use of autopilot on the uneventful leg led her to remark that "my long-range flying was becoming pretty sissy."[2] Fred often sat in the right seat of the cockpit, unless he was navigating from the rear cabin. After spending a night with the pilot Clara Livingston on her 1,600-acre plantation, Amelia and Fred hopped to Caripito, Venezuela, to refuel. Next they traveled to Paramaribo, Dutch Guinea, flying low and skirting rain squalls over hundreds of miles of dense jungle. On June 4 they landed at Fortaleza, Brazil, after a 1,628-mile leg that crossed the equator and various tributaries of the muddy Amazon River. Fred had hoped to douse Amelia with cold water to celebrate her first flight over the equator, but his hectic cockpit duties never gave him a chance to do so.

Upon landing at Fortaleza's excellent airport the Electra underwent an overhaul at Pan Am's facilities, receiving a complete inspection and washing down. From their hotel overlooking the harbor Amelia and Fred gazed down on the red-tiled roofs and busy streets of the thriving metropolis. With their ship in trusted hands, they were free to shop, explore the waterfront, and have their clothes laundered. For the entire trip Amelia was carrying only a few toiletries, five shirts, two pairs of slacks, a change of shoes, a working coverall, and a light raincoat.

Following a short hop on June 6, the Electra landed at Natal, Brazil, the standard jumping-off point for flights across the South Atlantic. Air France flew regularly scheduled mail runs across the ocean from Natal, and its pilots advised Amelia to defer her departure until the next day. She availed herself, too, of the weather forecasts provided by its two ships stationed mid-ocean. (This may have reinforced her belief that a meteorologist was aboard the *Itasca* to provide forecasts when in fact the cutter reported weather observations only—not forecasts.)

Before dawn the next day Amelia and Fred set off for Dakar, Senegal, a trying 1,900-mile flight in headwinds and in downpours so heavy they shook the plane. Cloud clover prevented Fred from taking a fix on their position until close to the African coast, at which point he advised Amelia on a course to Dakar.

Upon nearing Dakar, however, they encountered haze, low visibility, and fast-fading daylight. The plane's direction-finder was inoperative and Amelia could not get a bearing to Dakar. Amelia and Fred chose to fly north toward better weather and landed at St. Louis, Senegal. Despite Amelia's claim in her dispatch to the *Tribune* that she had turned north against Fred's advice, this appears to have been a joint decision. The successful 13-hour 22-minute crossing was Amelia's second flight over the equator and her third over the Atlantic.

On the following morning she and Fred flew the 163 miles to Dakar, where the plane underwent maintenance on its engines and flight instruments. Meanwhile they savored the local French cuisine. As Amelia commented, good food was found wherever the French settled. Whereas Amelia had said in one of her dispatches that she associated countries in South America with the pungent smells of fruit, meat, and tropical growth, she described western Africa in terms of its kaleidoscope of colors. "Bright raiment" adorned the people she encountered there and "their clothing contrasted gaudily with the neutral background of brown plains, bare hills, parched vegetation and drab dwellings."[3]

Over the following four days, the Electra hopped over central Africa, landing at Gao, French West Africa; Fort Lamy, French Equatorial Africa; and El Fasher and Khartoum in Sudan. In Eritrea, Amelia and Fred set down at Massawa before continuing to the city of Assab, along the Red Sea on June 14. Much of the route had traversed a sea of sand and rock—isolated deserts that had few signs of human habitation, with meandering trails in place of roads. The grueling flights, in blistering-hot weather, exhausted Amelia and Fred, who flew and navigated without help from the plane's radios. Either by Amelia's error or because the direction-finder needed repairs, she was unable to take bearings from any of the many radio stations that lay along her route. Fred wrote to his wife from Massawa, "From a navigational aspect our flights over the desert were more difficult than over water."[4]

The hurried global journey allowed little time for frivolities—or sleep. A typical day's schedule found Amelia and Fred up before dawn to fly and going to bed only after late-night dinners at their destinations. Usually they slept only five hours a night. With what time they had, maintenance on the Electra preempted all tourist activities. Occasionally there were local excursions, but all too often other duties claimed their spare time—speaking to local reporters, for example, or taking philatelic covers to be stamped at the post office. During the journey Amelia peppered her dispatches and letters home with a winsome longing to stay longer at sites she visited. There were few opportunities for personal telephone calls, but along the way Amelia sent letters to George that, he wrote, "would warm the heart of any husband." From India she wrote him: "I wish you were here. So many things you would enjoy. . . . Perhaps some day we can fly together to some of the remote places of the world—just for fun."[5]

BEFORE DAWN ON JUNE 15 the Electra lifted off for a nonstop flight over the Red Sea to skirt Arabia and fly on to Karachi, India (which would later become part of Pakistan). The 1,920-mile flight lasted slightly more than 13 hours and left Amelia tired and frustrated. She ascribed the delay to a jammed mixture-control lever that had forced her to reduce speed, as she was unsure of how much gasoline the right engine consumed. At Karachi Amelia's friend Jacques de Sibour greeted the vagabond travelers, congratulating Amelia for being the first person to fly nonstop from the Red Sea to India. Soon after, Jacques announced a telephone call from George, and he and Amelia chatted for a brief time. The next day Amelia cabled him her estimated time of arrival at Howland Island, though bad weather and mechanical problems en route would force unexpected delays. George, meanwhile, was brokering publicity deals for his wife that included radio broadcasts and lectures, and his interest in her welfare was not merely a husband's concern. The deals came with deadlines attached and hinged on when she would arrive at Honolulu and Oakland.

On the short layover at Karachi, Imperial Airways' mechanics serviced the Electra, and the Royal Air Force's technicians adjusted its instruments as best they could. The Cambridge exhaust gas analyzer, which was needed to obtain maximum fuel efficiency and was a critical instrument for the oceanic hops, was inoperative again. Later it was repaired in Bandoeng.

ON JUNE 16 GEORGE Putnam cabled the chief of naval operations to notify him of Amelia's expected arrival at Lae a week later. His cables also went out to the commandant of the Coast Guard and to Ruth Hamilton, the acting director at the Department of the Interior. Two days later, George alerted Richard Black, an official of the Interior department, of the radio frequencies Amelia would use inbound to Howland Island. George had appointed Black to be the Earhart representative aboard the *Itasca* and confirmed for him that Amelia would broadcast by radio telephone. He did not specify that the Electra would not send with Morse code because he was not familiar with its radio equipment.

On June 17 Amelia and Fred took off for Calcutta, a 1,390-mile flight offering diverse sights on the ground and in the air. At first, windblown sand and haze obscured the ground view, and a gaggle of black eagles soared into the plane's path at 5,000 feet, coming much too close for comfort. Shortly after, the Electra flew over vast plains, where it was tossed about by strong updrafts and engulfed by rain squalls. Approaching Calcutta they saw green and tan paddy fields below them, the tropical vegetation standing in contrast to Karachi's drier climate. At the city's Dum Dum airdrome, they were served afternoon tea under the shadow of the Electra's wing on the concrete apron. Unfortunately, as they soon discovered, their arrival coincided with the start of the monsoon season.

While they slept rain soaked the airdrome's grass field, preventing a takeoff with a full fuel load. Amelia decided on adding an interim refueling stop at Akyab, in Burma. During the early morning takeoff on June 18, the lightly fueled plane barely cleared the trees that bordered Calcutta's airdrome. After refueling at Akyab they made three attempts to leave in rain and low visibility, one in which they battled relentless monsoon rains that forced them to backtrack after a two-hour flight. The third attempt took place on June 19, and they headed for Rangoon, Burma, only 400 miles away. Approaching Rangoon, they saw the Shwe Dagon Pagoda with its "covering of pure gold a burnished beacon for wayfarers of the air," Amelia would recall.[6]

The monsoons had thwarted their plans to continue immediately to Bangkok. After Amelia and Fred accepted the invitation of the American Consul to stay at his home that night, he and a guide escorted them on a tour to the golden pagoda. There Fred refused to remove his shoes and socks and go inside. A world-traveler, Fred had probably seen Buddhas before, but whatever his reasons, Amelia climbed the countless steps unshod and without him.

During a break in the rains, the Electra winged its way to Bangkok, where it made a brief refueling stop before it headed out again, to Singapore. The journey over the Gulf of Siam, in blue skies with little puffs of cumulus clouds, saw Amelia and Fred scanning a mauve sea and marveling at the fair weather. They had left the monsoons behind and had moved on to an equatorial climate. After the Electra set down at Singapore's new multimillion-dollar airport, Amelia and Fred were greeted by their hosts, the American Consul General and his wife, with whom they stayed for the night.

Early in the morning on June 21, the Electra launched for Bandoeng, Java, crossing the equator for the third time during the trip. The plane passed over turquoise water with tiny islets dotted with palms and fringed by strips of beaches before it came upon the volcanic mountains jutting from Java's interior. Although they expected a short layover there, it lasted nearly a week because of repairs to the Cambridge instruments. At one point Amelia and Fred were in transit to their next stop, only to have to return to Bandoeng for additional repair work.

While waiting for the Dutch technicians to peg the source of the instruments' problems, Amelia and Fred stayed with friends of Fred and toured the neighboring city of Batavia (modern-day Jakarta), some three hours away by car. While there Amelia feasted on *ryst tafel*, whose twenty-one different courses included curried chicken, meat, eggs, fish, relishes, nuts, and vegetables. Regrettably the rich meal caused Amelia to suffer a severe, daylong attack of diarrhea.

The Electra left Bandoeng on the afternoon of June 27, its flight instruments in working order at last. It landed five hours later at Koepang, on the southern tip of Timor, in a grass field surrounded by a stone wall to keep out roaming pigs. There were no hangars, and assisted by amused locals, Amelia and Fred staked down their ship for the night.

BY THIS TIME *ITASCA'S* Commander Thompson was trying to work directly with Amelia to ascertain the frequencies she would use on the flight to Howland Island rather than relying on messages relayed by intermediaries. He also needed to know her expected time of departure from New Guinea. On June 23 the cutter operator sent an advance cable to Port Darwin, in Australia (her next stop after Koepang), with information about its radio equipment, including its direction-finder frequency range. The same day another advance cable was sent to Port Darwin and Lae, asking Amelia to "advise this vessel twelve hours prior to your departure from New Guinea full information regarding your desires in matter of radio frequencies and communication schedule. We will conform to any frequencies desired."[7] Two days later, on June 25, while Amelia and Fred were still in Java, George Putnam attempted to provide the Coast Guard cutter with answers to its requests. He informed Richard Black that the Electra would communicate on 500, 3105, and 6210 kilocycles by voice, but unknown to George the 500 kilocycle frequency could send code only, not voice. As a backup plan, the Navy would set up a high-frequency radio direction-finder on Howland Island, but its batteries wore down as Amelia was flying there, and it was of no use to her.

Adding to the uncertainty were the two time zones the Electra would cross en route to Howland, and *Itasca's* use of U.S. Navy time, which divided hourly time zones into two half-hour ones and thus did not conform to Greenwich Mean Time. As it worked out the Electra would depart at 0:00 hours GMT from Lae so that the elapsed time of the flight and GMT would coincide. The Electra would also cross the International Date Line.[8]

By now the three ships were in position, awaiting Amelia. The *Itasca* was off Howland Island, the U.S. Navy tug *Ontario* stood at sea about halfway between Lae and Howland, and the U.S. Navy seaplane tender *Swan* was positioned halfway between Honolulu and Howland.

FROM KOEPANG THE ELECTRA crossed the Timor Sea to Port Darwin, Australia, on June 28. There Amelia's and Fred's documents were subjected to a thorough review by the public health inspector and were found to lack an official U.S. Public Health stamp. Despite their travels through regions where malaria, yellow fever, and other diseases occurred, he allowed them entry provided they would remain on alert should any symptoms arise overnight. Then the head of the Darwin radio direction-finding unit pulled Amelia aside to discuss her equipment. He asked her why she had not used her receiver while approaching Darwin—its use was mandatory and he had sent her frequencies—and she admitted the unit had given her problems along the entire route. He worked with the receiver, found a blown fuse, and provided her with additional fuses to use in case the problem arose again. In Amelia's defense it must be noted the Bendix receiver was a new technology and would present occasional problems to all but the most experienced radio operators. Moreover, the Bendix did not have written instructions because manuals were not customary then; pilots learned by trial and error. Still, overly optimistic about Fred's celestial navigation, Amelia did not seem to appreciate the receiver's significance in locating Howland Island. Fred would guide her to the vicinity of the island, but it would be up to Amelia to locate it with the help of the Bendix.

AFTER A 1,200-MILE FLIGHT of nearly eight hours—"against head winds as usual," Amelia reported—the Electra reached Lae, New Guinea, on June 29.[9] Some 22,000 miles of the air journey were complete, with only 7,000 remaining. But the rigors of the strenuous schedule—almost forty days of flying—were taking a toll on Amelia. Her face was drawn and fatigued, and her figure was gaunt.

She hoped to take off for Howland within two days, but rain at Lae, coupled with Fred's need to calibrate his chronometers, forced a delay. She was becoming increasingly tense. "Radio misunderstanding and personnel unfitness probably will hold one day. Have asked Black for forecast for tomorrow. You check meteorologist on job as FN must have star sights," Amelia wired George on the thirtieth.[10] The radio problems were ongoing, but what she meant by "unfitness" is unknown, though she was likely referring to either her own fatigue or her navigator's hangover. The previous night Fred had downed several Scotch whiskeys while entertaining local pilots with stories of his flying exploits, although he apparently abstained thereafter.

While his wife was agonizing about the hazardous flight leg to Howland, George was still preoccupied with lining up her publicity commitments. "Is there likelihood Oakland arrival by Monday morning," read his cable to her.[11] She never saw this telegram. He also wired Richard Black to arrange good photographs of her arrival and to confirm that Amelia would broadcast on the NBC station upon her arrival at Honolulu.

Amelia's anxiety continued to grow, and the next day her dispatch to the *Herald Tribune* read in part: "'Denmark's a prison' and Lae, attractive and unusual as it is appears to two flyers just as confining. Lockheed stands ready for longest hop weighted with gasoline and oil to capacity."[12] The Electra was finally ready for its hop at day's end on the thirtieth, having undergone maintenance performed by Guinea Airways mechanics. Amelia signed off on the work done on the engines, instruments, and aircraft. In addition to the mechanical help extended to Amelia, the airfield's radio operator Harry Balfour assisted with the plane's radios and obtained time checks so that Fred's chronometers could be set with precision. But during Amelia's short test flight the morning of July 1, both she and Balfour missed an opportunity to figure out why she could not get a minimum signal on the direction-finder loop, with which Amelia could have homed in to the station at Lae. Neither understood that it could not take bearings on 7500 kilocycles. Though Balfour was an experienced radio operator, he was not familiar with the new Bendix receiver. Amelia also had Balfour cable the *Itasca* asking for a forecast and that it "report in English not code especially while flying."[13] During the considerable hours they spent with Balfour, Fred and Amelia had stressed neither of them could understand Morse code at any speed, beyond individual letters transmitted slowly. Balfour would almost certainly have been surprised to hear this.

From Fleet Air Base, Pearl Harbor, Amelia and Fred received a weather forecast dated July 1, the last they would get before departing. The radiogram predicted headwinds of 13-knots (about 15 miles per hour) and rain and clouds most of the way, conditions that might have prevented Fred from taking star sights to obtain a fix on their position after they left. Within a half hour of their departure, however, Harry Balfour received a new forecast calling for 25-knot headwinds en route to the *Ontario* and thereafter falling to 20 knots to Howland. If the forecast was accurate, the winds might have increased the Electra's flight time to Howland by an hour or more. But it was the first, more optimistic forecast on which Amelia and Fred based their gasoline consumption and groundspeed calculations. They had already lightened the plane as much they could—tossing all nonessential items from the plane, including some survival equipment. Amelia left behind flares, tools, smoke bombs, and spare parts. Reportedly the Electra carried life vests, a rubber raft, and a Very pistol, but this was not verified, although George Putnam would later insist they were aboard.

With the chronometers checked and the plane in good condition, Amelia wanted to leave Lae as soon as possible. On the far horizon Howland, Honolulu, and California beckoned, drawing the Electra closer to its goal: a successful world flight around the equator.

ON JULY 2, 1937, at 10:00 A.M. local time, 00:00 GMT, Amelia pushed the throttles to full power, and the plane, loaded with 1,100 gallons of gasoline, began its takeoff run on Lae's field.[14] Eyewitness accounts of the takeoff reported the plane using the entire 3,000-foot turf runway, and then sinking to five feet over the Huon Gulf before climbing to 100 feet and disappearing from sight. The airline's Lockheed pilots standing by were impressed with Amelia's handling of the difficult takeoff. Harry Balfour sent a priority message to *Itasca* with Amelia's local takeoff time and her expected time of arrival at Howland, eighteen hours later.

Amelia and Balfour had arranged a transmission schedule, but static interference prevented consistently good communication until early afternoon. Balfour also transmitted the latest weather forecast, but she did not acknowledge its receipt. On 6210 kilocycles Balfour heard several reports from Amelia, the last being received at 7:20 GMT. At that time, KHAQQ, Amelia's call sign, gave a position as latitude 4 degrees 33 minutes south, longitude 159 degrees 7 minutes east, and a reported height of 8000 feet over cumulus clouds with a wind of 23 knots.[15] During the entire flight, this was the only complete position report Amelia transmitted. Thus, after slightly more than seven hours, the Electra had traveled a distance of 741 nautical miles at an average groundspeed of 116 miles per hour. Considering the plane's excessive weight at takeoff, its climb to altitude, and the headwinds, the speed was reasonable and would increase over the remaining distance as fuel was used up and the Electra's gross weight decreased.

Two radio logs aboard *Itasca*, as well as a log maintained by the operator manning the Navy's direction-finder on Howland, recorded what little
communication with Amelia there was from 14:18 GMT to 20:14 GMT. But
only once during this entire time did Amelia acknowledge receiving signals
transmitted by *Itasca*: she could be heard but was not receiving the cutter's
transmissions. Yet they had been sent on all normally used wavelengths and
were received in Hawaii, San Francisco, and Samoa. Commander Thompson
of the *Itasca* later concluded that Amelia's receiver was malfunctioning.

To further complicate matters, Commander Thompson's radiomen
ignored the message from Amelia that Balfour had sent *Itasca* a few days
earlier, in which she specifically asked the cutter to avoid Morse code while
she was flying. Unaccountably, the cutter's radio operators often broadcast
in Morse code during this leg of the flight. Almost all mariners and long-
distance flyers communicated in the universal language of dots and dashes,
and for whatever reason they found it difficult to abandon. Furthermore,
Itasca maintained its time clocks according to the Navy's and Coast Guard's
tradition of operating at sea with half-hour zones, which did not conform to
GMT. When Amelia was broadcasting at quarter past the hour, for example,
clocks aboard *Itasca* read quarter to the hour. She was following the agreed-
upon schedule but the radio operators were not. Perhaps Amelia's instructions never reached them, though the cutter had logged her cable as having
been received.

What follows is a partially reconstructed record of the communication
between the Electra and *Itasca*. According to a later report, the Coast Guard
radio transcripts were "necessarily not complete due to the rapidity of events
and also due to the Earhart exclusive use of voice, only partially received."[16]
For hours *Itasca*'s radio operators and officers gave all their attention to the
inbound Electra, and the tension aboard was palpable, as thick as the heavy
humid air settling over the cutter. The operators were calling KHAQQ on
various frequencies in voice and code and requesting answers, but received
only one reply to their calls.

At 14:18 GMT, Amelia transmitted "cloudy and overcast"; at 15:15 she
reported "overcast, will listen on hour and half hour on 3105"; at 16:23 she
reported "partly cloudy"; at 17:44 GMT she requested she be given a bearing once she whistled into the microphone; and a few minutes later she

transmitted "about 200 miles out—approximately—whistling now," which *Itasca* received as poor reception.

At 18:15 GMT Amelia tried again: "Please take bearing on us and report in half hour. I will make noise in microphone—about 100 miles out." This transmission could be heard clearly on the cutter.

Good weather was prevailing at Howland: clear visibility, smooth seas, ceiling unlimited, and a light east wind of 7 knots. Shortly before the 18:15 transmission (at 6:45 A.M. local) *Itasca* started emitting heavy smoke from her boilers to aid Amelia in locating Howland, but in the glare of the rising sun she might have missed seeing it.

At 19:12 GMT Amelia transmitted, "We must be on you but cannot see you. But gas is running low. Been unable to reach you by radio. We are flying at altitude 1000 feet." Another *Itasca* log reported her as saying she was "running out of gas only ½ hour left." The message's signal strength indicated her plane was probably within 50 miles of the cutter. Amelia's statement that "gas is running low" could have meant she was close to using the reserve fuel set aside for a contingency plan whereby she and Fred would head toward another group of more recognizable islands. It is possible she had enough fuel aboard to fly for another two hours. She might have backtracked to the Gilbert Islands or flown on a southeast heading toward the Phoenix Islands, though she never transmitted any such change in plans.[17] Not knowing the actual headwinds or the Electra's rate of fuel consumption, one can only speculate about her course of action.

Sixteen minutes after her last transmission, at 19:28 GMT or 7:58 local, Amelia radioed, "We are circling but cannot hear you. Go ahead on 7500." This message also had a high signal strength. While the plane circled—or "drifted," as one radio operator said he had heard her say—Fred might have been trying to shoot the sun with his bubble octant to establish a position. He was apparently unable to do so, despite the excellent weather at Howland, which should have made a fix possible. It's conceivable the Electra was 30 miles west-northwest of Howland, where sailors saw cloud cover—conditions that might have prevented Fred from getting a fix.

In another attempt to contact Amelia, *Itasca* sent a series of the letter A in Morse code on 7500 kilocycles. At 19:30 GMT Amelia transmitted she had received the signals but was unable to get a "minimum" and asked *Itasca* to take a bearing on her and answer on 3105 using voice. But the 7500 kilocycle frequency was outside the design range of her receiver, and she would not have been able to use it to home in to the cutter. The *Itasca* had been monitoring its 500-kilocycle direction-finding equipment since night fell, but it never received signals from her on this frequency.

By now Amelia was overdue and the collective anxiety aboard the cutter was increasing with every passing minute. In the ship's small radio room, which was heating up rapidly as a hot sun beat down on the bridge, the radiomen were becoming panicked. For hours they had done everything possible to bring in Amelia, without success.

Twenty hours and fourteen minutes after the Electra left Lae, New Guinea, *Itasca* heard Amelia loudly and clearly: "We are on the line of position 157–337. Will repeat this on 6210 kilocycles. Wait—listening on 6210 kilocycles. We are running north and south."

This message was by voice on 3105 at high strength and all in the radio room heard it the same, though it was described as "hurried, frantic, and apparently not complete."[18] Nothing was heard on 6210.

Amelia and Fred had been flying back and forth on a north-south bearing trying to find the island. Were they looking in the wrong place? Amelia's charts showed Howland Island lying six miles farther east than its true location, and new hydrographic charts were not issued until June 1937.

On July 2, 1937, Fleet Air Base, Pearl Harbor, broadcast: "Amelia Earhart plane en route Howland Island...unreported since 2045 GCT July 2 and apparently down at sea position unknown. *Itasca* searching probable northwest sector off Howland Island."[19]

That same day the Secretary of the Navy in Washington, D.C., approved use of naval facilities to conduct what was to become the largest search to date for an aircraft lost at sea.

EPILOGUE

WITHIN THREE HOURS AFTER Amelia's last message, Commander Thompson ordered *Itasca* to an area about 40 miles northwest of Howland Island, reasoning the Electra had set down beneath the heavy cloud banks there. Upon arriving, the cutter's sailors reported 6-foot waves and seas teeming with sharks. Had Amelia attempted a ditching on the heaving breakers, it is likely the Electra would have broken apart on impact and quickly sunk. But if Thompson and his men thought she had met a watery death, they remained silent about it, and the cutter would continue to scour the seas in its hunt for the Electra. Four lookouts were posted at its crow's nest and bridge, and at night high-powered searchlights blazed forth. Its radio operators listened on various frequencies and steadily called the Electra. After *Itasca* sent an "all ships" alert, other ships and shore stations also kept a constant watch for the plane's signals, as did Pan American Airways' radio station at Mokapu Point near Honolulu.

On July 2 the Navy launched a PBY Catalina flying boat from Pearl Harbor, but a freak storm with snow and sleet 420 miles north of Howland Island forced its return to Hawaii. (Its use was risky anyway because it was designed to land in lagoons or sheltered harbors, not open seas in the South Pacific.) Meanwhile, in Honolulu the battleship USS *Colorado* was ordered to get underway as soon as possible, bringing its three catapult-launched float-planes to use for reconnaissance. The battleship would undertake a four-day voyage to the search area. The Navy tender USS *Swan,* at the Earhart guard station halfway between Howland Island and Honolulu, steamed south toward the search area, but it, too, was days away. In California the aircraft carrier USS *Lexington* was being readied along with its escort of three destroyers, but they and their sixty-seven scout planes would not arrive until July 12, ten days after the Electra disappeared. There and in Hawaii, shore leaves for the holiday weekend were canceled, leaving many a disgruntled sailor.

Shortly after the plane was reported missing, amateur radio operators began to claim they were hearing SOS broadcasts from the Electra. Hearing these claims, Paul Mantz believed the Electra might have reached land. The reports offered hope, and *Itasca* was called away to initiate a new search south of Howland Island. The Coast Guard and Navy were not able to authenticate any of the claims, however, and some operators later confessed they were hoaxes. After radio experts pointed out the downed plane could only transmit from land—there was no hand-crank electrical mechanism to power the radio—the bogus reports of transmissions began to dissipate.

At the Coast Guard headquarters in Oakland George Putnam kept a constant vigil, pacing back and forth and hardly sleeping. He assumed the plane was drifting or had landed on an atoll. He was sure its empty fuel tanks had enough buoyancy to keep the plane afloat, sufficient time to enable Amelia and Fred to escape with a rubber raft, food rations, and other equipment. His hopes were probably bolstered by a newspaper article giving two examples of landplanes floating long enough for their pilots to be rescued, one for eight days in the Atlantic, the other for seven days off the coast of Newfoundland.[1] He continually fired off telegrams to anyone he believed could help. As the weeks passed his desperation to find Amelia would reach the point that he sought the advice of clairvoyants and psychics.

On July 3 news of Amelia's disappearance shocked citizens worldwide. The headlines in American newspapers screamed "Miss Earhart Forced Down At Sea, Howland Isle Fears; Coast Guard Begins Search," "Amelia Down on Pacific; Rush Search," and "Radio Signals Heard from Earhart Plane."[2] As the hunt continued and hope began to fade, the media coverage would eventually ebb, but for days it was commonly believed they had survived.

On July 4 White House officials reported that President Roosevelt was following the search closely. His personal concern for the safety of Amelia escalated the effort, and he authorized a search that would involve ten ships, one hundred aircraft, and three thousand men.

On this same day George tried to comfort Fred Noonan's wife, Beatrice, who had joined him in Oakland. When he failed to stop her sobbing, he snapped: "It's this way, Bee. One of two things have happened. Either they were killed outright—and that must come to all of us sooner or later—or they are alive and will be picked up. Keep your chin up, Bee."[3] She promptly collapsed and was ordered to rest at home under the care of a physician.

By July 12 the *Colorado* had called off its hunt in the Phoenix Islands and was awaiting arrival of the *Lexington*. A day later the aircraft carrier reached its first search station, about 100 miles north of Howland Island, and search planes began to roar off the flight deck.

Back in the States, criticism had erupted over the exorbitant costs projected for the search, with politicians and civilians questioning why Amelia's flight warranted this expense. The *Christian Science Monitor* noted that the United States might possibly ban oceanic stunt flights as a result of Amelia's failed effort. The article cited her "inadequate radio preparation and insufficient coordination previous to the takeoff" as among the reasons why such flights might be prohibited. It went on to claim that the Department of Commerce granted permission for her second world attempt because of her public prominence and her close friendship with the Roosevelt family. There was no important reason for her flight, the article concluded, because the Pacific routes had already been flown by Pan American and other pioneers.[4]

As public censure grew, President Roosevelt felt it necessary to respond, and on July 20 he lashed out at newsmen reporting that the search had cost $4 million. He declared the money would have been spent on routine maneuvers and counted toward the time the aviators must spend in the air or the vessel at sea. He added that any citizen, rich or poor, would receive this sort of help.

Despite covering 250,000 square miles—an area the size of Texas—in every direction from Howland Island, the search had turned up no sign of the Electra or its occupants, and on July 18 it was abandoned. A little more than a month later, the Bureau of Air Commerce announced that the airfield on Howland Island was not practical for future flights. Despite being funded with American taxpayer dollars, the Howland runway built for Amelia would never see commercial use. The former BAC director Eugene Vidal, who had suggested Amelia refuel at Howland Island, later said she planned to land on a beach in the Gilbert Islands if she couldn't find Howland. No sign of Amelia had turned up during a 1937 search on these islands.

In November 1937 two hundred men and women would gather at Floyd Bennett Field in New York to pay tribute to Amelia with speeches and a flyover by several planes. At an Amelia Earhart Foundation banquet the following year Louise Thaden and Ruth Nichols praised Amelia as a great American pioneer. Eleanor Roosevelt was named honorary chairman of the national sponsors committee of the nonprofit foundation, which had been formed to conduct an expedition to look for Amelia. In 1940 it would hire a sea captain to search various Pacific islands during his scheduled yacht tour, but he uncovered no trace of the Electra. The foundation, beset by financial problems and mismanagement, soon dissolved. Even years later, aviator Jackie Cochran rarely talked about Amelia because she had been devastated by her death. Both the Ninety-Nines and Zonta International, organizations of which Amelia was a member, would establish scholarships in her name for women in aviation that continue to be awarded.

Not all pilots lauded Amelia. In August 1937 Laura Ingalls announced she would attempt new records to increase the prestige of women aviators, which was "endangered by the disappearance of Amelia Earhart."[5] Paul Mantz later told his grandson, Greg, that Amelia was not qualified to make the round-the-world flight. Greg said when Paul "left the team, he knew he was going to watch her kill herself."[6] Criticism of Amelia's flying skills had begun long before her last flight. She was not a methodical planner who gave attention to all possible outcomes, a talent inherent in the best long-distance flyers. She skimped on her radio navigation preparations—not learning the radio equipment nor comprehending its importance in locating Howland Island on her last flight. While Pan American pilots reported every half hour to aid in narrowing a search area should the aircraft go down, she gave only one position report en route to Howland and none while flying on another Pacific flight, from Hawaii to California. Time was her nemesis. Always rushing to fulfill her public commitments, Amelia failed to carve out enough time to focus and concentrate on the task at hand. All things considered, it was as if she willed herself to survive her earlier flights, but bravery and determination cannot replace the many hours of advance work needed to successfully accomplish a transoceanic crossing. The vast Pacific Ocean makes no allowances for navigation errors. But perhaps some recklessness is called for in all explorers. Courage and daring certainly are, and Amelia blazed trails in her "shining adventures," as she called them.

ON JULY 25 newspapers announced that George Putnam was offering a $2,000 reward for information "which would definitely clear up the mystery surrounding the disappearance" of Amelia and Fred.[7] For many months he kept faith that she would be found alive and continued to suggest new areas to be searched. By the end of the year, however, he had accepted her death. In 1939 he remarried, and in the Second World War he served overseas as an intelligence officer in the Army Air Corps. The time apart from his new wife strained the marriage, and she filed for divorce shortly thereafter. Meanwhile, he established his own publishing company, George Palmer Putnam, Inc., though he never again achieved the commercial success he had enjoyed earlier in his life. He sold the Rye, New York, house to help meet his considerable living expenses and maintain an image of prosperity. With his fourth wife, Margaret Haviland, he operated a hotel in Death Valley, California, until he died of kidney failure, in 1950.

AMY EARHART REMAINED ON the West Coast for nearly a decade, believing her daughter was alive and certain she would turn up in California. She was convinced that Amelia's last flight had been a spy mission for the U.S. government. (In later correspondence with Paul Mantz and Muriel Morrissey, Eleanor Roosevelt denied any knowledge of this.) A prolific correspondent, Amy wrote countless letters, up to forty a day, to her family and to fans of Amelia. Although George sent her a check every month and paid her medical bills, she refused to accept that her daughter had not left a substantial estate and remained financially irresponsible. Paul Mantz offered to loan her money—until he discovered her more than adequate allowance from George. Eventually she returned to Muriel in Medford, Massachusetts, where she died in 1962 at age ninety-five.

MURIEL ALSO LIVED A long life. She returned to a teaching career after her children grew up and spent her spare time in community work and maintaining her sister's legacy. She did not subscribe to any of her mother's "spy mission" theories and believed her sister had crashed in the Pacific. George and Muriel often corresponded, and later she said he had been of immense help to her and her mother after Amelia's death. She died in Medford in 1998 at age ninety-eight.

AMELIA EARHART HAS REMAINED in the popular consciousness as a beloved icon long after the achievements of other women pilots have faded into obscurity. George Putnam could never have arranged any better publicity for Amelia than what would later emerge. Over the following decades, interest in her would wax and wane, and popular interest in her story declined in the immediate years after her disappearance. Despite several attempts, George could not convince a Hollywood studio to make a movie of Amelia's life. However, as the Second World War progressed and aviation took on ever greater significance for Americans, movie moguls determined it was timely to produce such a film. Released in 1943, the fictionalized treatment of her life was titled *Flight for Freedom* and starred Rosalind Russell as the pilot Tonie Carter and Fred MacMurray as the navigator. While Tonie prepared to take off from Hawaii on a global flight, the U.S. government asked her to fly a secret mission and to deliberately crash to provide time for further preparations. The plot continued as she reversed course and landed secretly on a Pacific island, a subterfuge that allowed the military to conduct a search over Japanese territory.

The film provided the spark for Amelia's legend. Since then, numerous outlandish theories about her disappearance have proliferated. Among the better-known ones: that Amelia and Fred had been captured and executed by the Japanese on Saipan Island; that the Japanese compelled her to serve as Tokyo Rose; and that she survived, returned to the States, changed her name, and remarried. Another theory, still undergoing investigation, purports that the pair died as castaways on the island of Nikumaroro in the Pacific.

Our enduring fascination with Amelia is yet another example of the strong hold the dead have on the living. Some have asked why we won't let her go peacefully and accept that she drowned. Why revisit her demise? Therein lies a mystery, perhaps one greater than the specifics of her death. There is no question she had charisma, and George Putnam laid the groundwork for her popularity, but the universal appeal she engendered goes beyond that. And while the desire for fame and commercial gain drive the ongoing searches for her Electra and the definitive account of her fate, the many other pioneer pilots who disappeared over the Atlantic or Pacific have been forgotten while Amelia's celebrity burns brightly.

Amelia gambled on her last flight, as did many of her flying contemporaries who also perished. Before beginning the second transpacific flight, she gave George a handwritten note that in view of her disappearance is heartrending, yet timeless and apt today: "Please know I am quite aware of the hazards of the trip. Women must try to do things as men have tried. When they fail, their failure must be but a challenge to others."[8]

REFERENCE NOTES

ABBREVIATIONS

AE   Amelia Earhart
AOE   Amy Otis Earhart
GPP   George Palmer Putnam
MEM   Muriel Earhart Morrissey
IWASM International Women's Air and Space Museum, Cleveland, Ohio
MHS   Minnesota Historical Society, St. Paul, Minnesota
PSC   Purdue University Archives and Special Collections
SLRC   The Schlesinger Library, Radcliffe Institute, Harvard University

MANUSCRIPT COLLECTIONS AND PERSONAL PAPERS

Columbia University Oral History Collection

Muriel Morrissey
Ruth Nichols
Blanche Noyes

International Women's Air and Space Museum

Amelia Earhart Papers

Minnesota Historical Society

Otis Family Papers, P2031

Purdue University Archives and Special Collections

George Palmer Putnam Collection of Amelia Earhart Papers

Seaver Center for Western History Research, Los Angeles County Museum of Natural History

Amelia Earhart Collection

The Schlesinger Library, Radcliffe Institute, Harvard University

Amelia Mary Earhart

Amy Otis Earhart
Clarence Strong Williams

Texas Woman's University, The Woman's Collection, Oral History Collection

Interview with Edna Gardner Whyte, February 8, 1979

University of Wyoming, American Heritage Center

Eugene Vidal Collection, Accession #6013

U.S. Coast Guard

Itasca: Radio Transcripts Earhart Flight

U S. Navy

Naval History Division: Amelia Earhart Correspondence

Chapter 1   Atchison

1. MHS, Otis Family Papers, P2031. Alfred, born in 1827, came from a long line of distinguished ancestors, including Englishman John Otis. The first Otis to arrive in America, John had settled at Hingham, Massachusetts, in 1635, where he claimed house lots in the town's first land division.
2. SLRC, Notes by AOE.
3. MHS, Otis Family Papers, letter from Alfred G. Otis to George L. Otis, December 1852, no day given.
4. Kansas Historical Society Web site, http://www.kshs.org/index.htm.
5. MHS, Otis Family Papers, letter from Alfred G. Otis to George L. Otis, June 24, 1856.
6. Previous biographers, as well as Amy Otis Earhart and George Palmer Putnam, wrote that Alfred served in the Union Army. The author thanks the reference staff of the Hennepin County Library for their thorough research into records of Civil War soldiers. The name Alfred G. Otis did not appear in these or other records of soldiers at that time.
7. SLRC, Notes by AOE.
8. Several of Amy's stories exemplify her predilection to embellish the history of her family by reinventing or embroidering facts.
9. MHS, Otis Family Papers, letter from Alfred G. Otis to George L. Otis, April 16, 1856.
10. Morrissey, *Courage Is the Price*, p. 20.
11. SLRC, Notes by AOE.
12. *Ms. Magazine*, January 1977, Letters to the Editors, letter written by MEM.
13. Alfred Otis had earned $60 a month teaching in the early 1850s, and his request that Edwin earn $50 a month was not at all unreasonable.

14. Morrissey, *Courage Is the Price*, p. 25.

Chapter 2 Childhood

1. Mize, *A Song of Saints*, and author's correspondence with Mr. Mize.
2. Earhart, *The Fun of It*, p. 3.
3. Ibid., p. 7.
4. Thaden, *High, Wide, and Frightened*, p. 147.
5. SLRC, Notes by AOE.
6. Morrissey, *Courage Is the Price*, p. 28.
7. The State Historical Society of Missouri Web site, http://shs.umsystem.edu/index. shtml.
8. Earhart, *The Fun of It*, p. 3.
9. Earhart, *20 Hrs.*, p. 1.
10. Earhart, *Last Flight*, p. 84.
11. Earhart, *The Fun of It*, p. 8.
12. Morrissey, *Courage Is the Price*, p. 32.
13. Putnam, *Soaring Wings*, p. 29.
14. Earhart, *The Fun of It*, p. 9.
15. MHS, Otis Family Papers, letter from Amelia J. Otis to Charles E. Otis, March 6, 1906.
16. Earhart, *Last Flight*, p. 2.
17. Quoted from *Scientific American*, January 2007, "100 years earlier."
18. Codicils to the wills of Alfred G. and Amelia J. Otis, dated October 14, 1911, U.S. District Court, Atchison, Kansas.
19. Probate Papers of Amelia J. Otis and Alfred G. Otis, U.S. District Court, Atchison, Kansas; Consumer Price Index, Samuel H. Williamson, "Six Ways to Compute the Relative Value of a U.S. Dollar Amount, 1774 to Present," *Measuring Worth*, 2007; in *Courage Is the Price*, a biography of Amelia published in 1963, Muriel wrote of her grandparents' "million-dollar estate," and further commented that her mother's inheritance had been put in trust for twenty years or until Edwin's death. This was not true. The codicil restrictions had been limited to fifteen years and certainly did not mention Edwin's death. Why she made these claims is unclear, but perhaps the passage of time and her bitterness at her family's eventual squander of Amy's inheritance had dimmed her memory. Of course, it is possible Amy had presented these misstatements as facts.
20. Morrissey, *Courage Is the Price*, p. 78.
21. MHS, Otis Family Papers, letter from AOE to Charles E. Otis, March 18, 1913.

Chapter 3 On the Move

1. MHS, Otis Family Papers, letter from Charles Otis to Mark Otis, September 23, 1913.
2. Ibid.

3. MHS, Otis Family Papers, letter from James Otis to James Otis Dowrie, February 2, 1991.

4. SLRC, letter from AE to Virginia Park, March 7, 1914.

5. *Los Angeles Times*, February 22, 1959; Morrissey, *Courage Is the Price*, p. 97.

6. MHS, Otis family papers, Notes written by Charles Otis in 1907.

7. SLRC, letter from AE to AOE, March 1917.

8. SLRC, letter from AE to AOE, October 25, 1916; in 1917 Miss Sutherland unexpectedly married William Furbey Brown, a cowboy she had met on vacation. Amelia did not comment on the marriage.

9. SLRC, letter from AE to AOE, October 31, 1917.

10. Morrissey, *Courage Is the Price*, p. 101.

11. PSC.

12. Brooks-Pazmany, *United States Women in Aviation*, pp. 33–41.

13. Earhart, *The Fun of It*, p. 19.

14. A.E. later visited Ogontz to talk of her aviation career and was named an honorary member of the Class of 1930.

15. Web site, http://www.spartacus.schoolnet.co.uk/Wfurse.htm.

16. Earhart, *Last Flight*, p. 3.

17. Ibid., pp. 2–3; O. Allen, *The Airline Builders*, pp. 18–19; and various articles.

18. Earhart, *The Fun of It*, p. 23.

Chapter 4   Flying Lessons

1. Earhart, *The Fun of It*, p. 24.

2. Web site, http://www.csudh.edu/1910airmeet/event; Thomas F. Norton, *General Aviation News*, October 1, 2004; various magazine articles.

3. Earhart, *The Fun of It*, p. 24.

4. Ibid., p. 25.

5. Ibid.

6. Southern, *I Taught Amelia to Fly*; John Underwood, "Kinner: The Man and His Machines," *Air Progress Aviation Review*, n.d.

7. Earhart, *The Fun of It*, p. 26.

8. SLRC, Notes by AOE.

9. Earhart, *20 Hrs.*, p. 15; in 1929 Amelia asked Neta Snook Southern to join the Ninety-Nines, which she declined to do, and in 1937 Neta corresponded with Amy Earhart about her daughter's disappearance. She maintained contact with Amy for several years thereafter.

10. Earhart, *The Fun of It*, 35.

11. Southern, *I Taught Amelia to Fly*, p. 124.

12. Earhart, *20 Hrs.*, pp. 25–6.

13. *Los Angeles Examiner*, August 8, 1922.

14. Ruth Law's record appears in Brooks-Pazmany, *United States Women in Aviation*, p. 41; the Baroness's record was published in the *New York Times*, June 14, 1919. (She perished in an aircraft accident a month later.)

15. Earhart, *20 Hrs.*, pp. 29–30.

Chapter 5   To Boston

1. Morrissey, *Courage Is the Price*, p. 119.
2. The Gold Bug information was provided courtesy of Chris Ritter, librarian, Antique Automobile Club of America (AACA) Library & Research Center, Hershey, PA. His research specifies that the 1920 Gold Bug, the 6–45 model, was priced at $3,475.
3. Web site, http://www.randmcnally.com.
4. SLRC, Notes of AOE.
5. IWASM, letter from AE to Marian Stabler, October 1925.
6. Putnam, *Soaring Wings*, p. 47.
7. IWASM, letter from AE to Marian Stabler, October 1925.
8. Records of Denison House at the Web site http://oasis.lib.harvard.edu/oasis/deliver/~sch00182; Earhart, *20 Hrs.*, xxi.
9. Morrissey, *Courage Is the Price*, p. 133.
10. Ibid, p. 135.
11. IWASM, letter from AE to Marian Stabler, August 1, 1927.
12. *Boston Herald*, July 2, 1927.
13. PSC, letter from AE to Ruth Nichols, September 15, 1927.
14. Railey, *Touch'd with Madness*, p. 101.

Chapter 6   Preparations

1. Earhart, *The Fun of It*, p. 59.
2. Ibid.
3. Lindbergh's 1927 flight is depicted in Winters, *Anne Morrow Lindbergh*, pp. 39–41.
4. *The Literary Digest*, "The American Super-Girl and Her Critics," October 29, 1927, p. 52, 54–5, provided courtesy of http://www.oldmagazinearticles.com.
5. *Pioneer Press*, "Bulletin," May 4, 2002.
6. *Time*, March 26, 1928, "Aeronautics: Two Women."
7. Nichols, *Wings for Life*, p. 95–6.
8. Putnam, *Wide Margins*, p. 19.
9. Quoted in Lovell, *The Sound of Wings*, p. 78, from Ford, *The Time of Laughter*.
10. Putnam, *Wide Margins*, p. 293.
11. Railey, *Touch'd with Madness*, p. 104.
12. Earhart, *20 Hrs.*, p. 42; IWASM, letter from AE to Marian Stabler, June 1, 1928.
13. Quoted in Lovell, *The Sound of Wings*, p. 99, from *The Illustrated Love Magazine*, interview with AE, January 1932.

Chapter 7   Across the Atlantic

1. Earhart, *The Fun of It*, p. 84.

2. The previous pontoon-equipped flights included a 1922 journey from Lisbon across the South Atlantic to Rio de Janeiro, and portions of the 1924 Douglas Cruisers' circumnavigation flights.

3. Brice Goldsborough, "The Earth Inductor Compass," *Vintage Airplane*, April 2005, first printed in *Aero Digest*, June 1927.

4. Chapman, *Whistled Like a Bird*, pp. 99–100.

5. Ibid., p. 43, 67.

6. Ibid., p. 94.

7. George Putnam asked AE to keep a log of the flight and probably told her he would use these notes for a forthcoming book, which would eventually see release as *20 Hrs., 40 Min.* The portions of the log that appear in the book, however, do not always agree with the actual log because of word substitutions and deletions. To better depict and more accurately recreate the 1928 *Friendship* flight in the present book, the author used a copy of Amelia Earhart's actual flight log, provided courtesy of Mr. John Cahoon, Collections Manager at the Seaver Center for Western History Research, Los Angeles County Museum of Natural History, Los Angeles, California.

8. Earhart, *Friendship* flight log.

9. Ibid.

10. *New York Times*, June 4, 1928.

11. SLRC, Notes by AOE.

12. Earhart, *Friendship* flight log.

13. Ibid.

14. Ibid.

15. Ibid.

16. Formerly known as the *Columbia*, renamed in Miss Boll's honor.

17. Earhart, *Friendship* flight log.

18. *Flight*, June 14, 1928.

19. Earhart, *Friendship* flight log.

20. PSC, cable from Bill Stultz to Commander Byrd, June 13, 1928.

21. Earhart, *Friendship* flight log.

22. Putnam, *Soaring Wings*, p. 62.

23. Earhart, *Friendship* flight log.

24. Ibid.

25. Ibid.

26. Ibid.

27. Ibid.

28. Ibid.; in 1928, Cobh, County Cork, Ireland, was known by its English name, Queenstown.

Chapter 8   The Heroine

1. Colonel Hilton H. Railey, introduction to Briand Jr., *Daughter of the Sky*, p. xvi.

2. *New York Times*, June 19, 1928.

3. Ibid.

4. Ibid.

5. *New York American*, June 19, 1928.

6. *New York Times*, June 19, 1928.

7. PSC, cable from AE to Secretary of State Kellogg, circa 1928.

8. Earhart, *20 Hrs.*, p. 172.

9. Quoted in Lovell, *The Sound of Wings*, p. 127, from *Flight*, June 21, 1928.

10. Lady Bailey arrived home in London in January 1929. In their record flights, British aviators also sought to link parts of the British Empire. The French, Dutch, and other European pilots were also extending their reach into the mother country's colonies.

11. Naughton, *Lady Icarus*, p. 155; this letter to the editor from Frederick Guest titled "Lady Heath's Flight" was printed in the *Times* (London) on April 11, 1928.

12. *New York Times*, June 20, 1928.

13. *Flight*, June 28, 1928.

14. Siobhán Mulcahy, "Mary, the Woman Who Fell to Earth," *Ireland on Sunday*, March 2, 2003.

15. In July 1929, Bill Stultz and his two passengers perished in an aircraft accident that resulted from Bill's stunts at low altitude. It was later alleged that Bill had been drinking heavily before this flight.

16. *New York Times*, July 7, 1928.

17. PSC, circa 1928.

18. IWASM, letter from AE to Marian Stabler, August 16, 1928.

19. SLRC, letter from AE to AOF, August 26, 1928.

20. IWASM, letter from AE to Marian Stabler, August 16, 1928.

21. Ibid.

22. Chapman, *Whistled Like a Bird*, p. 119.

Chapter 9   The Vagabond

1. Amelia Earhart, "What Miss Earhart Thinks When She's Flying," *Cosmopolitan*, December 1928.

2. Web site, http://www.ameliaflight.com/flight.po, a 2001 flight re-creation of AE's 1928 journey across the States.

3. Ibid.

4. *New York Times*, September 1, 1928.

5. Rich, *Amelia Earhart: A Biography*, p. 119.

6. The term dead reckoning evolved from "deduced reckoning," obviously a better description.

7. Naughton, *Lady Icarus*, p. 142.

8. *New York Times*, September 15, 1928.

9. Cassagneres, *Ambassador of Air Travel*, p. 182.

10. Christopher Smart, "Amelia Earhart had unexpected layover in Utah," *Salt Lake Tribune*, October 19, 2009.

Chapter 10   Off and Running

1. Amelia Earhart, "Try Flying Yourself," *Cosmopolitan*, November 1928.

2. Naughton, *Lady Icarus*, p. 195.

3. Thaden, *High, Wide, and Frightened*, p. 147.

4. Putnam, *Soaring Wings*, p. 79.

5. Charles F. Downs II, "Celebrating the Wright Brothers' First Flight," *Prologue*, Winter 2003, Vol. 35, No. 4, www.archives.gov/publications/prologue/2003/winter/aero-conference-1.html.

6. Chapman, *Whistled Like a Bird*, p. 130.

7. Ibid., p. 132.

8. *New York Times*, July 30, 1929.

9. Lady Heath had arrived in the United States in late 1928 to begin a six-month lecture tour, but, according to biographer Lindie Naughton, Heath "found that most of her engagements had been cancelled owing to 'lack of interest,' with Amelia Earhart replacing her." This was the result of Putnam's machinations, wrote Naughton. See Naughton, *Lady Icarus*, p. 194.

10. *New York Times*, March 29, 1929.

11. Lovell, *The Sound of Wings*, p. 144.

12. Despite several attempts, the author was unable to obtain Amelia Earhart's file from the airman certification branch of the Federal Aviation Administration. Apparently the contents of the file were lost or are restricted. Thus the author could not verify Earhart's flight hours except through Earhart's papers and personal correspondence with friends, which included Eugene Vidal.

13. Smith, *Aviatrix*, pp. 158–9.

14. Amelia Earhart, "Are American Women Holding Aviation Back?" *Liberty*, February 13, 1937.

15. Winters, *Anne Morrow Lindbergh*, pp. 63–4.

16. Ibid., p. 64; PSC, letter from AE to AML dated May 8, 1929.

17. Gore Vidal, "Love of Flying," *New York Review of Books*, January 17, 1985.

18. R. Allen, *Revolutions in the Sky*, p. 225.

19. Interview with Edna Gardner Whyte, Texas Woman's University, The Woman's Collection, Oral History Collection, February 8, 1979, pp. 45–6; Smith, *Aviatrix*, p. 169.

20. *New York Times*, July 23, 1929.

21. As background material for the Women's Air Derby of 1929, the author referred to various pages in the following books: Jessen, *Powder Puff Derby of 1929*; Naughton, *Lady Icarus*; Schultz, *Pancho*; Thaden, *High, Wide, and Frightened*; Veca and Mazzio, *Just Plane Crazy*; and various newspaper clippings.

22. *New York Times*, August 19, 1929.

23. *Atlanta Constitution*, August 27, 1929.

24. Mark J. Price, "National Air Races Enthrall Thousands in 1929," *Akron Beacon Journal*, August 24, 2009; and various newspaper clippings.

25. Information about Amelia's glider accident appeared in *Soaring* magazine, "Clio's Wings," by Raul Blacksten, November 2008; this was the same Frank Hawks who had piloted on Amelia's first flight, in Los Angeles.

Chapter 11   Faster

1. F. Allen, *Since Yesterday: The 1930s in America*; Claire Suddath, "The Crash of 1929," *Time*, October 29, 2008.
2. See Winters, *Anne Morrow Lindbergh*, pp. 75–7, for further details of AE's visit and the article.
3. Backus, *Letters from Amelia*, letter from AE to AOE, November 22, 1929, p. 85.
4. Morath, *High Flyers*, pp. 85–7; in correspondence with the FAI's Marcel Meyer, executive officer of records, on March 16, 2009, the author was told that women's records were introduced in 1928. The first FAI-ratified feminine record was set on July 28, 1929, by Madame Maryse Bastié for endurance.
5. Veca and Mazzio, *Just Plane Crazy*, letter From AE to Bobbi Trout, February 13, 1929, p. 87.
6. Backus, *Letters from Amelia*, p. 85.
7. SLRC, letter from AE to AOE, 1931, no day.
8. Backus, *Letters from Amelia*, undated letter from AE to AOE, p. 86.
9. SLRC, Notes by AOE.
10. Chapman, *Whistled Like a Bird*, p. 154.
11. Ibid., p. 157.
12. Ibid., p. 167.
13. Putnam, *Soaring Wings*, p. 74.
14. *New York Times*, August 5, 1930; Barnes's record attempt did not appear in the list of FAI ratified flights.
15. *New York Times*, August 6 and 17, 1930.
16. Gore Vidal, "Love of Flying," *New York Review of Books*, January 17, 1985.
17. Eugene Vidal Collection, Accession 6013, Box 40, American Heritage Center, University of Wyoming.
18. SLRC, letter from AE to AOE, September 16, 1930; SLRC, letter from AE to AOE, October 2, 1930.
19. SLRC, letter from AE to AOE, October 13, 1930.
20. Nancy Porter, director, *The American Experience: Amelia Earhart*, PBS video, WGBH/Boston, Nancy Porter Productions, 1993.
21. Rich, *Jackie Cochran*, p. 66.
22. PSC, letter from AE to GPP, February 7, 1931.
23. Putnam, *Soaring Wings*, p. 75.
24. Backus, *Letters from Amelia*, letter from AE to AOE, February 22, 1931, p. 107.

Chapter 12   The Autogiro

1. An aircraft stalls when its wings lose lift, which can also result in a spin. Even today, spins at low altitude are a leading cause of aircraft accidents.
2. Andrew King, "Blades of Glory: The Pitcairn Autogiro," *EAA Sport Aviation*, January 2010; author interview with certified flight instructor Mr. F. Lee Bradshaw—an instructor in helicopters and gyroplanes, along with many other aircraft—who explained the aerodynamics of autogiros.

3. *New York Times*, April 9, 1931.

4. Charnov, *From Autogiro to Gyroplane.*

5. Ibid., p. 79; in the note 9 on page 96, Mr. Charnov refers to an interview with Pitcairn company pilot George Townson, who claimed to have had "words" with Earhart and that "she was an impatient pilot."

6. *New York Times*, June 13, 1931.

7. Ibid., June 20, 1931; Amelia's position as vice president of the NAA, along with the influence of the NAA president, Senator Hiram Bingham, working on her behalf, may have prevented the more drastic action of a ninety-day grounding—a pilot's nightmare.

8. On July 19, 1931, the *New York Times* published an article by Amelia in which she stated that her autogiro was the first to go to the Pacific Ocean and back.

9. Experimental Aircraft Association, "Oral Interview with John 'Johnny' Miller," online video clip, http://www.eaa.org/apps/timelessvoices/VoicesDetails.aspx?VoicesID=385.

10. The accident in Camden was mentioned in Butler, *East to the Dawn*, p. 260.

11. Putnam, *Soaring Wings*, p. 209.

12. PSC, aircraft records for the autogiro. Possibly her first autogiro was written off after the September accident since she put together a statement dated October 19, 1931, testifying she had flown it approximately 150 hours and 40 minutes. She based this on her records because the machine's aircraft and engine logbooks were lost at the time of the crash.

Chapter 13   Second Crossing

1. Earhart, *The Fun of It*, p. 210.

2. It is unknown who this backer was.

3. *New York Times*, May 29, 1932.

4. Lew Holt, "How Many Will Die Flying the Atlantic this Season," *Modern Mechanics and Inventions*, August 1931, an article with pictures and descriptions of these instruments. According to Holt, in 1931 Ruth Nichols's plane was equipped with these instruments, as well as a variable pitch propeller and a warning instrument to indicate when ice was forming on the wings.

5. Nichols, *Wings for Life*, p. 209.

6. IWASM, letter from AE to Louise Thaden, May 18, 1932.

7. Nancy Porter, director, *The American Experience: Amelia Earhart*, PBS video, WGBH/Boston, Nancy Porter Productions, 1993.

8. After Amelia's flight, George Putnam smoothed over the lack of approval with American government officials; Amelia was issued a passport several days after she arrived in London.

9. That same day, the captain of a fifty-ton German flying boat, the DO-X, decided to delay departing from Newfoundland to the Azores until the following day, the twenty-first.

10. Moolman, *Women Aloft*, p. 65.

11. *New York Times*, May 21, 1932.

12. *San Diego Union*, May 21, 1932.

13. Her barograph would confirm her altitude levels, she told a reporter right after the flight. In *Soaring Wings*, p. 106, GPP wrote that she entered a spin in flight and used a barograph to determine her altitude loss. Unfortunately, her barograph did not turn up after the flight and it is unknown what became of it. The FAI did not ratify Amelia's transatlantic flight as a feminine distance record, so we can assume her barograph was lost or malfunctioned. Therefore, Amelia's flight did not supersede Ruth Nichols's ratified feminine distance record of October 25, 1931, a 3182.65 kilometer flight. (The FAI used Charles Lindbergh's barograph to substantiate his world-record 5809-kilometer distance flight of May 21, 1927.)

14. PSC, AE Flight Log, May 1932.

15. *New York Times*, May 22, 1932.

16. "Address of Miss Amelia Earhart," National Society, Daughters of the American Revolution, Forty-Second Continental Congress, April 21, 1933.

17. Discrepancies abound about her actual flight time because of time zone differences and because apparently Amelia calculated her time based on making landfall, not the actual landing. Based on newspapers, including the *San Diego Union* and the *Boston Globe* (both dated May 22, 1932), this is the actual time. Had her barograph survived, her time aloft would have been clearly indicated on the instrument.

Chapter 14 Celebrity

1. Pilots and passengers in airships had flown the Atlantic often; as noted in the previous chapter, AE's distance record was unofficial, not having been ratified by the FAI because her barograph was either lost or it malfunctioned.

2. Pan American Airways would inaugurate service across the Pacific using flying boats in late 1935, and four years later it would begin transatlantic flights.

3. *New York Times*, July 3, 1932.

4. *Boston Herald*, May 24, 1932.

5. *New York Post*, May 21, 1932.

6. *New York World-Telegram*, May 22, 1932.

7. Quoted in Lovell, *The Sound of Wings*, p. 190; *The Aeroplane*, May 25, 1932.

8. *Boston Sunday Globe*, May 22, 1932; *Los Angeles Times*, May 1932, unknown day.

9. *New York Times*, June 1, 1932.

10. George Putnam, "Forgotten Husband," *Pictorial Review*, December 1932.

11. Annie Brown, "Struggles of Pioneering Pilot Amelia Who Wanted the World," *Daily Record* (UK), November 14, 2009.

12. *Oakland Tribune*, August 21, 1932.

13. *New York Times*, August 26, 1932.

14. SLRC, Letter from AE to Commander Clarence S. Williams, September 6, 1932.

15. The average monthly wage in 1932 was about $135.

16. Backus, *Letters from Amelia*, letter AE to AOE, November 4, 1932.
17. Ibid., December 24, 1932.

Chapter 15   The Treadmill

1. SLRC, Letter from AE to AOE, February 13, 1933.
2. *New York Times*, April 21, 1933.
3. "Address of Miss Amelia Earhart," National Society, Daughters of the American Revolution, Forty-Second Continental Congress, April 21, 1933.
4. Ibid.
5. Today, women represent 15 percent of the armed forces and fly fighter jets, helicopters, tankers, and other aircraft for the military.
6. *New York Times*, November 11, 1933.
7. C. Smith, *Amy Johnson*, p. 321.
8. Ibid., letter from Amy Johnson to her father, p. 326.
9. MHS, Letter from AE to Croil Hunter, Northwestern Airways, March 9, 1933, 148.K.17.8 (F), Box 19, Northwest Airlines, Inc., corporate records.
10. Soon the agency was renamed the Bureau of Air Commerce.
11. MHS, Letter from GPP to Croil Hunter, Northwestern Airways, October 9, 1933, 148.K.17.8 (F), Box 19, Northwest Airlines, Inc., corporate records.
12. Eugene Vidal Collection, University of Wyoming, American Heritage Center.
13. SLRC, various newspaper advertisements.
14. *New York Times*, March 21, 1934.
15. Peterson and Glab, *Rapid Descent*, p. 27.
16. Quoted in Rich, *Amelia Earhart*, p. 155.

Chapter 16   Aloha

1. Stephen Joiner, "Hollywood's Favorite Pilot," *Air & Space*, October/November 2007.
2. Ibid.
3. The Vega's radio, its call sign KHABQ, transmitted on 3105 and 6210 kilocycles; Amelia's Vega was registered as NR-965Y.
4. Clarence S. Williams, "What Happened to Ulm," *Los Angeles Times Sunday Magazine*, December 30, 1934.
5. Leslie Ford, "A Flier in Sugar," *The Nation*, January 30, 1935.
6. Backus, *Letters from Amelia*, Letter from AE to AOE, January 6, 1935, p. 164.
7. SLRC, Associated Press, January 12, 1935.
8. Amelia Earhart, "My Flight from Hawaii," *National Geographic*, May 1935.
9. *Los Angeles Evening Herald and Express,* January 12, 1935.
10. SLRC, Unidentified newspaper clipping.
11. A year earlier, in 1934, Sir Charles Kingsford Smith and navigator Patrick Gordon Taylor had flown the same flight route in three hours less. The two men made the

first west-east flight from Hawaii in 15 hours, which was the last leg in their journey
from Australia.

12. *New York Times*, January 13, 1935.
13. PSC, Letter from Louise Thaden to AE, January 12, 1935.

Chapter 17   Mexico

1. SLRC, Letter from GPP to AOE, February 11, 1935.
2. Dwiggins, *Hollywood Pilot*, p. 86.
3. Earhart, *Last Flight*, p. 18.
4. "Philatelists Fly into Rage over Flyer's Stamp Corner," *Newsweek*, May 11, 1935.
5. Ibid.
6. Earhart, *Last Flight*, p. 18
7. *New York Times*, May 9, 1935.
8. Briand Jr., *Daughters of the Sky*, p. 130.
9. PSC, Telegram, Eugene Vidal to AE, May 9, 1935.
10. Interview with Edna Gardner Whyte, Texas Woman's University, Oral History Collection, Number 28, February 8, 1979.
11. Quoted in Rich, *Amelia Earhart*, p. 204.
12. Reginald M. Cleveland, "Safety in Air Travel," *New York Times*, May 12, 1935.
13. SLRC, Pasadena Community Playhouse Advertisement, June 23, 1935.
14. *New York Times*, September 13, 1935 and July 12, 1935.
15. Morath, *High Flyers*, p. 205.
16. *St. Paul Pioneer Press*, October 6, 1935.

Chapter 18   The Flying Laboratory

1. Earhart, *Last Flight*, p. 27.
2. Ibid., p. 27.
3. "Al Williams Rips Earhart 'Stunt' Flight," *Cleveland Press*, March 31, 1937.
4. Roy Blay, "Amelia Earhart's Last Flight," *Lockheed Horizons*, May 1988.
5. Although first registered as X16020, for its global flight the aircraft was registered as NR16020.
6. Roy Blay, "Amelia Earhart's Last Flight," *Lockheed Horizons*, May 1988.
7. The lower-frequency 3105-kilocycle radio waves are used at night because they reflect better from the ionosphere than do the higher-frequency 6210-kilocycle radio waves.
8. See Long and Long, *Amelia Earhart: The Mystery Solved*, for additional information about the radio equipment.
9. Dwiggins, *Hollywood Pilot*, p. 73.
10. Ibid., p. 96, undated letter from GPP to Paul Mantz.
11. SLRC, letter from GPP to AOE, January 16, 1937.
12. Flynn, *The Roosevelt Myth*, p. 423, note; according to a study made in 1940 by Flynn, Eleanor Roosevelt earned $1.2 million during the first seven and a half years

of her husband's presidency. Over a fifteen-year period, Flynn determined, she earned a minimum of $3 million from books, lectures, and radio programs. (These are not present-day dollars.)

13. Aviator Ruth Nichols and AE corresponded in early 1936 about their plans for world flights. Nichols was one of many aviators, including male pilots, who were hampered in their flight attempts by a lack of financial backing.
14. *New York Times*, April 20, 1936.
15. *New York Times*, May 14, 1936.
16. PSC, letter from GPP to Eleanor Roosevelt, June 1936.
17. Earhart, *Last Flight*, p. 25.
18. Ibid.
19. PSC, letter AE to President Roosevelt, November 10, 1936.
20. PSC, telegram AE to President Roosevelt, January 7, 1936.
21. *New York Times*, February 12, 1937.
22. Earhart, *Last Flight*, p. 30.
23. Quoted in Roy Blay, "Amelia Earhart's Last Flight," *Lockheed Horizons*, May 1988.
24. PSC, *Herald Tribune* cables to GPP, March 15 and 16, 1937.
25. "The Cabinet: Vidal Out," *Time*, March 8, 1937.
26. The Golden Gate Bridge would officially open on May 27.

Chapter 19   Luke Field

1. Dwiggins, *Hollywood Pilot*, p. 91.
2. In *East to the Dawn*, p. 379, Susan Butler wrote that Paul's landing that day was so hard that the "impact weakened the landing gear. Amelia was not happy." In an endnote reference in this same book, on p. 461, Butler wrote that Amelia told author Janet Mabie she laid the blame for the hard landing on Paul.
3. *Boston Post*, United Press International release dated March 18, 1937; in addition, Air Corps personnel reported Paul's landings had been satisfactory at Wheeler and at Luke.
4. SLRC, Associated Press release dated March 18, 1937.
5. *New York Times*, March 21, 1937.
6. Ibid.; Earhart, *Last Flight*, p. 40.
7. As quoted in the *San Diego Union* on March 23, 1937, from the *Honolulu Star Bulletin*, March 22, 1937.
8. Earhart, *Last Flight*, p. 40.
9. Dwiggins, *Hollywood Pilot*, p. 90.
10. It is possible that as the right turn began Amelia had been overcorrecting for the left-turning tendency of propeller torque by applying too much right rudder, which would have begun a turn to the right. She should have known not to change the power setting on the throttles in this situation. This procedure, which required a fine touch, was not at all advised by any but the most experienced pilots. She was new to the Electra and had not allowed sufficient time to learn its capabilities and

performance characteristics. (The author's analysis of the accident was based on an extensive review of documents and on her interviews with experienced pilots who have many hours of piloting and instructing in multi-engine aircraft. She especially wishes to thank retired Pan American Airlines pilot Mr. Lyle Wheeler, whose decades of experience as a pilot and instructor proved of enormous help to her. The flight instructor Mr. Jim Hanson also helped with a review.)

11. Nancy Porter, director, *The American Experience: "Amelia Earhart,"* PBS video, WGBH/Boston., Directed by Nancy Porter, Nancy Porter Productions, 1993.
12. Al Williams, "Al Williams Rips Earhart 'Stunt' Flight," *Cleveland Press*, March 31, 1937.
13. "Mourning Becomes Electra," *Time*, March 29, 1937.
14. *New York Times*, March 22, 1937.
15. *Boston Post*, March 26, 1937.
16. PSC, letter from GPP to Helen Reid, March 24, 1937.
17. PSC, letter from GPP to AE, circa 1937.
18. Ibid.
19. Earhart, *Last Flight*, p. 43.
20. PSC, note from AE to Paul Mantz, April 8, 1937.
21. Long and Long, *Amelia Earhart: The Mystery Solved*, p. 290.
22. Quoted in Lovell, *The Sound of Wings*, p. 255, from a speech given by author Frederick Goerner at the Amelia Earhart Symposium at the Smithsonian Institution, Washington, D.C., 1983.
23. Rich, *Jackie Cochran*, pp. 68–9.
24. Thaden, *High, Wide, and Frightened*, p. 150.
25. PSC, *McCall's* magazine cover, May 1937.
26. *New York Times*, May 16, 1937.

Chapter 20   The Last Flight

1. PSC, telegram sent by Carl Allen to the *New York Herald Tribune* on July 3, 1937, commenting on his interview with AE that had occurred in Oakland, CA, circa March 1937.
2. Earhart, *Last Flight*, p. 57.
3. Ibid., p. 81.
4. Ibid., p. 88.
5. Putnam, *Wide Margins*, p. 292.
6. Earhart, *Last Flight*, p. 117.
7. PSC, *Itasca* cable to AE, June 23, 1937.
8. See Long and Long, *Amelia Earhart: The Mystery Solved*, for additional information about the time zones and radio equipment installed in the Electra and on *Itasca* and Howland Island.
9. Earhart, *Last Flight*, p. 129.
10. PSC, telegram from AE to GPP, June 30, 1937.

11. PSC, telegram from GPP to AE, June 30, 1937.

12. PSC, telegram from AE to *Herald Tribune*, July 2, 1937.

13. Quoted from *The Chater Report*, correspondence from Mr. Eric Chater, manager of Guinea Airways, to Mr. M. E. Griffin, July 25, 1937, which included a report of the telegram sent by AE to the *Itasca* on June 30.

14. Ibid.; Mr. Chater reported that the Electra carried 1,100 gallons of fuel at takeoff.

15. Ibid.; the report included Amelia's radio transmission.

16. PSC, USCG radio transcripts report of the Earhart flight to Howland Island.

17. Ric Gillespie, director of the International Group for Historic Aircraft Recovery, has led several Earhart search expeditions to Nikumaroro Island, which is south of Howland Island.

18. PSC, USCG radio transcripts report of the Earhart flight to Howland Island.

19. Ibid.

Epilogue

1. *New York Times*, July 3, 1937.

2. Respectively, these appeared on July 3, 1937, in the *New York Times*, *Ludington Daily News*, and *Spokane Daily Chronicle*.

3. *Time*, July 12, 1937.

4. *Christian Science Monitor*, July 14, 1937.

5. *New York Times*, August 16, 1937.

6. Stephen Joiner, "Hollywood's Favorite Pilot," *Air & Space*, October/November 2007.

7. *Los Angeles Times*, July 25, 1937.

8. PSC, Note from AE to GPP, circa 1937.

BIBLIOGRAPHY

Allen, Frederick Lewis. *Only Yesterday: An Informal History of the 1920s.* New York: Harper & Row, 1931; New York: Bantam, 1946.

———. *Since Yesterday: The 1930s in America.* New York: Perennial Library, 1972. First published 1939 by Harper & Row.

Allen, Oliver E., and the editors of Time-Life Books. *The Airline Builders.* Alexandria, VA: Time-Life Books, 1981.

Allen, Richard Sanders. *Revolution in the Sky: The Lockheeds of Aviation's Golden Age.* Atglen, PA: Schiffer, 1993. Revised edition.

Backus, Jean L. *Letters from Amelia: An Intimate Portrait of Amelia Earhart.* Boston: Beacon Press, 1982.

Bell, Elizabeth S. *Sisters of the Wind: Voices of Early Women Aviators.* Pasadena, CA: Trilogy Books, 1994.

Boeing Company, The. *A Brief History of the Boeing Company.* Chicago: The Boeing Company, 2006.

Briand Jr., Paul L. *Daughter of the Sky.* New York: Duell, Sloan and Pearce, 1960.

Brooks-Pazmany, Kathleen. *United States Women in Aviation: 1919–1929.* Washington, DC: Smithsonian Institution Press, 1991.

Butler, Susan. *East to the Dawn: The Life of Amelia Earhart.* Reading, MA: Da Capo Press, 1999.

Campbell, Mike, and Thomas E. Devine. *With Our Own Eyes: Eyewitnesses to the Final Days of Amelia Earhart.* Lancaster, OH: Lucky Press, 2002.

Cassagneres, Ev. *Ambassador of Air Travel: The Untold Story of Lindbergh's 1927–1928 Good Will Tours.* Missoula, MT: Pictorial Histories Publishing Co., 2006.

Chapman, Sally Putnam. *Whistled Like a Bird: The Untold Story of Dorothy Putnam, George Putnam, and Amelia Earhart.* New York: Warner Books, 1997.

Charnov, Bruce H. *From Autogiro to Gyroplane: The Amazing Survival of an Aviation Technology.* Westport, CT: Praeger, 2003.

Downey, Kirstin. *The Woman Behind the New Deal: The Life of Frances Perkins, FDR's Secretary of Labor and His Moral Conscience.* New York: Nan A. Talese/Doubleday, 2009.

Dwiggins, Don. *Hollywood Pilot: The Biography of Paul Mantz.* New York: Doubleday & Co., 1967.

Earhart, Amelia. *Friendship* flight log, June, 1928. Seaver Center for Western History Research, Los Angeles County Museum of Natural History, Los Angeles, California.

———. *The Fun of It: Random Records of My Own Flying and of Women in Aviation.* New York: The Junior Literary Guild; Brewer, Warren & Putnam, 1932.

———. *Last Flight.* New York: Harcourt, Brace & Co., 1937.

———. *20 Hrs., 40 Min.: Our Flight in the Friendship.* New York: Arno Press, 1980.

Falloon, Jane. *Throttle Wide Open: A Life of Lady Bailey, Irish Aviatrix.* Dublin: The Lilliput Press, 1999.

Fédération Aéronautique International (FAI). Records Feminine, Miss Amelia Earhart (Etats Unis) and other aviators. Paris.

Flynn, John T. *The Roosevelt Myth.* New York: The Devin-Adair Company, 1948.

Ford, Corey. *The Time of Laughter.* Boston: Little Brown, 1967.

Gillespie, Ric. *Finding Amelia: The True Story of the Earhart Disappearance.* Annapolis, MD: Naval Institute Press, 2006.

Hopkins, George E. *Flying the Line: The First Half Century of the Air Line Pilots Association.* Washington, DC: The Air Line Pilots Association, 1982.

Jablonski, Edward. *Atlantic Fever.* New York: The Macmillan Company, 1972.

Jessen, Gene Nora. *Powder Puff Derby of 1929: The True Story of the First Women's Cross-Country Air Race.* Naperville, IL: Sourcebooks, Inc., 2002.

Lomax, Judy. *Women of the Air: The Remarkable Story of the Women Who Pioneered the Skies from Balloons to Voyager.* New York: Dodd, Mead & Company, 1987.

Long, Elgen M., and Marie K. Long. *Amelia Earhart: The Mystery Solved.* New York: Touchstone, 1999.

Lovell, Mary S. *The Sound of Wings: The Life of Amelia Earhart.* New York: St. Martin's Press, 1989.

Mackersey, Ian. *Jean Batten: The Garbo of the Skies.* London: Macdonald, 1990.

Mize, W. Richard. *A Song of Saints.* Atchison, KS: Rector, Wardens and Vestry of Trinity Episcopal Church, 1989.

Moolman, Valerie, and the editors of Time-Life, Inc. *Women Aloft.* Alexandria, VA: Time-Life Books, 1981.

Morath, Pierre. *High Flyers 1905–2005: A Century of Sporting Achievement in the Air.* Quart, Italy: Musumeci S.p.A., 2005.

Morrissey, Muriel Earhart. *Courage Is the Price.* Wichita, KS: McCormick Armstrong Publishing Division, 1963.

Morse, Joseph Laffan, editor in chief. *The Universal Standard Encyclopedia.* An abridgement of *The New Funk & Wagnalls Encyclopedia.* New York: Standard Reference Works Publishing Co., 1956.

Naughton, Lindie. *Lady Icarus: The Life of Irish Aviator Lady Mary Heath.* Dublin: Ashfield Press, 2004.

Nichols, Ruth. *Wings for Life.* Philadelphia: J. B. Lippincott Co., 1957.

Oakes, Claudia M. *United States Women in Aviation 1930–1939.* Washington, DC: Smithsonian Institution Press, 1991.

Peterson, Barbara Sturken, and James Glab. *Rapid Descent: Deregulation and the Shakeout in the Airlines.* New York: Simon and Schuster, 1994.

Pope, Frances, and Arthur S. Otis. *Elements of Aeronautics.* New York: World Book Co., 1941.

Putnam, George Palmer. *Soaring Wings.* New York: Harcourt, Brace & Co., 1939.

———. *Wide Margins.* New York: Harcourt, Brace & Co., 1942.

Railey, Hilton Howell. *Touch'd with Madness.* New York: Carrick & Evans, Inc., 1938.

Rich, Doris L. *Amelia Earhart: A Biography.* Washington, DC: Smithsonian Institution Press, 1989.

———. *Jackie Cochran: Pilot in the Fastest Lane.* Gainesville, FL: University Press of Florida, 2007.

Scharf, Lois, and Joan M. Jensen. *Decades of Discontent: The Women's Movement, 1920–1940.* Boston: Northeastern University Press, 1987.

Schultz, Barbara Hunter. *Pancho: The Biography of Florence Lowe Barnes.* Lancaster, CA: Little Buttes Publishing Co., 1996.

Smith, Constance Babington. *Amy Johnson.* London: Collins, 1967.

Smith, Elinor. *Aviatrix.* Thorndike, ME: Thorndike Press, 1981.

Southern, Neta Snook. *I Taught Amelia to Fly.* New York: Vantage Press, 1974.

Strippel, Dick. *Amelia Earhart: The Myth and the Reality.* New York: Exposition Press, 1972.

Thaden, Louise. *High, Wide, and Frightened.* New York: Stackpole Sons, 1938.

Veca, Donna, and Skip Mazzio. *Just Plane Crazy: Biography of Bobbi Trout.* Santa Clara, CA: Osborne Publisher, 1987.

Ware, Susan. *Still Missing: Amelia Earhart and the Search for Modern Feminism.* New York: W. W. Norton & Company, 1993.

Winters, Kathleen C. *Anne Morrow Lindbergh: First Lady of the Air.* New York: Palgrave Macmillan, 2006.

INDEX